W9-BKF-492

Also by Bruce Pandolfini:

Chess Openings:

TRAPS AND ZAPS

By Bruce Pandolfini

A FIRESIDE BOOK
Published by Simon & Schuster
New York   London   Toronto   Sydney   Tokyo   Singapore

Rockefeller Center
1230 Avenue of the Americas
New York, New York 10020

Copyright © 1989 by Bruce Pandolfini

Designed by Stanley S. Drate/Folio Graphics Co. Inc.

Manufactured in the United States of America

20   19   18   17   16   15   14

Library of Congress Cataloging in Publication Data

Pandolfini, Bruce.
   Chess openings : traps and zaps / by Bruce Pandolfini.
      p.   cm.
   "A Fireside book."
   Includes indexes.
   1. Chess—Openings.   I. Title.
GV1450.P29   1989
794.1'22—dc19   88-28976
                                           CIP

ISBN 0-671-65690-2

for Roselyn

Acknowledgments

My thanks go to chess master Bruce Alberston, who contributed invaluably in research, analysis, ideas, and judgments. Larry Tamarkin made the diagrams. I would also like to thank Idelle Pandolfini, Carol Ann Caronia, Julian Adler, Deborah Bergman, George Wen, Roz Levin, Bonni Leon, and Ellen Pluta, as well as Paul's Lounge (46 Third Ave.), where Bob and the crew helped conceive the book, Instant Copy (43 Third Ave.), where Scott and other chess fans photocopied it, and Ben & Jerry's (41 Third Ave.), where Peter, Scott and Shwan kept it going with ice cream and coffee. Finally, I would like to thank my editor, Laura Yorke, who really made the whole thing possible, and whose insight, patience and intelligence were essential to the project.

Contents

Introduction   **xiii**

Algebraic Notation   **xxi**

1 The Early d2–d4 Complex   **1**
Center Game (1–6) / 3
Center Gambit (7–8) / 9
Danish Gambit (9–16) / 11
Goring Gambit (17–18) / 19
Scotch Gambit (19–22) / 21
Scotch Game (23–32) / 25

2 The Sister Openings   **35**
Bishop's Opening
  (33–39) / 37
Vienna Game (40–54) / 44

3 The King's Gambit   **59**
King's Gambit Accepted
  (55–67) / 61
King's Gambit Declined
  (68–74) / 74
Falkbeer Counter-Gambit
  (75–80) / 81

4 Unusual Openings 88

Damiano Defense (81–83) / 91
Latvian Counter-Gambit
(84–86) / 94
Queen's-Pawn Counter-Gambit
(87–90) / 97
Alapin Opening (91–95) / 101
Ponziani Opening (96–101) / 106

5 The Knight's Game 112

Philidor Defense (102–107) / 115
Petroff Defense (108–113) / 121
Three Knights Game
(114–116) / 127
Four Knights Game
(117–120) / 130

6 The Italian Complex 134

Hungarian Defense
(121–123) / 137
Paris Defense
(124–126) / 140
Giuoco Piano (127–138) / 143
Evans Gambit (139–141) / 155
Two Knights Defense
(143–148) / 159

7 The Ruy Lopez   **165**
Without 3. . . a6 (149–181) / 167
With 3. . . a6 (182–202) / 200

Glossary   **221**

Sources   **233**

Tactical Index   **237**

Opening Index   **239**

Introduction

As a chess teacher I am often asked the following question: Is it better to survey all aspects of the game at once to lay a solid overall foundation, or is it more advantageous to study certain areas of chess intensively from the start, possibly to the temporary neglect of other matters?

If time were not a factor, the idea of "all and everything" would be an acceptable one for the average chess player. But the solution for the pragmatic player who is looking to increase his playing strength rapidly with as little as an hour a week to practice has to be different. As a chess teacher, my number-one priority is to actually help my students improve their level of play. When they want to do so in a reasonably short time period, the most practical advice I can give them is to concentrate on a few things, mainly opening moves and principles. Once they have built up this specialized but powerful arsenal, they can fill in the gaps and broaden their knowledge.

Of the three traditional phases in the game of chess—the opening, the middlegame, and the endgame—the opening is always the most significant to the average player. That's because every game has an opening, and therefore certain opening principles are important to every game. You've got to play the opening to get to the middlegame or endgame, and in fact many chess games end in the opening phase simply because the other two phases don't exist if you lose the game in ten moves.

There is a second practical advantage to studying the opening before the middlegame and endgame. Openings are easier to remember, since the starting position is always the same. Middlegame and endgame positions, to the contrary, almost never crystallize exactly the way you've seen them before in a book.

Of course, since most openings can go from ten to fifteen or more moves, even the same variation can change considerably from game to game. Nevertheless, any player may see the first moves of an opening play out many times, especially when he is playing White and exerts greater influence over the course of play.

By repeating the same openings for White and the same defenses for Black over and over, you come to a deeper understanding of the effects of these moves. Soon you gain greater familiarity with your opponent's reasonable responses, thereby achieving the mastery to exploit erroneous play in *actual* chess games, as opposed to what happens in books. You don't have to be a psychologist to realize that winning encourages more participation, more reading, and further development. The process is generally self-rewarding.

One might conclude that the opening is the easiest phase in which to develop prowess. Alas, this is not so! Too many players study the opening almost religiously, by rote, and misuse the versatile and adaptable tools it puts at their disposal. Too often, the only reference material available consists of a certain type of opening manual that charts numerous moves, with little or no commentary. This approach is useful for experienced players because it provides notes on who played a variation in what tournament or match, and which side stood better in the final position. What typically it doesn't supply is analysis of the moves— why some are recommended, while others aren't even considered. Nor does this approach explain how to proceed with the game once the variation is completed. Such information may be needed to move ahead.

Some opening books offer analysis but still leave you hanging if your opponent doesn't play according to Hoyle. Suppose he or she tries an offbeat line or blunders? What do you do then? Since amateurs don't always play the best moves, isn't it more sensible to review the mistakes that tend to occur repeatedly in their own games? Learning to recognize illogical play, and to pounce on it is accomplished through systematic study of inconsistent moves and how to counter them.

Mistakes like these are often the results of violating opening principles. One such arch sin probably familiar to most average players is that of bringing out the Queen early to grab an unimportant enemy pawn, and in return neglecting the development of other pieces and the castling of the King. Learn how to exploit such foolishness in an opponent and watch your success ratio go up.

Opening Principles

The purpose of the opening is to mobilize your entire army rapidly by activating a different piece on each turn, gaining moves by attacks and threats and forcing your opponent to waste time defending himself. You should also castle quickly to safeguard your King from potential danger and to clear the path for the Rooks and Queen shifting along the front rank.

As you bring out your pieces in the opening, you should try to set problems for your opponent on each turn. The goal is to prevent him from completing his own development and from safely castling his King. If you're lucky, he may not even survive an opening against your mounting threats. Don't let him get away. Hound his King until real concessions are made or you win material or you get the big prize: checkmate. This strategy is bound to work against an opponent who flagrantly violates opening principles that he either doesn't know or brushes aside if he does.

To develop a general understanding of what the opening should accomplish, you need numerous examples showing how your opponent's violation of principles can ruin his game. The material must demonstrate corresponding cause-and-effect relationships. The side making the error shows what to avoid, while the side exploiting the mistake shows how to play well. This is better than reviewing errorless chess games between two masters who seldom make the mistakes that are instructive to a casual player. At the same time, examples portraying one player's taking advantage of another's errors are more useful to the student than games between amateurs where neither side capitalizes on the enemy's missteps.

The "Traps and Zaps" Approach, and How to Use this Book

This "crime and punishment" approach to learning the openings has been very effective. In *Chess Openings: Traps and Zaps,* I offer a collection of 202 short openers where proper play in the beginning phase is violated. The winning player, often in fewer than ten moves, must punish his opponent's mistakes or simple failure to abide by sound opening principles.

I have arranged the games according to groups of openings. Every example is introduced by the name of the overriding tactic used to get a winning position, such as "In-Between Move" in example 1 (page 3). This is followed by the name of the opening, which in example 1 is "Center Game." In all these examples, both sides begin by moving their King-pawn two squares. The moves leading to the key position of the diagram, where a winning shot is to be found, are given in algebraic notation.

In example 1 the opening moves are: 1. e4 e5 2. d4 exd4 3. Qxd4 Nf6 4.Bg5 Be7 5. e5. After the diagram is a cue indicating who moves first, given in example 1 as "Black to move." I recommend learning these opening moves by playing them on a real chessboard and sitting on the side of the board for the player whose turn it is, indicated by the cue under the diagram. For example 1, therefore, turn the board so that you have Black.

If you don't have a ready chessboard, look at the diagram and imagine you're playing an actual game. However you reach the diagrammed position—by playing out the moves or simply by pretending you're sitting at a real chessboard according to the diagram—spend a couple of minutes in that situation, seeking a strong move. Try to analyze what's wrong with your opponent's last play. Look for ways to threaten his King, especially by combining such a threat with an attack against another unit. In other words, look for double attacks, the golden key to a winning advantage. This exercise will sensitize you to find similar tactics in your own games.

After engaging in this task, whether you've solved the problem or not, turn to the "Scenario." It sets the theme, gives the winning continuation, and presents the reasoning behind the moves. Following the Scenario is the "Interpretation." It explains why the loser went wrong, how he could have avoided the trap, and what he should have done instead. Important principles and useful guidelines are included to reinforce the lesson of each opening example.

Such themes as the failure to develop rapidly and effectively or neglecting King safety occur in numerous examples. These repetitions are important in order to see how only a few principles really determine the course of most openings. Understand them in their various guises, and you will actually start to play better chess and reach a viable middlegame against virtually anyone. By carefully digesting and evaluating the book's examples, you will also be arming yourself to fend off any foe. No one will be able to trounce you in the opening ever again.

All the examples in this book are short games drawn from the vast pool of double King-pawn openings. They are often less than ten moves and easy to remember. Later, with more experience, you will be in a better situation to expand your opening repertoire. By understanding very well some of the principles of double King-pawn openings, eventually you will master the principles of all openings with greater ease and success.

The material is arranged in seven chapters, each constituting a block of openings. A discussion of that section's openings introduces each chapter, explaining their differences and similarities. The chapters are related, yet stand as individual entities. You can read from page one, chapter after chapter, or you can focus on just the openings or group of openings that interests you. Arranged in logical sequence, the organization mainly follows historical development and moves from simpler positions to more complicated ones.

For those wishing to bone up on tactics, an alternative approach is to play over situations of similar attacking ideas, which are listed in the Tactical Index at the back of this book under categories such as pins, forks, discoveries, skewers, and so on. And should you find an unfamilar technical term, or one you may have forgotten, you can review its definition in the Glossary. Finally, another back-of-the-book listing, Opening Name Index, includes most known double King-pawn openings and the textbook moves characterizing them. Check this if you want to see the "textbook" versions of the more common scenarios this book covers.

Some Important General Comments

As you read along, you may wonder why this book contains such emphasis on double King-pawn openings. In other words, why do all the examples in this book begin with White playing his King-pawn from e2 to e4, and with Black ritually responding with his King-pawn from e7 to e5?

The reason is quite simple. Double King-pawn openings stress the principles of open games. Open games, open positions, and open centers facilitate piece activity, King safety, and central movement.

A game, position, or center is generally open if at least two pawns—one for White and one for Black—are exchanged off the board, so that the pieces can move freely and quickly through the center. Double King-pawn openings either lead to an exchange of central pawns (usually White's d-pawn for Black's e-pawn) or retain the possibility of such an exchange right into the middle game. The opposite of an open game is a closed game, where the center is typically blocked and immobilized by four interlocked pawns, two of White's and two of Black's. In such a game, an exchange of central pawns is unlikely.

Open games are direct and immediate, and much easier to understand than closed games. Closed games are subtler and slower, and therefore harder to understand and play. Open games bristle with attacks, threats, and traps. Closed games demand long-term plans and deliberate maneuvers, and they often intimidate beginners. Closed games cannot really be comprehended without considerable experience, whereas open games require much less preparation. So openings that generally produce open positions obviously have more practical value to the student than those of any other kind.

Because double King-pawn openings tend to produce open positions—direct, clear, and easy to understand—it is fairly standard thinking that the study of openings should start with them. What you must know to play better chess is illustrated powerfully in double King-pawn openings.

Unless you have unlimited study time, I do not recommend that you try to learn all openings at once. There are just too many, and at a general level the principles that predominate in one group seem to contradict the principles emphasized in another. (This is not always so at a higher level.)

So if different opening systems are studied simultaneously, it's easy to become confused. It takes time to employ new concepts that appear antithetical to those already learned.

Quick victories are a lot of fun and usually remembered, especially when you are on the winning side. I am reminded of the succinct description of learning given by the Czech educator Jan Amos Komensky (1592–1670): "Through play, knowledge." Can there be a more cogent chess lesson than refuting your opponent's illogical error and winning a game in ten moves? You will find 202 ways to do just that in this book. So win away—and be brilliant.

Algebraic Notation

The games in this book are given in algebraic notation, which is a system to record chess moves used throughout the world. The essence of each example can be grasped without playing out the moves, by examining the diagrammed position and reading the descriptive comments in the Scenario and Interpretation. But you will improve faster if you learn the simplified algebraic notation offered here. The system works as follows:

- The board is regarded as an eight-by-eight graph with sixty-four squares in all.
- The files (the rows of squares going up the board) are lettered a through h, beginning from White's left.
- The ranks (the rows of squares going across the board) are numbered 1 through 8, beginning from White's nearest row. You can therefore identify any square by combining a letter and a number, with the letter written first (see Diagram A). For example, the square on which White's King stands in the original position is e1, while the original square for Black's King is e8. All squares are always named from White's point of view.

Black

a8	b8	c8	d8	e8	f8	g8	h8
a7	b7	c7	d7	e7	f7	g7	h7
a6	b6	c6	d6	e6	f6	g6	h6
a5	b5	c5	d5	e5	f5	g5	h5
a4	b4	c4	d4	e4	f4	g4	h4
a3	b3	c3	d3	e3	f3	g3	h3
a2	b2	c2	d2	e2	f2	g2	h2
a1	b1	c1	d1	e1	f1	g1	h1

A

White

Symbols You Should Know

K   King
Q   Queen
R   Rook
B   Bishop
N   Knight

Pawns are not symbolized when recording the moves. But if referred to in discussions, they are named by the letter of the file occupied. Thus a pawn on the c-file is a c-pawn. A pawn on c5 is the c5-pawn. If a pawn makes a capture, one merely indicates the file the capturing pawn starts on. If a White pawn on b2 captures a Black pawn, Knight, Bishop, Rook, or Queen on a3, it is written **bxa3**. In indicating a capture, the square captured is named, not the enemy unit. To distinguish like pieces, or sometimes for emphasis, the names of pieces may be linked to the occupied square by a hyphen. A Knight occupying c3 is the c3-Knight, a Bishop occupying g4 is the g4-Bishop, and so on. (A further distinction between Kingside and Queenside is sometimes useful. A Knight starting the game on the Queenside squares b1 or b8 is a Queen-Knight. A Bishop beginning on the Kingside squares f1 or f8 is a King-Bishop.)

Other Symbols You Should Know

×	capture
+	check
0-0	castles Kingside
0-0-0	castles Queenside
!	good move
!!	very good move
?	questionable move
??	blunder
?!	risky move but worth considering
!?	probably a good move but unclear
1.	White's first move

1. . .   Black's first move (when appearing independently of White's

2.   White's second move

2. . . .   Black's second move

(1–0)   White wins

(0–1)   Black wins

Reading the Line Score of a Game

Consider the shortest chess game possible. The four moves of this game are given in Diagrams B through E.

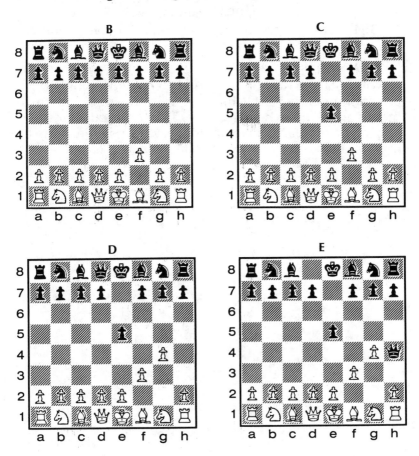

The same game could be written:

> **1. f3? e5   2. g4?? Qh4** mate

1. f3?	means that White's first move is pawn to f3. The question mark after the move indicates that it is not good. This move is shown in Diagram B.
e5	means that Black's first move is pawn to e5. This move is shown in Diagram C.
2. g4??	means that White's second move is pawn to g4, which is a blunder. This move is shown in Diagram D.
Qh4 mate	means that Black's second move is Queen to h4, which is mate. This move is shown in Diagram E.

Note that the number of the move is written only once, appearing just before White's play. In this book, the main moves are given in **boldface** type. The analyzed alternatives appear in regular type. Sometimes these suggestions are in parentheses.

CHESS OPENINGS:

TRAPS AND ZAPS

1

The Early d2-d4 Complex

Center Game
Danish Gambit
Goring Gambit
Scotch Gambit
Scotch Game

The openings of Chapter 1 are characterized by an early advance of White's d-pawn to d4, which pries open the center while also opening lines for rapid deployment of the pieces. For the developing student, this group of openings is an excellent training ground in tactics and active piece play.

In the *Center Game* (1. **e4 e5** 2. **d4 exd4** 3. **Qxd4**) White contents himself with knocking out the e5-pawn, Black's foothold in the center. White then regains this pawn by capturing on d4 with his Queen. Such an early Queen move is theoretically a liability, and after 3. . . . Nc6, White indeed must back the Queen out of the center, losing time. Despite this drawback, the Center Game offers White reasonably good chances, and Black must play energetically in midcourt to secure equality.

The *Danish Gambit* (1. **e4 e5**. 2. **d4 exd4** 3. **c3 dxc3** 4. **Bc4 cxb2** 5. **Bxb2**) is an entirely different kettle of fish. Here, White sacrifices two pawns to accelerate development. This is not a humble opening, and if White fails to generate sufficient attacking possibilities, he will

will simply be two pawns down with no compensation. Black, lacking development, must defend carefully. Rather than clinging too greedily to his extra pawns, he should return one or both of them to mobilize his forces. Otherwise, White's attack becomes irresistible.

The *Goring Gambit* (1. **e4 e5** 2. **Nf3 Nc6** 3. **d4 exd4** 4. **c3**) is closely related to the Danish Gambit, with the accent again on expeditious development. Here, White generally restricts himself to sacrificing only one pawn, thus minimizing much of the risk entailed in the Danish. Black, in theory, ought to be able to grab the pawn and endure White's attack. In practice, however, it's not so easy to keep White off his back.

The *Scotch Gambit* (1. **e4 e5** 2. **Nf3 Nc6** 3. **d4 exd4** 4. **Bc4**) resembles the Goring Gambit, with the sacrifice of a single pawn for speedy development. Exactly what constitutes a Scotch Gambit is not so clear to the casual player. In practice, this opening almost always transposes into other openings: Two Knights Defense, Max Lange Attack, Giuoco Piano, and even the Goring Gambit. It is often perceived as a transitional opening leading to a complex of related openings. One might play it to disguise one's true intentions.

The *Scotch Game* (1. **e4 e5** 2. **Nf3 Nc6** 3. **d4 exd4** 4. **Nxd4**) is White's attempt to enjoy the benefits of the Center Game without incurring its disadvantage: the premature exposure of White's Queen. With a pawn on e4 and a Knight on d4, White has the makings of a powerfully centralized game, and Black must conscientiously combine development and counterattack before White consolidates these assests into a concrete, permanent advantage. In theory, Black can pound away at squares e4 and d4, shaking White's grip on the center and ultimately achieving the freeing advance of his Queen-pawn from d7 to d5. This spirited thrust will allow Black to enter the middlegame on an even keel.

1

IN-BETWEEN MOVE

Center Game

1. e4	e5
2. d4	exd4
3. Qxd4	Nf6
4. Bg5	Be7
5. e5?	

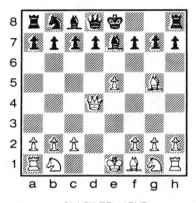

BLACK TO MOVE

Scenario: White wants to attack the f6-Knight, but he overlooked **5. . . . Nc6,** assailing White's Queen and e-pawn. There are three safe squares for the Queen that also defend the pawn: c3, e3, and f4. If 6. Qc3, then 6. . . . Bb4 pins White's Queen to its King. If 6. Qe3, then 6. . . . Ng4 7. Qe4 (or 7. Bxe7 Qxe7 8. Qe4 Ngxe5) 7. . . . Ngxe5 gains the e5-pawn. And if 6. Qf4, then 6. . . . Nh5 7. Qf3 (or 7. Bxe7 Qxe7 wins the e-pawn next move) 7. . . . Bxg5 8. Qxh5 Bc1 9.Nd2 Bxb2 10. Rb1 Bxe5 puts Black two pawns ahead.

Interpretation: White's second move, d2-d4, is designed to take control of the center, but the plan could backfire. White's Queen can be sucked into the central zone prematurely, after which it is subject to harassment from Black's developing army. Instead of the unprepared advance 5.e5, White should have brought out his b1-Knight, defending his e4-pawn. Afterward, he may be able to castle Queenside. Don't start attacking if you can't follow through with muscle. First build your game by rapid development. Then feast on your opponent's targets and weaknesses. Moreover, don't rely too much on the Queen. Before bringing it out, develop a couple of minor pieces.

2

PIN

Center Game

1. e4   e5
2. d4   exd4
3. Qxd4   Nc6
4. Qa4   Nf6
5. Nc3   d5
6. Bg5   dxe4
7. Nxe4   Qe7
8. 0-0-0   Qxe4

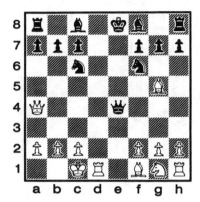

WHITE TO MOVE

Scenario: Black's Queen seems protected by his f6-Knight, but not forever. White disrupts with 9. **Rd8 + !**. Black's c6-Knight can't take White's Rook because it's pinned to Black's King by White's Queen. If 9. . . .**Kxd8** (or 9. . . .Ke7   10. Qxe4 +) 10. **Qxe4**, then Black's f6-Knight, now in a pin, cannot take the Queen back. Black says good-bye to his Queen.

Interpretation: If your King is still uncastled, avoid opening the center, giving your opponent some access to your fettered monarch. And at the very least, don't initiate risky captures that aid the enemy's attack. Black gauged that his Queen was adequately guarded by the f6-Knight after 8. . . .Qxe4, but he neglected to consider what White's Rook check could do. Before inaugurating a combination or sequence of moves, try to evaluate the consequences of all your opponent's reasonable checks. They could force you to change your plans completely.

3

IN-BETWEEN MOVE

Center Game

1. e4	e5
2. d4	exd4
3. Qxd4	Nc6
4. Qe3	g6
5. Nc3	Bg7
6. Nd5	Nge7
7. Ne2	d6
8. Bd2	Bxb2
9. Bc3	Bxa1

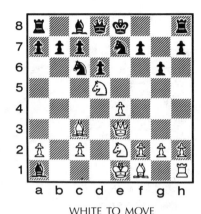

WHITE TO MOVE

Scenario: Black probably expects White to take his dark-square Bishop, which has grabbed White's Rook, but life isn't always tit for tat. Rather than capture on a1, White's rude Knight intercedes with a check, 10. **Nf6+**. After the obligatory 10. . . . **Kf8**, White ends Black's torment with 11. **Qh6** mate.

Interpretation: When you've flanked your King's Bishop, you probably can't exchange it away without incurring Kingside weaknesses. Especially vulnerable are the squares traveled by the Bishop—for Black, the dark squares. The f6 and h6 squares are already weakened here by the g7-pawn's early advance. Once Black's dark-square Bishop also is shut out, those squares become indefensible. That's why it's prudent to think hard before exchanging the flanked King's Bishop, even if it wins a pawn. If you can get away with it, fine; but here, White actually wins by exploiting the undefended f6 with a Knight and also the abandoned h6 with his Queen. Be chary about early, impulsive pawn moves since they ususally bring on enemy attack. As Marcus Aurelius put it, "What is not good for the swarm is not good for the bee."

4

MATING ATTACK

Center Game

1. e4	e5
2. d4	exd4
3. Qxd4	Nc6
4. Qe3	Bb4+
5. c3	Ba5
6. Bc4	Nge7
7. Qg3	0-0
8. h4	Ng6

WHITE TO MOVE

Scenario: Black has castled into a furious assault. No prisoners are taken after 9. **h5**, driving away Black's Kingside shelter. If the g6-Knight flees to e7, then 10. Bh6 capitalizes on a debilitating pin. So Black continues 9. . . .Nge5, when 10. Bg5! pushes Black's Queen to a meaningless square, 10. . . .Qe8, making it impossible for that piece to lend defense from f6. And here came more surprises, for 11. Bf6 g6 12. hxg6 Nxg6 is refuted by 13. Qxg6+! hxg6 14. Rh8 mate.

Interpretation: Black's troubles were manifold. Though tactically the early b4-Bishop check works out fine, it weakens Black's Kingside, especially the square g7. In the final position, White's dark-square Bishop runs roughshod over g7 and h8, made possible by Black's aloof dark-square Bishop placement. The King-Knight's defensive abilities are also not so good from square e7. It would have been more enterprising to develop this piece to f6. Black, too, castles into a powerful attack force spearheaded by the h-pawn. Moving it up, White introduces his h1-Rook with deadly effect. Near the end, White's c4-Bishop holds the key, for it pins Black's f7 pawn, preventing it from capturing on g6. It's amazing that Black lasts even fourteen moves.

5

FORK

Center Game

1. e4   e5
2. d4   exd4
3. Qxd4   Nc6
4. Qe3   Nf6
5. Bc4   Ne5
6. Bb3   Bb4 +
7. c3   Bc5
8. Qg3?

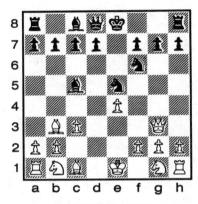

BLACK TO MOVE

Scenario: Black lays a trap, and White falls into it. White's Queen is history after 8. . . . **Bxf2 + !**, forking White's King and Queen. No matter what White answers, his Queen goes: (A) 9.Qxf2 Nd3 +, Knight-forking White's King and Queen; (B) 9. Kxf2 Nxe4 +, again Knight-forking White's royal pair.

Interpretation: White bought a couple of bad raps here. First, he should have answered Black's fourth-move b4-Bishop check by 5. Bd2. It's usual to respond to a premature check by the King-Bishop by blocking with a pawn. That compels the Bishop to move again to save itself, which causes your opponent to waste a turn. So White naturally responded with 7.c2-c3. This mechanical move weakened the d3 square, leaving it without pawn protection. In one of the winning lines, Black's e5-Knight exploits this square. White could have avoided loss of his Queen even after that, however, for there was no need to play 8.Qe3-g3. The simple retreat 4. Qe3-e2 would have averted disaster. One might play White's final blunder, 8. Qe3-g3, because it is natural to move the Queen aggressively, since its great power is always uppermost in the mind. But in the opening, the Queen's value actually makes it a liability. Bring it out early and your opponent can attack it and force you to waste time saving it. Don't develop the Queen early without a good reason.

6

REMOVING THE GUARD

Center Game

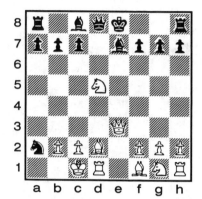

WHITE TO MOVE

1. e4	e5
2. d4	exd4
3. Qxd4	Nc6
4. Qe3	Nf6
5. Nc3	Be7
6. Bd2	d5
7. exd5	Nb4
8. 0-0-0	Nfxd5
9. Nxd5	Nxa2 +

Scenario: White's move, 10. **Kb1**, is forced, but it wins. Black has to save his threatened a2-Knight, 10. . . . .**Qxd5**, but after 11. **b3 Nb4**, White flings an unexpected shock at his adversary: 12. **Qxe7 +!** **Kxe7** 13. **Bxb4+ Ke6** 14. **Bc4**. In the end, White stays a piece ahead.

Interpretation: Black got terribly greedy while his King was in the center, where White's S.W.A.T team could get at it. Knight-pawns and Rook-pawns tend to bring on a hullabaloo. Too often, taking them means putting your pieces out of play, wasting time, and pushing your King out on a high wire. Black was doing fine until he got sidetracked by White's a2-pawn. But a simple recapture on d5 restores his excellent chances.

7

TRAPPED PIECE

Center Gambit

1. e4	e5
2. d4	exd4
3. Bc4	Qh4
4. Qe2	Bb4 +
5. c3	dxc3
6. bxc3	Bc5
7. Nf3	Qh5

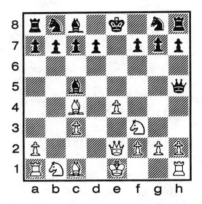

WHITE TO MOVE

Scenario: Black's Queen wobbles on the board's edge—an area where her mobility is restricted. White tackles her poor position with a series of troublesome threats. The starting move is 8. **g4!**. Black can try to save his Queen in several ways: (A) 8. . . .Qg6 9. Ne5, and after Black's Queen moves, White's Knight takes on f7 and then on h8; (B) 8. . . .Qxg4 9. Bxf7 + Kf8 (if instead 9. . . .Kxf7, then 10. Ne5 + forks King and Queen) 10. Rg1 Qh3 11. Rg3, and Black's Queen falls; (C) 8. . . .Qh3 9. Bxf7 + Kf8 10. Rg1, followed by 11. Rg3, again trapping and winning Black's Queen.

Interpretation: Inexperienced players are prone to early Queen sorties. They get it out there for impractical reasons. In the opening, the odds are a developed Queen will become a liability instead of a strength, so often the Queen is best left well enough alone on its home square in the early stages. Naturally, this rule like any other has limitations and exceptions. Black's third move, Qd8-h4, though respectable, suggests that Black does not understand how to use his Queen. His real error came at move 7, when his Queen treaded into no-man's-land. Had he played Qh4-e7 instead, the chances in the position would have been about even. In the opening, don't bring out your Queen early without clear and specific reasons. Try to develop your minor pieces first. As an old West Fourth Street (New York) park player used to say, "The Queen is a symphony. Play your preludes first."

8

MATING ATTACK

Center Gambit

1. e4	e5
2. d4	exd4
3. Nf3	Bb4 +
4. c3	dxc3
5. bxc3	Bc5
6. Bc4	d5
7. Bxd5	Qf6
8. Bg5	Qg6

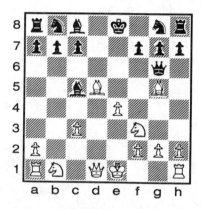

WHITE TO MOVE

Scenario: Black has put his head into the lion's mouth and the jaws are about to close. After 9. **Bxf7 + ! Kf8** (getting mated by 9. . . .Qxf7 10. Qd8 and losing the Queen by 9. . . .Kxf7 10. Ne5 + are not particularly appealing to Black either) 10. **Qd8 + Kxf7** 11. **Ne5 + Ke6**, White has the convenient 12. **Qd5** mate.

Interpretation: Black did some questionable things and White answered with a mating attack. Black's Bishop-check on move 3 was not lucrative, since the piece had to move again after it was attacked. Better to get out the King-Knight first instead of the King-Bishop (remember, Knights before Bishops). And why budge the Queen on move 7? Even though it would not greatly improve his game, Black should have developed his g8-Knight instead. The Queen should be handled like fine china. It must receive careful development. You may think the Queen is the one piece you know how to use, but you're probably wrong. How can you understand the Queen when the pieces that truly constitute the Queen's power—the Rook and Bishop—escape your notice? Chess is pure reason; you can't get anywhere without reason in chess. "As it isn't, it ain't. That's logic," said Tweedledee in Lewis Carroll's *Alice in Wonderland*.

9

MATING ATTACK

Danish Gambit

1. e4	e5
2. d4	exd4
3. c3	dxc3
4. Bc4	Bb4
5. bxc3	Be7?

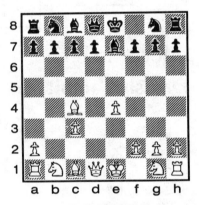

WHITE TO MOVE

Scenario: Black's last move, 5. . . . Be7, is a bleating mistake, for he could not afford to block the e7 square because his Queen might have had needed access to protect f7. White forces a winning game by 6. **Qd5**, when Black can't defend f7 with 6. . . . Nh6, for White merely captures the h6-Knight with his c1-Bishop; and Black can't recapture on h6 because mate at f7 would still be menaced. Black can avoid mate, 6. . . . **d6**, but after 7. **Qxf7+ Kd7** 8. **Qf5+ Ke8** (the blunder 8. . . . Kc6 permits 9. Qb5 mate) 9. **Bf7+ Kf8** 10. **Be6+ Nf6** 11. **Bxc8**, White is a piece ahead.

Interpretation: If you have extra material, sometimes you can give some of or all of it back and end up with an equal or better position. When your opponent takes back your material, he must cede at least one move to do that. If you can build your game while he's capturing, you should wrest away the initiative. If the position is reasonable, at the very least you will blunt his attack. Black might have taken some of the sting out of White's assault if he had essayed 4. . . . d7-d5. That gives back a pawn, but in exchange Black opens the c8-Bishop's diagonal and forces White to block d5 with either the c4-Bishop or the e4-pawn. White could also capture on d5 with his Queen, but that leads to a Queen trade, which is frowned upon when one is materially behind.

10

DOUBLE ATTACK

Danish Gambit

1. e4	e5
2. d4	exd4
3. c3	dxc3
4. Bc4	cxb2
5. Bxb2	Bb4 +
6. Kf1	Nf6
7. e5	d5
8. Bb5 +	Bd7

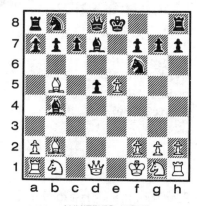

WHITE TO MOVE

Scenario: Black didn't peer far enough ahead. He saw that on 9. Bxd7 + he has 9. . . . Nxd7, saving his Knight. He also perceived that 9. exf6 enables him to strike back with 9. . . . Bxb5 +. What he didn't see, however, was White's remote Queen roundabout 9. **Qa4!**. This shot defends the b5-Bishop while placing two of Black's pieces, the b4-Bishop and f6-Knight, under the gun. Black must lose at least a piece.

Interpretation: Black's fifth move, 5. . . . Bb4 +, was not the best. After sidestepping this Bishop-check, 6. Kf1, Black was confronted with problems. He needed to defend his g-pawn, secure his b4-Bishop out there by itself, and develop his game more. He should have returned the extra pawns to establish a dynamically balanced position. Instead of the risky 5. . . . Bb4+, Black should have inserted the counterthrust 5. . . . d7-d5. After 6. Bxd5, he could play 6. . . . Nf6. If White didn't react vigorously from here (6. Bxf7+), Black could even have gotten the upperhand. Use your advantages. If you have material in exchange for your opponent's attack, don't be afraid to surrender the material to come away with the initiative. In the opening, the ability to attack generally outweighs the extra pawn. It's often the other way around in the endgame, but you don't get that far if you're mated in ten moves. "You cannot find a medicine for life when once a man is dead"—Ibycus.

11

SKEWER

Danish Gambit

1. e4	e5
2. d4	exd4
3. c3	dxc3
4. Bc4	cxb2
5. Bxb2	Bb4+
6. Kf1	Nf6
7. e5	d5
8. Bb5+	Nd7

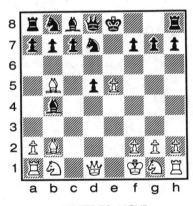

WHITE TO MOVE

Scenario: Black is temporarily two pawns ahead but it's White's move, a critical reality here for the second player. After 9. **Qg4**, White double-attacks the g7-pawn and b4-Bishop. Black could guard both by 9. . . . **Bf8**, though 10. **e6! fxe6** 11. **Qh5+ Ke7** (he could also lose handily with 11. . . . **g6** 12. **Qh3 Rg8** 13. **Qxe6+**, followed by capturing the Rook on g8) 12. **Ba3+ c5** 13. **Bxc5+!**

Nxc5 14. **Qg5+** skewers King and Queen, picking up Black's Queen on the next move.

Interpretation: White is too well developed for Black to get away unscathed if he tries to hold the gambited material this way. Best for Black is 8. . . . c6. White's ninth move, Qd1-g4, is an attempt to refute Black's fifth move, Bishop's check Bf8-b4+. White's Queen sally attacks both points made vulnerable by Black's Bishop move: the g7-pawn and the b4-Bishop itself. With White's Queen and two Bishops bearing down on Black's naked King's position, a deadly attack is inevitable. You can't neglect development and the King's safety in the opening. Avoid pointless checks as you would a bad habit—which is what they are.

12

SAVING BY CAPTURING

Danish Gambit

1. e4	e5
2. d4	exd4
3. c3	dxc3
4. Bc4	cxb2
5. Bxb2	Nf6
6. e5	Qe7
7. Qe2	d5

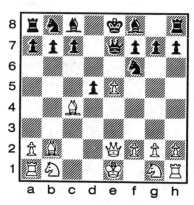

WHITE TO MOVE

Scenario: White wins a piece forthwith: 8. **exf6**, attacking Black's Queen. If Black answers 8. . . . gxf6, then White has a free move to ply his c4-Bishop to safety, leaving him a piece up. And if Black responds 8. . . . Qxe2+, looking to capture White's c4-Bishop after trading Queens, White disappoints him by taking Black's Queen, then on e2, with his c4-Bishop, thus getting the Bishop out of trouble. Black winds up a piece down.

Interpretation: In chess, forces and circumstances that prevail on one move may vary with the next. Black thought he could save himself by first exchanging Queens and then capturing his booty, the c4-Bishop, not realizing that the very action that wins the Bishop—the Queen trade—provides the means for that Bishop's salvation. From move to move, you have to approach the resulting position as if seeing it for the first time, even though you envisioned the outcome on the previous move. What you previewed may bear little relation to reality. "There is many a slip 'twixt the cup and the lip"—ancient proverb.

13

MATING ATTACK

Danish Gambit

1. e4	e5
2. d4	exd4
3. c3	dxc3
4. Bc4	cxb2
5. Bxb2	Nf6
6. Nc3	Bb4
7. Ne2	Nxe4
8. 0-0	Nxc3
9. Nxc3	Bxc3
10. Bxc3	0-0

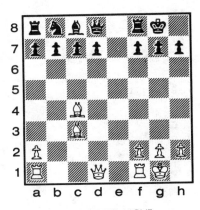

WHITE TO MOVE

Scenario: Black has grabbed one pawn too many, and now White's position is a honed attacking machine. Mate happens after 11. **Qg4 g6** 12. **Qd4.** Since Black's f7-pawn is pinned by White's c4-Bishop, Black cannot block out White's Queen and Bishop battery along the a1-h8 diagonal. Mate follows shortly on either g7 or h8.

Interpretation: The best way to break White's mounting assault in this line is to sacrifice a pawn or two back, as in the line 5. . . .

d5 6. Bxd5 Nf6 7. Bxf7+ Kxf7 8. Qxd8 Bb4+ 9. Qd2 Qxd2+ 10. Nxd2. The position is then materially even, with Black having more pawns on the Queenside and White having more on the Kingside. Essentially, the asymmetrical position has achieved dynamic balance, and both players have a chance to win. Sometimes having an extra pawn or two means being able to surrender the additional material at your opponent's expense in position. Afterward, the situation may be materially even, but you might have the better game. For example, you may come away with the initiative, especially if your opponent has to sacrifice a few moves to win back the material he sacrificed earlier.

14

FORK

Danish Gambit

1. e4	e5
2. d4	exd4
3. c3	dxc3
4. Bc4	cxb2
5. Bxb2	d5
6. Bxd5	Nf6
7. Nc3	Nxd5
8. Nxd5	c6?

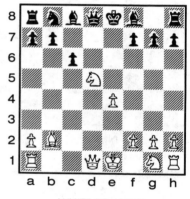

WHITE TO MOVE

Scenario: Black's last pawn push is deceptively playable. After 9. Nf6!+ gxf6 10. Qxd8+ Kxd8 11. Bxf6+, White wins the h8-Rook next move, putting him an exchange up (White would have a Rook for a minor piece). A mistake is 9. . . . Ke7, for real trouble brews with 10. Ba3+ Ke6 11. Qg4+ Kxf6 12. e5+ Kxe5 13. Nf3+ Kf6 14. Qg5+, when 14. . . . Ke6 15. Qe5+ Kd7 16. 0-0-0+ Bd6 17. Qxd6+ Ke8 18. Qxd8 is mate.

Interpretation: Black reasons the pressure on his game would lessen after trading his f6-Knight for White's light-square Bishop.

When under attack, the principle suggests trading pieces to reduce the power of the enemy's assault force. Superficially consistent with this is the advance 8. . . . c7-c6. Black hopes to drive back White's d5-Knight and then reduce his opponent's threats considerably by trading Queen for Queen along the d-file. Unfortunately, White is able to sacrifice his Knight with a gain of time, enabling a Queen-trade to take place under conditions more favorable for White than Black anticipated. Black thereby lacks time to waste on pawn moves. Instead of 8. . . . c7-c6, he should develop a new piece, say 8. . . . Nb8-c6, which will also defend his Queen, though White can still attack afterward. If you accept an opening gambit, you might have to skate on thin ice to survive to a middlegame.

15

SKEWER

Danish Gambit

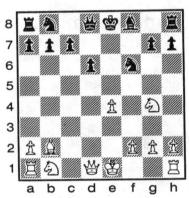

1. e4	e5
2. d4	exd4
3. c3	dxc3
4. Bc4	cxb2
5. Bxb2	d6
6. Nf3	Bg4
7. Bxf7 +	Kxf7
8. Ne5 +	Ke8
9. Nxg4	Nf6

WHITE TO MOVE

Scenario: Black can kiss this game good-bye. After 10. **Nxf6 + gxf6** 11. **Qh5 + Ke7** (or 11. . . . Kd7 12. Qf5 +, and White devastates on the next move with Bb2xf6) 12. **Bxf6 +! Kxf6** 13. **Qh4 +**, White forces Black's King off the h4-d8 diagonal, skewering the opposing Queen.

Interpretation: Black really does himself wrong in this example. He grabs a couple of pawns while sacrificing development, and instead of giving a pawn or two back to complete his own development and blunt White's attack, he tries the premature Bishop sortie 6. . . . Bc8-g4. The principle is "Knights before Bishops," meaning that one should generally activate at least one Knight before moving a Bishop. Of course this guideline cannot be followed rigidly, and some opening systems do break this principle without incurring problems, but it is still something to heed. By violating the principle here, Black postpones the chance to castle Kingside, and that earns him real trouble. Once White's Queen checks at h5, Black is clearly losing.

16

DEFLECTION

Danish Gambit

1. e4	e5
2. d4	exd4
3. c3	dxc3
4. Nxc3	Bb4
5. Qd4	Nc6
6. Qxg7	Qf6
7. e5	Ne4

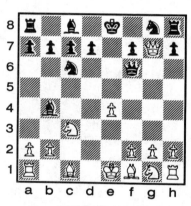

WHITE TO MOVE

Scenario: Black has found a way to save his h8-Rook—temporarily. After 7. **Bh6!**, Black has two unsatisfactory captures of the h6-Bishop. Both 7. . . . Qxh6   8. Qxh8 as well as 7. . . . Nxh6   8. Qxf6 win big material for White. So Black continues 7. . . . **d6**, whereupon White garners a piece by 8. **Qxf6 Nxf6   9. Bg7**, forking Black's f6-Knight and h8-Bishop.

Interpretation: Normally, one doesn't act wisely bringing one's Queen out early, but after Black's premature Bishop development, 4. . . . Bb4, White's Queen counter 5. Qd4 assails the b4-Bishop and the g7-pawn it abandoned. That g7 square proved to be Black's bête noire, for both White's Queen and dark-square Bishop later on enjoyed occupying it. Black played 4. . . . Bf8-b4 hoping to trade pieces, which is the recommended course of action when ahead in material. Thus, on move 5, Black should exchange his Bishop for the c3-Knight. But all exchanges must be reasonable, and certainly not made in violation of principle. The guideline is "Knights before Bishops." Thus, better than moving his dark-square Bishop, Black should centralize his Knight, Nb8-c6. Such a move would also prevent White's Queen from utilizing the center, avoiding and nullifying the possibility of White's winning tactic.

17

FORK

Goring Gambit

1. e4	e5
2. Nf3	Nc6
3. d4	exd4
4. c3	dxc3
5. Nxc3	Bb4
6. Bc4	Nf6

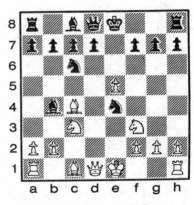

WHITE TO MOVE

Scenario: Just when Black thought he had significant pressure against White's c3, he finds that his opponent forces the win of material. After 8. **Qd5**, Black must—and he can't—satisfactorily deal with the mate threat at f7 and somehow save his unprotected and menaced e4-Knight. It's not in the chess pieces, and White gains the e4-Knight.

Interpretation: Black's 5. . . .Bb4 is somewhat ambitious, since White has a considerable initiative at that point. Black might have played more conservatively with 5. . . .d7-d6, opening the light-square Bishop's diagonal and guarding against and ef-e5 push. Black courted further trouble by playing 6. . . .Ng8-f6. His final move, 7. . . .Nf6-e4?, just loses a piece without compensation. He had to play 7. . . .d7-d5. The best way to refute a gambit is rapid, purposeful counterdevelopment. Development for development's sake will not do it.

18

FORK

Goring Gambit

1. e4	e5
2. Nf3	Nc6
3. d4	exd4
4. c3	dxc3
5. Nxc3	Bc5
6. Bc4	d6
7. Qb3	Qd7
8. Nd5	Na5

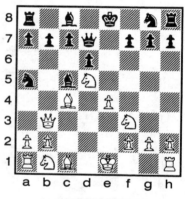

WHITE TO MOVE

Scenario: Black's last move may look good, for it double-attacks White's Queen and c4-Bishop. But Black has two vulnerable points: the unguarded a5-Knight and g7-pawn. White answers 9. **Qc3!**, menacing both captures. Black must save his Knight, 9. . . .Nxc4, but rather than recapture, White plunders the Kingside with 10. **Qxg7.** After 10. . . .Qg4 11. **Qxh8 Qxg2** 12. **Qxg8+! Qxg8** 13. **Nf6+**, White soon emerges the exchange ahead.

Interpretation: Black plays 8. . . .Na5, wishing to trade pieces, for he is a pawn ahead. When up material, do exchange pieces to emphasize your advantage and to reduce the possibility of counterattack. The fewer pieces your opponent has, the harder it is for him to develop attacking compensation. The reasoning in playing 8. . . .Na5 is sound, but it places a Knight on an undefended square on the edge. And Black has an additional weakness at g7, which is no longer guarded by the dark-square Bishop, now outside the pawn chain at c5. Black's real error is that he's not ready for hand-to-hand combat; he's too undeveloped. Don't get into heavy fighting until your King is safe and your pieces are ready for action. The counterattack could kill you. "Then the Grasshopper knew it is best to prepare for days of necessity"—Aesop.

19

KING HUNT

Scotch Gambit

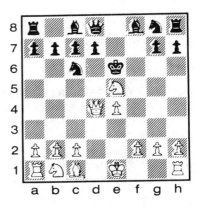

1. e4	e5
2. Nf3	Nc6
3. d4	exd4
4. Bc4	Na5?
5. Bxf7+	Kxf7
6. Ne5+	Ke6
7. Qxd4	Nc6?

WHITE TO MOVE

Scenario: How many moves can Black afford to waste in an opening? He's moved his c6-Knight three times to be where it could get after one move. Black's King has had it: 8. **Qd5+ Kf6** 9. **Qf7+ Kxe5** 10. **Bf4+ Kxe4** 11. **Nc3+ Kd4** 12. **Qd5 mate.**

Interpretation: Black's Knight-jaunts on moves 4 and 7 ceded two important tempi to his opponent. At least Black could have stopped White's menaced d5-Queen check by 7. . . .c7-c6 or 7. . . .Ng8-f6. Kings shouldn't lead the charge in any kind of war. In chess, once a King is separated from its supporting forces, mate is almost always inevitable. "They are no kings, though they possess the crown"—Daniel Defoe.

20

MULTIPLE ATTACK

Scotch Gambit

1. e4	e5
2. Nf3	Nc6
3. d4	exd4
4. Bc4	Bc5
5. Ng5	Nh6
6. Qh5	Ne5?

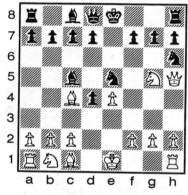

WHITE TO MOVE

Scenario: White sacrifices a pawn to speed development. Black has as many pieces out as White, but they are not all as well disposed: two lined up on the 5th rank and the other on the edge at h6. White pierces Black's veneer with 7. **Ne6!**, when 7. . . . **dxe6** 8. **Qxe5** points out Black's disarray and attendant helplessness. White then threatens to capture on c5, g7, and h6—any of which would put White a piece ahead. There is no defense to all three forays.

Interpretation: On his sixth move, instead of defending with a Knight already in play, moving it a second time, Black would better have brought out a new piece. He should have defended f7 by 6. . . . Qe7, which includes an element of counterplay against White's e4-pawn as well. Time is so critical in the opening that you absolutely cannot waste a single move. Unless the position dictates otherwise, try to transport a different piece on each move, to increase the potential of your entire corps. It takes little to swing the pendulum one way or the other, and an extra developed piece might provide the push.

21

SKEWER

Scotch Gambit

1. e4	e5
2. Nf3	Nc6
3. d4	exd4
4. Bc4	Bc5
5. 0-0	Nge7
6. Ng5	d5
7. exd5	Ne5?
8. Bb3	h6
9. Ne4	Bb6
10. h3	Nxd5?

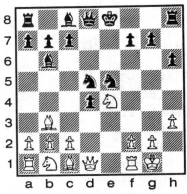

WHITE TO MOVE

Scenario: White is already securely positioned: he is castled and not immediately endangered. The center of the board is clear of pawns. Because Black's King is uncastled and his pieces loose and flimsily placed, White's initiative spells disaster for him. The winning move is 11. **Qh5!**, garnering a piece. If Black's e5-Knight moves, his d5-Knight could be double-attacked and captured. He can't protect the e5-Knight with his f-pawn because White's Queen pins it to its King. If Black's Queen guards the e5-Knight from e7, then the d5-Knight hangs to White's b3-Bishop. Bye-bye, piece.

Interpretation: Moving Black's King-Knight to e7 meant the f7 square would be difficult to guard. This later gave White the chance for a decisive coup. Note that Black couldn't have safely castled on move 6. White then would gain advantage by moving his Queen to h5, or by exchanging Bishop and Knight for Rook and pawn on the f7 square. After the last capture, White's Queen forks Black's King at f7 and his c5-Bishop, ensuring superiority. It was a serious error for Black to put his Knight on e7. If he had tried to follow with 7. . . .Nxd5, then 8. Qf3 would give White a tremendous attack.

22

UNPIN

Scotch Gambit

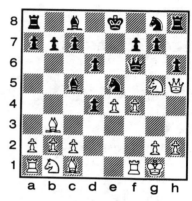

BLACK TO MOVE

1. e4	e5
2. Nf3	Nc6
3. d4	exd4
4. Bc4	Bc5
5. 0-0	d6
6. Ng5	Ne5
7. Bb3	h6
8. Qh5	Qf6
9. f4	

Scenario: White has ignored Black's possible discovered check along the a7-g1 diagonal. He also may think his g5-Knight is not endangered because Black's h-pawn—the unit attacking it—is pinned and not so free to capture. White has evaluated wrongly: 9. . . .d3+ 10. **Kh1 g6** (now Black's Queen defends the h8-Rook) 11. **Qd1 hxg5** 12. **fxe5** (to regain his lost piece) 12. . . .**Rxh2+!** 13. **Kxh2 Qh8+** 14. **Kg3 Qh4+** 15. **Kf3 Qg4** mate.

Interpretation: White overreacted. Just because Black protected f7 on move 6 with a piece already out, instead of bringing out a new piece by 6. . . .Nh6, doesn't mean he necessarily has violated basic opening principles. Moving the c6-Knight again didn't really lose time because White has to waste a move in turn to save his c4-Bishop. Opening principles are helpful aids, but not always absolutes. If chess teachers seem to present them as categoricals, it's only because their fine points are misty. When are they to be followed and when transgressed? Learning how to apply such guidelines is a real art. "Logical consequences are the beacons of wise men"—Thomas Huxley.

23

MATING ATTACK

Scotch Game

1. e4   e5
2. Nf3   Nc6
3. d4   exd4
4. Nxd4   Nge7
5. Nc3   g6
6. Bg5   Bg7
7. Nd5   Bxd4

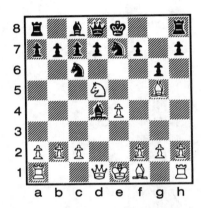

WHITE TO MOVE

Scenario: Right now, Black's vulnerable dark squares are barely held up by the d4-Bishop, but nothing lasts forever. After 8. **Qxd4! 0-0** (8. . . . Nxd4 9.Nf6+ Kf8 10. Bh6 mate) 9. **Nf6+ Kh8** 10. **Ng4+ Nxd4** 11. **Bf6+ Kg8** 12. **Nh6**, Black is mated.

Interpretation: Black hopped his g8-Knight to e7 rather than f6 to keep open the h8-a1 diagonal for his dark-square Bishop. This gave White a freer hand in the center, and pressured Black at once by 6. Bg5 and 7. Nd5. After White sacrificed his Queen for Black's dark-square Bishop, Black's position dismantled, even with his King castled. White's attack proceeded unabated on the dark squares. In the final position, White has taken full advantage of Black's dark-square weaknesses, occupying f6 with a Bishop and h6 with a Knight. Black would have been more sagelike to have developed his King's Bishop along the f8-a3 diagonal, through the center. By posting it on the flank as he did, he weakened his position and wasted time.

24

PROMOTION

Scotch Game

1. e4	e5
2. Nf3	Nc6
3. d4	exd4
4. Nxd4	Be7
5. Bc4	Nf6
6. 0-0	Nxd4
7. Qxd4	d6
8. f4	b6
9. e5	d5
10. Bb5 +	Bd7

WHITE TO MOVE

Scenario: Black thinks he has trick up his sleeve, but first he loses his shirt: 11. **exf6 +** Bc5 (Black was counting on this pin to salvage the game) 12. **Re1 +** Kf8 13. **fxg7 +** Kg8 14. **gxh8/Q**, and Black goes down to mate. He could have been mated just as well on the final move if White had promoted to a Rook instead of a Queen.

Interpretation: You can't neglect development, waste time, or make moves that fuel your opponent's attack in the opening and expect to survive. Black's fourth move, Bf8-e7, is passive but OK, though he later moves the piece again. Black's sixth move, Nc6xd4, moves the Queen-Knight for the second time and is a positional blunder. It doesn't lose material but it lures the White Queen to a powerful central square invulnerable to a shoo-in. Rather than castling on his eighth move, Black plays a totally unnecessary pawn move, b7-b6, guarding c5 and hoping that White doesn't see the possibility of later moving the e7-Bishop to c5, pinning White's Queen. Finally, Black's d6-d5 ninth move, a wild Queen-pawn exercise for the second time, loses a piece. *Time* is what counts in the opening. Don't waste it. "You can ask me for anything you like, except time"—Napoleon Bonaparte.

25

TRAPPED PIECE

Scotch Game

1. e4   e5
2. Nf3   Nc6
3. d4   exd4
4. Nxd4   Qh4
5. Nc3   Nf6
6. Nf5   Qh5

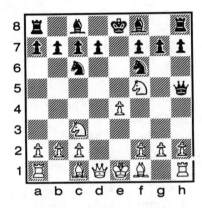

WHITE TO MOVE

Scenario: If you're going to bring out your Queen early, you better be prepared for the consequences. Black's most powerful piece is in hot water after 7. **Be2**, for the retreat 7. . . . Qg6 drops the Queen to 8. Nh4. So Black must cede a piece, 7. . . . .Ng4 8. **Bxg4**, to extricate his Queen.

Interpretation: Black's fifth move is a blatant error. Better was 5. . . . Bf8-b4, pinning the c3-Knight and threatening 6. . . . Qxe4+. The actual move he uses to attack the e4-pawn, Ng8-f6, is milk-toasty enough to give White a chance to grab the offensive with Nd4-f5, which quickly assails the adventurous Black Queen. The f6-Knight poses another difficulty: it blocks the Queen's h4-d8 diagonal retreat. The moral of the story is, if you must walk on the wild side and violate a principle, you'd better play perfectly thereafter. There's no more room for mistakes in this game. The player on the other side probably "never overlooks a mistake, or makes the smallest allowance for ignorance," as Thomas Huxley tells us.

26

MATING ATTACK

Scotch Game

1. e4	e5
2. Nf3	Nc6
3. d4	exd4
4. Nxd4	Qh4
5. Nb5	Bc5
6. Qf3	Nf6
7. Nxc7 +	Kd8
8. Nxa8	Re8
9. Bd3	Nxe4
10. 0-0	

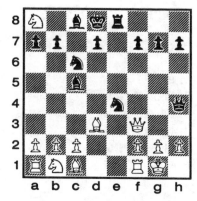

BLACK TO MOVE

Scenario: White has won Black's a8-Rook, but the rest of his ship is sinking swiftly. He has no useful retort to 10. . . .Nxf2, which threatens discovery mayhem. If 11. **Rxf2**, then 11. . . .**Re1 +** 12. **Bf1 Nd4** 13. **Qxf7 Ne2 +** 14. **Kh1 Rxf1 +** 15. **Rxf1 Ng3** is mate. (Black could reverse the pattern by first playing 14. . . .Ng3 +, when 15 Kg1 Rxf1 is also mate.)

Interpretation: This is funny. Black brings out his Queen early but White has to pay for it. That's partly because it's White who has expended time gaining material while neglecting development and King's position. After Black's eighth move, Rh8-e8, Black has five developed pieces to White's two. Moreover, though Black has moved his King, it's actually White's that is the more endangered King, even after castling. All this is easy to understand. White won the a8-Rook, but his g1-Knight needed five moves to get to a8. What chessplayer could recover from that much time loss in an opening? The extra Rook means nothing if you get mated. "I wasted time, and now doth time waste me"—*King Richard II*, William Shakespeare.

27

MATING ATTACK

Scotch Game

1. e4	e5
2. Nf3	Nc6
3. d4	exd4
4. Nxd4	Bc5
5. c3	Nf6
6. Bg5	0-0
7. Bc4	Qe7
8. 0-0	Qxe4
9. Bxf6	gxf6
10. Bd3	Qh4

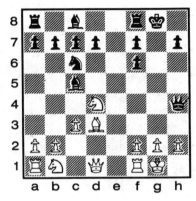

WHITE TO MOVE

Scenario: Black grabs a pawn with his Queen, and now the Queen goes. After 11. **Nf5 Qg5** 12. **h4 Qf4** (12. . . . .Qg6 drops the lady to 13. Ne7+) 13. **g3**, Black's Queen is practically homeless. If she abandons control of g4, say by 13. . . . .Qe5, then 14. Qg4+ mates next move at g7. Black must dump his Queen to thwart mate.

Interpretation: It's the same old story, the fight for the love glory of pilfering a pawn with a Queen. Except this battle almost always ends badly. When Black wins the e4-pawn, 8. . . . .Qxe4, he allows White to mess up his Kingside by 9. Bxf6 gxf6. With the g-file leading clearly to Black's King available to White's Queen, and with White's d3-Bishop and d4-Knight ready to join in, Black's poor Queen plops. The business of the opening is to mobilize the forces, not to hunt pawns; to ensure your King's position, usually by castling; and to build a playable middlegame. Mavericks who avoid these steps, choosing to propel the Queen outward at the start for an onslaught on enemy pawns, had better try some magic spells if they want to get away with it.

28

IN-BETWEEN MOVE

Scotch Game

1. e4   e5
2. Nf3   Nc6
3. d4   exd4
4. Nxd4   Bc5
5. Be3   Qf6
6. c3   Qg6
7. Qe2   Nf6

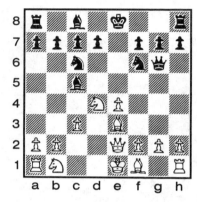

WHITE TO MOVE

Scenario: What's happening? Doesn't White win a piece by capturing on c6, uncovering an attack to Black's c5-Bishop? But wait; Black has a *zwischenzug*, saving the Bishop—or does it? After 8. **Nxc6 Bxe3**, White has his own in-between move: 9. **Ne5**. No matter how Black deals with the attack on his Queen, White emerges a piece ahead.

Interpretation: In most exchange situations, the second player responds to his opponent's capture by immediately capturing back—piece for piece, pawn for pawn, and so on. If you don't take back, your opponent extricates his capturing unit, and you've gained whatever was captured for nothing. The principle is to get at least as much in value as what you give up. Sometimes, however, you may delay recapturing if you can play another move that forces your opponent into a controlled response. After he answers your compelling in-between move, you may then have the time to complete the postponed recapture. The problem sets in when your in-between move isn't really effective and your opponent can save his endangered unit with a gain of time. You might just come away with an empty bag.

29

PIN

Scotch Game

1. e4	e5
2. Nf3	Nc6
3. d4	exd4
4. Nxd4	Bc5
5. Be3	Qf6
6. c3	Qg6
7. Qe2	Qxe4?

WHITE TO MOVE

Scenario: White's win starts with a capture and a discovery: 8. **Nxc6**, unveiling a discovered attack to the c5-Bishop. If Black then plucks away White's c6-Knight, White captures Black's c5-Bishop for nothing. Black could play a desperado, 8. . . .**Bxe3**, trying to get equal value for his dark-square Bishop before capturing White's c6-Knight, except for a problem: White can let Black's dark-square Bishop sit on e3 for at least one extra move after it captures there because it's pinned to his Queen by White's Queen. Black can't move the Bishop without losing his Queen. So White continues 9. **Nd4** and probably collects Black's dark-square Bishop next move.

Interpretation: Black makes three moves with his Queen, the last a blunder of sheer greed. In the opening, the emphasis should be on moving the central pawns, developing minor pieces, castling early, and working toward a safe but playable middlegame position of dynamic possibilities. On occasion, pawn-hunting with your Queen will sniff out bait, but it does absolutely nothing to nurture your opening position. To filch a pawn with your Queen, you usually have to make a three-move investment: one move to bring it out, one to capture the pawn, and one to bring your Queen back to everyday life. If you can expend that much time and get away with it you're lucky.

30

DISCOVERY

Scotch Game

1. e4   e5
2. Nf3   Nc6
3. d4   exd4
4. Nxd4   Bc5
5. Be3   Qf6
6. c3   Nge7
7. Nd2?   Nxd4
8. e5   Qxe5?

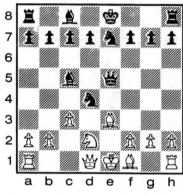

WHITE TO MOVE

Scenario: Black has really overlooked something. He doesn't see that 9. **cxd4 Bxd4** 10. **Nc4** attacks Black's Queen while also adding a second menace to Black's d4-Bishop. The Knight's movement from d2 to c4 has unveiled the file-power of White's Queen. Black loses his dark-square Bishop.

Interpretation: With correct play, White should lose a pawn in this variation, since moving his Knight from b1 to d2 weakens White's control over d4. After 8. e5, Black should eschew 8. . . .Qxe5? in favor of 8. . . .Nc2+. White takes the intruding Knight, 9. Qxc2, which allows Black to capture the King-pawn, 9. . . .Qf6xe5. With deliberate play, Black should retain his additional pawn and derive advantage, but Black fell asleep at the board. He blissfully captured the e5-pawn, possibly never considering White's reason for the sacrifice. If he had, he might have realized that White's e4-e5 advance was not a sacrifice but rather a trap. *Caveat emptor*—Let the buyer beware!

31

DISCOVERY

Scotch Game

1. e4	e5
2. Nf3	Nc6
3. d4	exd4
4. Nxd4	Nf6
5. Bg5	Be7
6. Nf5	d5
7. exd5	Ne5
8. Nxe7	Qxe7
9. Bxf6	

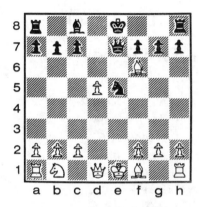

BLACK TO MOVE

Scenario: White has just captured a Knight on f6 and is threatening Black's Queen. Surely Black must recapture on f6, but Black need not agree, for 9. . . . Nf3 is double check and mate. If White tries to answer the checks by capturing either of Black's attacking pieces—his Queen or his Knight—he remains in check from the other one.

Interpretation: Don't take your opponent for granted. Perfunctory responses will not work. Even on "obvious" recaptures, or moves that seem practically forced, you still must step carefully to make sure you're not falling into a trap. White plays this opening far too automatically. He pins Black's f6-Knight, but he really shouldn't be developing his Queen's Bishop so early. Better to move out the Queen's Knight, instead. He attacks g7 and the e7-Bishop by jumping his Knight to f5, but in the opening he really shouldn't be moving the same piece so many times (three times and then a fourth move later). He would spend his time better to get out new pieces, to mobilize his entire army. It was unnecessary to capture on f6, when instead he could have saved himself by developing his King-Bishop to e2, screening the e-file, and preparing to remove his King from the center by castling. No one can survive all those wrong turns. "Wrong cannot right the wrongs that wrong hath done"— John Oxenham [William Arthur Dunkerley]

32

MATING ATTACK

Scotch Game

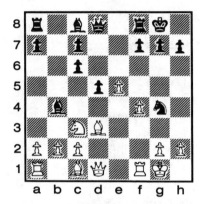

BLACK TO MOVE

1. e4	e5
2. Nf3	Nc6
3. d4	exd4
4. Nxd4	Nf6
5. Nc3	Bb4
6. Nxc6	bxc6
7. Bd3	0-0
8. 0-0	d5
9. e5	Ng4
10. f4	

Scenario: The last move, 10. f2-f4, irreparably damages White's game. He has no satisfactory answer to 10. . . . **Qh4,** threatening mate at h2. So White has to reply 11. **h3,** but 11. . . . **Bc5 +** 12. **Kh1 Qg3** is bad news to White. If 13. hxg4, to stop mate at h2, then 13. . . . Qh4 is mate. White must give up his Queen, 13. **Qxg4 Bxg4,** to ward off imminent mate.

Interpretation: A less risky move 9 for White would have been to trade e-pawn for d-pawn. Instead, he pushes the precarious 9. e4-e5, further separating his e-pawn from supporting forces. Once the venturesome pawn is attacked, 9. . . . Nf6-g4, White had better protect it with his Queen-Bishop, 10. Bc1-f4. But pushing the f-pawn, 10. f2-f4?, to defend the e-pawn can only lose. The resulting weaknesses along the a7-g1 diagonal and to the square g3 bring White's sudden demise. Pushing the f-pawn is sometimes desirable in that it either supports a Kingside attack or clears a path in front of the f1 (f8 for Black) castled Rook. Negative to this advance is its exposure of the g1-a7 (a2-g8 for Black) diagonal to a Bishop or Queen check. Be certain about all pawn moves. You can't take them back. "Nor all your piety nor wit shall lure it back to cancel half a line . . ."—Edward Fitzgerald, *Rubáiyát of Omar Khayyám.*

The Sister Openings

Bishop's Opening
Vienna Game

The *Bishop's Opening* (1. **e4 e5** 2. **Bc4**) and the *Vienna Game* (1. **e4 e5** 2. **Nc3**) are two sides of the same coin. While each opening has a distinct character, both overlap in several confluent variations.

A typical case is the Frankenstein-Dracula Variation (1. e4 e5 2. Nc3 Nf6 3. Bc4 Nxe4 4. Qh5), where White's second and third moves can easily be reversed and still reach the same position after the fourth move. (This variation is so named because the sudden twists and unexpected turns lead to "monstrous possibilities.")

The Bishop's Opening stems from the early days of chess science, after the game's rules were reformed in the late fifteenth century. It was then that the powers of the Bishop and Queen were enhanced, creating the awesome weapons of today's chess pieces. Swift attacks against the f7 square were the order of the day, and the Scholar's Mate (1. e4 e5 2. Bc4 Bc5 3. Qh5 d6 4. Qxf7 mate) was very popular. Even today, it remains the most often played beginning sequence for initiates.

Experienced players now understand, however, that White's Queen sortie to square h5 is premature. If Black fights back shrewdly, White's early Queen move should backfire. Nevertheless, the intrusion of White's Queen to h5 hovers in the background of the Bishop's Opening, and especially in the Frankenstein-Dracula Variation, when Black must ply incisive play to counteract it.

The Vienna Game is more recent. It is not that White's second move, Knight on b1 to c3, was unknown in early times. In recorded chess, it actually predates White's second move in the Bishop's Opening—Bishop on f1 to c4— by almost a thousand years. But for some reason, it was not really taken up until the mid-nineteenth century.

In the 1850s a group of Viennese masters, led by Carl Hammpe, began to explore the Vienna Game's intricacies. Since then, the Vienna has acquired supporters all over the world. Rudolf Spielmann (1833–1942) in Austria, Weaver Adams (1901–63) in America, and Alexander Konstantinopolski (born 1910) in Russia are three of its leading proponents in this century.

On the surface, White's second move, Nb1-c3, is an unassuming development toward the center, strengthening White's control of the e4 and d5 squares. White can choose to develop in the same quiet manner, moving his pieces to solid squares without intending to attack Black's e5-pawn. But usually White opens fire against e5 by advancing his f-pawn from f2 to f4. With White's pawn advance, the board becomes animated in the center and violent actions and counteractions ensue. In the lines where White follows with the Bishop on f1 to c4, the paths of the Bishop's Opening and Vienna Game merge into one superhighway.

33

FORK

Bishop's Opening

1. e4   e5
2. Bc4   Bc5
3. c3   Nc6
4. d4   d5?

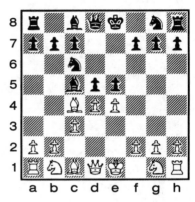

WHITE TO MOVE

Scenario: With the Black pieces, the player doesn't have time for aggressive actions comparable to White's in the opening. This is Black's universal disadvantage in every game. After 5. **exd5 Na5** 6. **dxc5 Nxc4** 7. **Qa4 +**, White soon captures Black's c4-Knight with his Queen, putting himself a piece ahead.

Interpretation: White's Queen has the double-attacking capability in having an open d1-a4 diagonal. By moving to a4, White's Queen gives check while attacking additionally along the 4th rank. Black's c4-Knight is a sitting duck. If you're thinking of similar central operations with your King still stuck in the center, consider the effect that enemy Queen checks will have on your game. Can your opponent check your King and combine that threat with an attack to another piece? If yes, you might be able to answer both attacks with one move and get safely away, but it's likely you won't. Be aware of double-attacks, especially from the enemy Queen. "The Queen, the Queen, can be very mean"—Bonaparte Altgeld.

34

Bishop's Opening

1. e4	e5
2. Bc4	Nf6
3. d3	Be7
4. f4	exf4
5. e5	Ng8
6. Nc3	d6
7. Bxf4	dxe5
8. Qh5	g6
9. Qxe5	Nf6

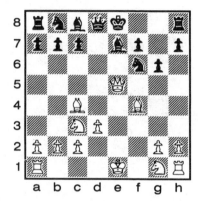

WHITE TO MOVE

Scenario: Black's Kingside weaknesses are irreparable. White penetrates with 10. **Nd5**, menacing winning Knight-captures on c7 and f6. Black's f6-Knight can't take White's d5 invader because his h8-Rook then hangs to White's Queen. So Black answers 10. . . .**Nbd7**, which loses to 11. **Nxc7+**. Black can't do better at this point than to sacrifice his Queen. If he doesn't, 11. . . .**Kf8** 12. **Bh6+ Kg8** 13. **Bxf7+! Kxf7** 14. **Qe6** is mate.

Interpretation: After Black's passive third move, Bf8-e7, he should never have followed with the exchange 4. . . .e5xf4, surrendering the center. Black's subsequent loss of time, having to retreat his f6-Knight after White's pawn push, 5. e4-e5, was difficult to overcome. A further time waste was the capture 7. . . .d6xe5, which Black thought would be answered by White's taking back on e5 with his f4-Bishop. The *zwischenzug*, 8. Qh5, threatening intrusion at f7, exposed the hopeless state of Black's uncoordinated position. Once Black pushed his g-pawn to stop the f7-threat, he weakened his dark squares, notably f6 and h6. White immediately mauled these holes and Black had no adequate defense. If Black had "world enough and time," perhaps he could escape. But no one can squander several moves in the opening and avoid defeat.

35

FORK

Bishop's Opening

1. e4   e5
2. Bc4   Nf6
3. d3   c6
4. Qe2   Be7
5. Nf3   0-0
6. Nxe5?

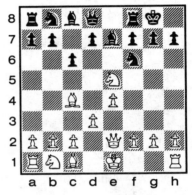

BLACK TO MOVE

Scenario: White's pawn-grabbing costs him a piece. After 6. . . . Qa5 +, however White blocks the a5-e1 diagonal, he has no way to save his e5-Knight. Black's Queen swipes it in next move.

Interpretation: The main way to win material in chess is to give some kind of double-attack or threat, leaving your opponent in a situation where, with one move, he is unable to adequately cope with both attacks. Double-attacks are particularly effective when one of the two attacked objects is the enemy King. Making the King live longer takes precedence over everything else, and it freezes the action. It's illegal to ignore a check. Because of its unusual power, the Queen tends to be the piece that gives most double-attacks. If you, as White, think of capturing an enemy unit on e5 with your f3-Knight while your King is still in the center and the a5-e1 diagonal is clear, make sure Black's Queen cannot check at a5. To reinforce this, remember that this can only happen if Black's c-pawn has moved earlier and does not block Black's 4th rank. You may be able to prepare capturing on e5 by developing a Knight to c3 or by castling. Thereafter, if e5 still is unguarded, maybe you can safely capture there.

36

MATING ATTACK

Bishop's Opening

1.	e4	e5
2.	Bc4	Nf6
3.	d3	c6
4.	Nf3	d5
5.	Bb3	dxe4
6.	Ng5	Bc5
7.	Nxf7	Qb6
8.	Nxh8?	

BLACK TO MOVE

Scenario: White's last move, 8. **Nxh8?**, is a real lemon. Change that move to castling, and White is winning. Now Black wins by 8. . . .**Bxf2+** 9. **Kf1 Bg4** 10. **Qd2 e3** 11. **Qc3 e2** mate. Of course, White could avert mate by sacrificing his Queen, but that only prolongs the agony, as Fred Reinfeld used to say.

Interpretation: White doesn't have to lose if he plays his eighth move sagaciously and gets his King to safety. But greed avails, and many players confronted with the possibility of capturing a Rook for free can't think about the consequences. As a safeguard, White should ask himself why Black, on move 7, left his h8-Rook hanging, subject to capture. Why didn't he try to save it? Unless you pose such a question, how will you know if your opponent has made an honest mistake or has set a trap? Take time for a deliberate approach that can avoid errors and save games. Get into your opponent's head; probe his moves and plans. Then you are equipped to make proper decisions.

37

IN-BETWEEN MOVE

Bishop's Opening

1. e4   e5
2. Bc4   Nf6
3. d4   exd4
4. Nf3   Nxe4
5. Qxd4   Nd6
6. 0-0   Nxc4

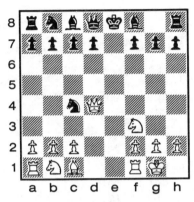

WHITE TO MOVE

Scenario: Since Black has captured White's Bishop, should White take back? No, not here, for 7. **Re1 + Be7** 8. **Qxg7 Rf8** 9. **Bh6** ensures that White will be able to win Black's f8-Rook for nothing, since Black's e7-Bishop is pinned along the e-file and incapable of defending f8. White at least winds up the exchange ahead, trading a minor piece (worth about three pawns) for a Rook (worth about five pawns).

Interpretation: The moves 1. e4 e5   2. Bc4 Nf6   3. d4 exd4   4. Nf3 constitute Ourousoff's Gambit. The same position could be reached by starting with Petroff's Defense, 1. e4 e5   2. Nf3 Nf6   3. d4 exd4   4. Bc4. It helps to know not only your openings but also how one opening can transpose into another. Two different openings actually can produce the same position later on. In this example, Black's fourth move, Ne4-d6, is an outright error. Better was 4. . . .Ne4-f6, which generally does not block the movement of the d-pawn. If the center-pawns can't move, it might cost considerable time to release and develop the pieces sitting on the back rank, if a player can do it at all. Black's poor development is indicated by his moving the same Knight four times in his first six moves. This is not desirable. On each move, try profitably to move a different piece. "In every enterprise consider where you would come out"—Publilius Syrus.

38

MATING ATTACK

Bishop's Opening

1. e4	e5
2. Bc4	Nf6
3. d4	exd4
4. Nf3	Nxe4
5. Qxd4	Nd6?
6. 0-0	Nc6
7. Re1 +	Ne7
8. Bb3	f6

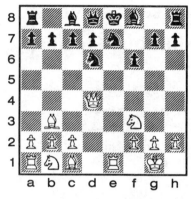

WHITE TO MOVE

Scenario: Black's last move, 8. . . .f7-f6, is intended to prevent the incursion of White's f3-Knight. But it's terribly weakening, especially along the b3-g8 diagonal. White's 9. **Qd5** threatens to play his c1-Bishop to f4 and to follow with a capture of Black's d6-Knight, leaving Black's f7 square vulnerable to White's Queen. Should Black try to thwart this by 9. . . .g5 White could still break through with 10. **Nxg5! hxg5** 11. **Bxg5**. White now has two threats: Bg5-f4 and Bg5-f6. Black could try to activate his h8-Rook, 11. . . .**h6**, but with 12. **Nc3!**, Black realizes that 12. . . .hxg5 13. Ne4 Nxd5 14. Nxd6 is mate. After 12. . . .**Rh7** 13. **Qg8 hxg5** (or 13. . . .Rg7 14. Nd5 Rxg8 15. Nf6 mate) 14. **Qxh7**, Black has no defense to the coming 15. **Qg6 +**. He's lost.

Interpretation: This is a rather complicated example with a number of side variations. On move 5, Black retreated his e4-Knight to d6, which blocked his d7-pawn. The result was that Black's Queenside pieces never got the chance to develop. Don't move pieces to squares that block your center-pawns. Black can't develop his Kingside pieces in this line either, for with the e7-Knight pinned by White's e1-Rook and the g7-pawn pinned by White's Queen, no real movement can occur in this sector. When developing your pieces in the opening, make sure they don't step on each other's toes. Do so by "untwisting all the chains that ties the hidden soul of harmony"—John Milton.

39

MATING ATTACK

Bishop's Opening

1. e4	e5
2. Bc4	Nf6
3. d4	exd4
4. Nf3	Nxe4
5. Qxd4	Nd6
6. 0-0	Nc6
7. Re1 +	Ne7
8. Bb3	f6
9. Qd5	g5

WHITE TO MOVE

Scenario: This is an extension of the previous example, number 38. You could win in this position by 10.**Bf4!** or you could win equally impressively with 10. **Bf4!** If Black tries to stop the looming capture on d6 by 10. . . . **gxf4,** he gets mated by 11. **Qh5 + Nf7** 12. **Qxf7** (or even 12. **Bxf7**). Black could avoid immediate mate after 10. Bf4 with 10. . . . c6, but that loses the d6-Knight and more after 11. Qxd6 gxf4 12. Qxf6. How, for one, does Black save his h8-Rook?

Interpretation: It's easy to see how Black loses here. He's all blocked up, tied down, and yet exposed. His d6-Knight blocks the movement of the d-pawn, so he can't develop his Queenside pieces in time or bring forces to his Kingside defense. His e7-Knight is pinned, preventing the use of his Queen and f8-Bishop. Finally, his Kingside pawns have moved, so they can't block potential checks and attacks. Black is truly helpless to save himself. In the opening, especially if you have Black, develop quickly, effectively, and harmoniously. There's really no other way.

40

MATING ATTACK

Vienna Game

1. e4   e5
2. Nc3   Bc5
3. Bc4   Ne7
4. d3   Nbc6
5. Qh5   0-0
6. Bg5   Qe8
7. Nf3   Ng6

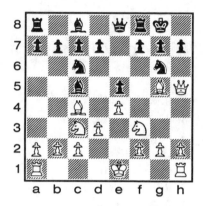

WHITE TO MOVE

Scenario: Black's last move relinquished control over d5, allowing White's c3-Knight entrée, 8. **Nd5.** The threat is to capture on c7, forking Black's Queen and a8-Rook. So Black defends c7, 8. . . . **Bb6.** A deeper plan emerges after 9. **Nf6+! gxf6** 10. **Bxf6.** How does Black stop White's Queen from playing to h6 and then g7, mating? Even the self-immolating **10. . . . Qe7,** offering Black's Queen as a deterrence to mate, cannot dissuade White. White just continues **11.Ng5,** and mate rears up shortly.

Interpretation: Black's early mistake was to develop his g8-Knight to e7 on his 2nd rank instead of f6 on his 3rd rank. By not guarding h5, Black left that square safe for White's Queen. The second error, 7. . . . **Ng6,** was irretrievable. Once White's c3-Knight entered d5 with tempo, Black's position became untenable. Correct was 7. . . . d6 followed by 8. . . . Be6, upgrading Black's d5 hold. Black lost because he moved an already developed piece—his Kingside Knight—instead of continuing to bring out other, undeveloped pieces. Especially in the opening, mobilize all the pieces. Don't wage war with skeleton forces. "Git thar fustest with the mostest . . ."—General Nathan Bedford Forest.

41

UNPIN

Vienna Game

1. e4   e5
2. Nc3   Nc6
3. f4   d6
4. Nf3   a6
5. Bc4   Bg4
6. fxe5   Nxe5?

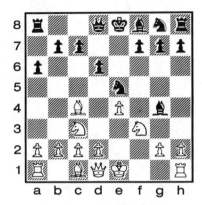

WHITE TO MOVE

Scenario: Black has walked right into a version of Legal's unpin tactic. White's f3-Knight, pinned by Black's g4-Bishop to White's d1-Queen, is able to move off the pinned d1-h5 diagonal, exposing the Queen to capture. Why can White's Knight safely move? Because if his Queen is captured, he forces mate—Legal's Mate—using three minor pieces. Thus, 7. **Nxe5! dxe5** 8. **Qxg4** nets White a whole minor piece.

Interpretation: White's winning tactics hinge on a key point: Black's inability to capture White's Queen once the pinned f3-Knight moves. If, after 7. Nxe5, Black does capture, 7. . . . Bxd1, then 8. Bxf7+ Ke7 9. Nd5 is Legal's Mate, named after the French master Sire de Legal (1702–92), who is said to have been Philidor's teacher. Legal was the first in a recorded game to play this attack. The tactic works when Black (and less often White) has prematurely brought out his Queen-Bishop, creating a pin on the enemy King-Knight. This early pin might work with Black's King-Knight on f6, defending g4. Black's irrelevant pawn move, 3. . . . a7-a6, squandered an important tempo. The early pin, 5. . . . Bc8-g4, was also a poor choice. Safer is 6. . . . Be7, guarding the potential g5 invasion point. Finally, Black doesn't have to recapture on move 6 with his c6-Knight. If he takes on e5 with his d6-pawn, White could not play Legal's tactic successfully, for 6. fxe5 dxe5 7. Nxe5? can then be answered by 7. . . . Nxe5, defending his g4-Bishop, so that White's Queen can't take it.

42

MATING ATTACK

Vienna Game

1. e4	e5
2. Nc3	Nc6
3. f4	Bc5
4. Nf3	d6
5. f5	Nf6
6. h3	d5
7. Nxe5	Nxe4
8. Nf3	

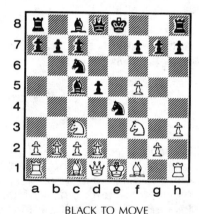

BLACK TO MOVE

Scenario: White thinks his f3-Knight holds the fort, which it does until Black's 8. . . .Qh4 +!. Then White's game plunges. The obvious 9. Nxh4 Bf2 + 10. Ke2 Nd4 + 11. Kd3 Nc5 mate could give anyone Knight-mares.

Interpretation: White wastes too much time and creates too many holes to last in this one. His fifth move, f4-f5, shuts out Black's light-square Bishop, but it's unnecessary then—one move down the drain. The other costly expenditure is the next move, h2-h3, played to keep Black's King-Knight out of g4. But it leaves g3 unprotected, so that White will not be able to safely block at g3 a timely check along the e1-h4 diagonal because White's h-pawn can no longer protect that square. Too many pawn moves in the opening waste time and weaken squares. Do confine pawn movements to those in the center, maximizing your development.

43

KING HUNT

Vienna Game

1. e4   e5
2. Nc3   Nc6
3. f4   exf4
4. Bc4   Qh4 +
5. Kf1   Bc5
6. g3?   fxg3
7. Nf3

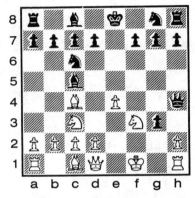

BLACK TO MOVE

Scenario: White's stumbling forces cannot help his King escape Black's mating attack: 7. . . . .g2 +   8. Kxg2 (or 8. Ke2 Qf2 +   9. Kd3 Nb4 mate) **Qf2 +**   9. **Kh3 d5** discovered mate. This is a criss-cross mate, where the diagonal powers of Black's Queen (e1-h4) and Queen-Bishop (c8-h3) cross.

Interpretation: After Black takes White's f-pawn of f4, he's in a stronger position to Queen-check at h4: White is unable to safely block the check at g3. A more prudent fourth move for White would be to develop the g1-Knight to f3, guarding against the h4-check. White, of course, plays 6. g2-g3? to stop mate at f2, but a safer way is simply 6. Qe1, offering a Queen trade to dissipate Black's attack. But even after that defense, Black stands well.

44

MATING ATTACK

Vienna Game

1. e4	e5
2. Nc3	Nc6
3. Bc4	Bc5
4. Qg4	Qf6?
5. Nd5	Qxf2 +
6. Kd1	Kf8
7. Nh3	Qd4
8. d3	Bb6
9. Rf1	Nf6

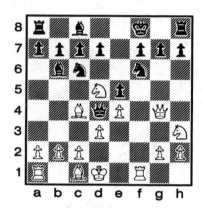

WHITE TO MOVE

Scenario: There are plenty of tactics here, but a sure winner is 10. Rxf6!, when the automatic recapture 10. . . .gxf6 is followed by 11. Bh6 + Ke7 12. Qg7, threatening a mess of squares, including f6, f7, and h8. A reasonable try is 10. . . .**d6**, but that is repelled by 11. **Qxg7 +! Kxg7** 12. **Bh6 + Kg8** 13. **Rg6 + hxg6** (or 13. . . .fxg6) 14. **Nf6** mate. With options coming out of his ears, White also mates by 13. Ne7 + Nxe7 14. Bxf7. Take your pick.

Interpretation: Black's fourth-move Queen's defense, Qd8-f6, appeared ominous, though it induced the time-gaining entrance, 5. Nc3-d5. Black did win a pawn with check, and forced White's King to move, losing the right to castle. But the exorbitant price Black had to pay was a displaced Queen, helpless to safeguard his King. To have your Queen out of play in the opening when you need it is too big a price to pay. Don't go pawn-grabbing. Develop, secure your King, and then perhaps you can start to plunder.

45

DISCOVERY

Vienna Game

1. e4   e5
2. Nc3   Nc6
3. Bc4   Bc5
4. Qg4   Bf8
5. Nf3?

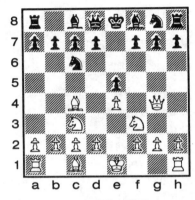

BLACK TO MOVE

Scenario: White's previous move is an egregious oversight. He now loses his c4-Bishop to the discovery 5. . . . d5. White must save his Queen, after which Black captures the hapless Bishop.

Interpretation: In the position just before Black wins a piece of 5. . . . d7-d5, White has four pieces developed to Black's one. Normally, that type of lead in development should be decisive, but it's not if some of those developing moves are mechanical, without clear purpose. One such automatic development is 5. Ng1-f3. White was able to get away with bringing out his own Queen as early as move 4 because of the threat to capture Black's weakened g7-pawn. After Black retreats his c5-Bishop to f8 to defend the g7-pawn, with a loss of time for him, White needs to reposition his Queen out of the c8-Bishop's diagonal line of attack. A good deployment is back to g3, observing Black's e5-pawn. But White didn't, and therein lies the problem. Don't just perfunctorily develop. Bring out your pieces in a constructive coordinated manner. "The plan's the thing wherein I'll catch the skulking King"—a misquote from Shakespeare's *Hamlet*.

46

MATING ATTACK

Vienna Game

1. e4	e5
2. Nc3	Nf6
3. Bc4	Bc5
4. d3	d6
5. f4	Ng4?
6. f5!	Nf2
7. Qh5	0-0
8. Nf3	Nxh1

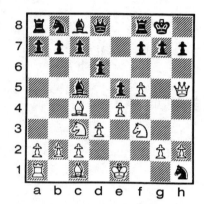

WHITE TO MOVE

Scenario: Proceeding at what seems a snail's pace, White's attack gets there nonetheless by 9. **Ng5.** After Black wards off mate at h7 with 9. . . .**h6,** White forges ahead with 10. **Nxf7 Rxf7** (Black doesn't really have a good alternative) 11. **Qxf7+ Kh8** (or 11. . . .Kh7 12. Bg5!, when the Bishop is immune to capture because of White's various mating responses) 12. **f6,** and Black is helpless against several different mating attacks.

Interpretation: In the final position after 12. f6, Black loses if he captures on f6 with his Queen. White simply checks with his Queen at g8. And if Black answers 12. . . .gxf6, then 13. Bxh6 menaces 14. Qg7 mate. Meanwhile, Black can't sit back and do nothing after 12. f6 because White threatens 13. Qxg7 mate. Black is so lost by move 12 that White has other ways to win, too. For example, both 12. Bg5 (12. . . .Qxg5 permits 13. Qg8 mate and 12. . . .hxg5 allows 13. Qh5 mate) as well as 12. Bxh6 gxh6 13. f6 will also succeed. Black's big error in this example is the misuse of the King-Knight. It makes four moves, giving White three extra moves to build an attack. Try not to move the same piece too many times in the opening. You have different weapons. Try to ready them all. None of them is vestigial.

47

MATING ATTACK

Vienna Game

1. e4	e5
2. Nc3	Nf6
3. Bc4	Nxe4
4. Bxf7 +	Kxf7
5. Nxe4	Nc6
6. Qf3 +	Kg8

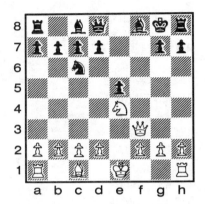

WHITE TO MOVE

Scenario: Clearly, Black's King is not really well placed. There is the blatant b3-g8 diagonal leading to Black's King. A White Queen check at b3 doesn't work, however, for Black has the insertion d7-d5. The winning key is 7. **Ng5!**, menacing mating checks at f7 and d5. If Black answers 7. . . . Qxg5, then White mates by Qd5. No better are 7. . . . Qe7 or 7. . . . Qf6, for after 8. Qd5 +, Black must insert his Queen losingly at e6 to stop mate. White's g5-Knight then captures it.

Interpretation: When Black temporarily sacrifices his Knight, 3. . . . Nxe4, he expects to answer 4. Nxe4 with 4. . . . d5, forking c4-Bishop and e4-Knight. This tactic—by which the King-Knight is sham-sacrificed to eliminate the enemy e-pawn, followed with a d-pawn fork to regain the sacrificed piece—is called the "fork trick." It's purpose is to clear away the enemy King-pawn to get a freer hand in the center. Black here should have continued 5. . . . d5!, instead of 5. . . . Nc6. This is the logical way to follow a fork-trick tactic; and in this instance, it would have given Black new defensive resources, for his c8-Bishop could then participate. If you can, move both center-pawns reasonably early in the game. Otherwise your pieces will be hindered from getting into action.

48

KING HUNT

Vienna Game

1. e4	e5
2. Nc3	Nf6
3. Bc4	Nxe4
4. Qh5	Nd6
5. Bb3	Be7
6. d3	0-0
7. Nf3	Nc6
8. Ng5	h6
9. h4	Ne8?

WHITE TO MOVE

Scenario: Black has castled into a gathering White storm. It's a hurricane after 10. Nxf7 Rxf7 (otherwise Black loses his Queen) 11. Qxf7+ Kh7 12. Qg8+ Kg6 13. h5+ Kf5 14. Qh7+ Kg4, when 15. Qe4 is mate.

Interpretation: Black can improve his play at several points. Rather than castle into a powerful attack on move 6, Black could develop his Queen-Knight to c6, a useful move. It's best not to castle on the side where your opponent has attacking possibilities. Another difficult, though almost forced decision is Black's eighth move, h7-h6. This pawn move stops the h7-mate threat, but weakens the g6-square. Instead, Black might have tried exchanging the e7-Bishop for White's g5-Knight. This is worth considering, for it reduces White's attack force without incurring weak squares. Nevertheless, after 8. . . .Bxg5 9. Bxg5 Qe8 (or 9. . . .Ne7), White has the predatory 10. Nd5. Of course, Black can't take White's g5-Knight, 9. . . .hxg5, for 10. hxg5 opens the h-file so that the h1-Rook can back up White's invading Queen. Black might stay in the game, however, if he essays 9. . . .Nd4!, which offers possibilities of trading d4-Knight for b3-Bishop or of blocking the Bishop's diagonal at e6. Even if you're under furious attack, you don't have to lie down and die. Fight back. It just may work. "Victory in spite of terror, victory however long and hard the road"—Winston Churchill.

49

MATING ATTACK

Vienna Game

1. e4	e5
2. Nc3	Nf6
3. Bc4	Nxe4
4. Qh5	Nd6
5. Bb3	Be7
6. d3	0-0
7. Nf3	Nc6
8. Ng5	h6
9. h4	Ne8?
10. Nd5	Nf6

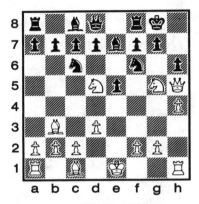

WHITE TO MOVE

Scenario: This example is the same as the previous one, except White wins with a different tenth move, 10. **Nd5.** In the previous position, the winning shot was 10. Nxf7. In this one, White follows through with 11. **Qg6!.** If, as in a famous game played by (White) Jacque Mieses (1865–1954) against an unsuspecting opponent, Black captures White's Queen, 11. . . . . **fxg6,** then White mates by 12. **Nxe7+ Kh8** 13. **Nxg6.**

Interpretation: White's victory is not really convincing. Instead of the inexact 10. . . . . Nf6, Black could have posed some problems for White with 10. . . . . Nd4. And even after 10. . . . . Nf6 11. Qg6, Black had the superior 11. . . . . Kh8 defense. White then has nothing better than 12. Nxf7+ Rxf7 13. Qxf7, putting him ahead by a mere exchange (a Rook for a minor piece). Black obviously didn't consider the consequences of taking White's Queen, because if so, he would have seen he was getting mated in two moves. Greed blinds him to the truth. Even in the worst position, if you keep your eyes open you may find surprising resources. Don't accept a sacrifice when you're not forced to, and you may coerce your opponent into some real concession elsewhere.

50

KING HUNT

Vienna Game

1. e4	e5
2. Nc3	Nf6
3. f4	exf4?
4. e5	Qe7
5. Qe2	Ng8
6. Nf3	d6?
7. Nd5	Qd8
8. exd6 +	Be6
9. Nxc7 +	Kd7
10. Ne5 +	Kc8

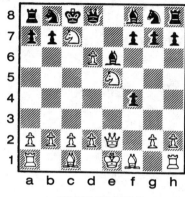

WHITE TO MOVE

Scenario: Instead of materialistically expropriating Black's a8-Rook, White eyes better with 11. **Nxe6!**, going for Black's throat. After 11. . . .fxe6 12. **Qc4+ Nc6**, White has the further surprise 13. **Qxc6 +!**. The neat conclusion is 13. . . .bxc6 14. **Ba6 + Kb8** 15. **Nxc6** mate. Oh, the wonderful things that minor pieces can do!

Interpretation: Much could be different with this game. Black shouldn't have exchanged 3. . . .exf4?, for that abandons the center and permits White the pawn-spiking 4. e4-e5. Try to maintain equal footing in the center in the opening. A further error is 6. . . .d7-d6, for that permits White at a favorable later time to exchange e-pawn for d-pawn, uncovering a discovery to Black's King along the e-file. Black could answer 7. Nd5 with 7. . . .Qd7 (instead of 7. . . .Qd8), but that's not good either after 8. exd6 +, constraining Black to cede a piece on e7, for 8. . . .Kd8 loses the Queen to 9. dxc7 +. After 7. . . .Qd8 8. exd6 +, Black can play 8. . . .Kd7, but that's dealt with by 9. Ne5 + at once, when Black must at least drop his Queen. The combination of Black's early surrender of the center and his unsound use of the Queen incurs a losing game.

51

FORK

Vienna Game

1. e4   e5
2. Nc3   Nf6
3. f4   exf4?
4. e5   Qe7
5. Qe2   Ng8
6. Nf3   Nc6
7. d4   d6?

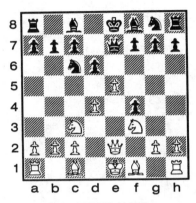

WHITE TO MOVE

Scenario: Black's last move asks for trouble. After 8. **Nd5**, Black's Queen must move off the e-file, allowing White the possibility of a discovered check to Black's King. Otherwise, staying on the file by 8. . . . Qe6 would lose the Queen to a c7-fork of King and Queen. If Black therefore answers 8. . . . **Qd8** (8. . . . Qd7 comes to the same thing) White infiltrates with 9. **Nxc7 + !**, when Black can't play 9. . . . Qxc7 because of 10. exd6+, attacking Black's Queen and King simultaneously. Since Black can't safely take White's c7-Knight, Black loses a Rook for nothing.

Interpretation: Black does several undesirable things. First he cedes the center, 3. . . . e5xf4, when White gets to assail Black's f6-Knight by 4. e4-e5. Thereafter, Black's pin on White's e-pawn, 4. . . . Qd8-e7, really comes to nought because of White's counter 5. Qd1-e2, breaking the e-file pin. Later, Black's Queen becomes badly misplaced at e7, where it can be driven away by White's d5-Knight incursion. At e7, the Queen also blocks in the f8-Bishop. Black cannot in the end survive his last blunder, 7. . . . d7-d6?. This mistake allows White to open the e-file by an exchange of pawns. Don't give away your center. Don't rely too much on your Queen. Don't open the center when your King may be endangered and you are poorly developed.

52

MATING ATTACK

Vienna Game

1. e4   e5
2. Nc3   Nf6
3. f4   d5
4. fxe5   Nxe4
5. Nf3   Nc6
6. a3   Bc5
7. d4

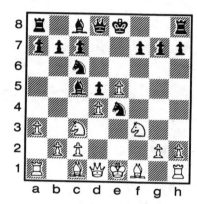

BLACK TO MOVE

Scenario: One little move can be critical in an opening. Waste it, and you lose. Black shows White his mistake by 7. . . . **Nxd4!**, when 8. **Nxd4** is silenced by 8. . . .**Qh4+** 9. **g3 Nxg3** 10. **Nf3 Bf2+!** 11. **Kxf2 Ne4+** 12. **Ke3 Qf2+** 13. **Kd3** (for 13. Kf4 g5 mate) 13. . . . **Nc5** mate. So after 7. . . . **Nxd4!**, White has nothing better than 8. Nxe4 dxe4, leaving Black a good center-pawn ahead.

Interpretation: The tactics in this opening story are tricky. If after 7. . . . Nxd4! 8. Nxd4 Qh4+ White answers 9. Ke2, then 9. . . . Qf2+ 10. Kd3 Qxd4+ 11. Ke2 Bg4+ 12. Ke1 Qf2 is mate. If White answers 8. . . .Qh4+ 9. g3 Nxg3 with 10. hxg3, both 10. . . . Qxh1 and 10. . . . Qxg3+ give Black a strong attack. In the main line, 10. . . . Bf2+! sets up a winning double-check after White captures the f2-Bishop. If White turns down the Bishop, fleeing his King to d2, then 11. Kd2 Qf4+ 12. Kd3 Bf5+ is no bowl of cherries for White, either. White got himself into this mess by the ineffectual pawn push, 6. a2-a3?. Shy away from useless pawn moves in your own games. They waste time in the opening that is badly needed for development.

53

FORK

Vienna Game

1. e4   e5
2. Nc3   Nf6
3. f4   d5
4. fxe5   Nxe4
5. d3   Bb4
6. dxe4   Qh4+
7. g3?

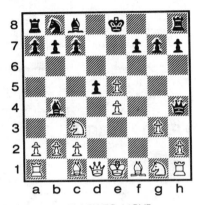

BLACK TO MOVE

Scenario: Black can win with either of two moves. He could unnecessarily insert 7. . . . Bxc3 + 8. bxc3 and then follow with 8. . . . Qxe4 +, forking White's King and h1-Rook. Or he could play more directly 7. . . . Qxe4 +, forking the same two pieces right away, for he needn't fear White's c3-Knight, which is pinned by Black's b4-Bishop. White loses the h1-Rook, leaving Black an exchange ahead (a Rook for a minor piece).

Interpretation: White cannot safely play 7. g2-g3. Instead he must bite the bullet and move his King, 7. Ke1-e2. He can no longer castle; his pieces will have trouble developing, and he will still be menaced, but he doesn't lose the exchange and he may be able to defend himself. Black's best would be to exchange on c3, 7. . . . Bxc3 8. bxc3, removing the e4-pawn's protection, and then to check on g4, 8. . . . Bc8-g4+. After 9. Nf3, Black gains back the piece with 9. . . . dxe4, attacking the pinned f3-Knight. Whenever the f-pawn has moved early in the game, beware of possible enemy Queen checks on the h-file. These may be especially effective if the Queen check also attacks vital points along the rank. A Black Queen at h4 could doubly attack e1 and e4. A White Queen at h5 hits both e8 and e5. If such an attack arises, be extra careful about blocking the Queen check with the g-pawn, for when the Queen moves to the e-file, a new double-attack will be given to your King and cornered Rook.

54

UNPIN

Vienna Game

1. e4	e5
2. Nc3	Nf6
3. f4	d5
4. fxe5	Nxe4
5. d3	Qh4 +
6. g3	Nxg3
7. Nf3	Qh5
8. Nxd5	Kd8

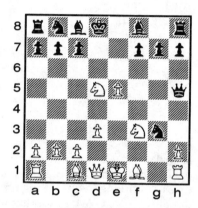

WHITE TO MOVE

Scenario: Black's fifth-move Queen-check inaugurated the Oxford Variation of the Vienna Game, which is now considered unsound. After 9. **Nf4 Qg4** (or 9. . . .Qh6 10. Ne2, followed by capturing on g3) 10. **Bh3**, Black's Queen is a vagrant. Note 10. hxg3 allows Black to escape by 10. . . .Qxg3 +. If Black continues from the main line with 10. . . .**Nxh1** 11. **Bxg4 Bxg4**, he still will not have enough for his Queen, since the h1-Knight is trapped. White will win it generally after Qe2, Be3, and castling Queenside.

Interpretation: If Black pursues this dangerous line, on move 8 he does better capturing White's Rook on h1 than defending c7 with his King. Upon playing his King to d8, he has to drop at least a piece. Against a bevy of coordinating minor pieces (Bishops and Knights), a Queen may not fend very well. If it's threatened, it must move, wasting time. Here it costs Black the game. Instead of heading into the Oxford Variation, Black does better exchanging Knights on c3. His chances thereafter are reasonable.

3

The King's Gambit

King's Gambit Accepted
King's Gambit Declined
Falkbeer Counter-Gambit

The *King's Gambit* (1. **e4 e5**   2. **f4**) recalls the romantic era of the last century. Adolf Anderssen and Paul Morphy reigned supreme, gambits were in fashion, and swash-buckling attacks on the enemy King were the way players oriented themselves on the chessboard.

In our century the King's Gambit was placed on a more positional footing and two recent World Champions, Boris Spassky and Bobby Fischer, included the King's Gambit in their arsenal of opening weaponry. Fischer, in fact, won every game in which he had the White pieces with the King's Gambit. His only loss with this opening occurred with the Black pieces against, as you can guess, Boris Spassky.

Two fundamental opening concepts motivate the King's Gambit: to seize the central terrain and to place the enemy King in jeopardy by pressuring his most vulnerable point, the f7 square. Once Black accepts the Gambit (2. . . .**exf4**), his e-pawn, decoyed to f4, lays the groundwork for White's later expansion with the Queen-pawn, moving d2 to d4. And if White can manage to eliminate the Gambit pawn on f4, he has a ready-made assault force against f7 in the c4-Bishop and the f1-Rook, so placed after Kingside castling.

Of the various defensive methods at Black's disposal, most involve returning the gambit pawn. But until Black's King reaches safety, usually by castling, he had better hang on to the f4-pawn, to keep the f-file blocked up. As long as Black's f4-pawn remains, the f-file stays closed and Black's f7 weakness is less assailable.

Not every chessplayer cares for the complicated King's Gambit. Those who disdain hand-to-hand combat, preferring quiet positional play, might consider declining the Gambit with **2. . . .Bc5.** Even Aron Nimzovich's recommendation to beginning students, **2. . . .d7-d6,** is reasonable, despite its hemming in of Black's f8-Bishop. Another way for Black to decline the Gambit is the *Falkbeer Counter-Gambit,* **2. . . .d5   3. exd5 e4.** With this counterattack, Black tries to steal White's thunder, offering a pawn of his own in a role reversal, with White defending and Black attacking. It, too, like the King's Gambit itself, is not for the feint-hearted.

55

SKEWER

King's Gambit Accepted

1. e4   e5
2. f4   exf4
3. Kf2? Qh4 +
4. Kf3?

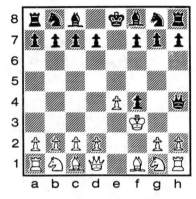

BLACK TO MOVE

Scenario: Black wins handily by 4. . . . Qh5 + , which skewers White's King and Queen. To save the Queen, White must respond 5. g4, when Black, by capturing en passant, 5. . . . fxg3 + , gives a discovered check to White's King. After White's King moves to safety, Black gains White's Queen for nothing.

Interpretation: White's third move, 3. Ke1-f2, is a blunder. Why move the King if you don't have to? White may be hoping for some weird tactical possibilities, where Black's Queen winds up on the e-file and gets pinned to its King. But none of this is forced. Once the mistake is made, however, White should answer 3. . . . Qh4 + with 4. g3, playing for complications and a compensating attack. The game might go, for example, 4. . . . fxg3 + 5. Kg2 gxh2 6. Nf3, when, if Black's not careful, White might develop some counterplay. Even 4. Kf2-e2—though insufficient—is better than the ridiculously bold 4. Kf3?. Particularly in the King's Gambit, White should avoid endangering his King any more than necessary. With the f-pawn already moved up, White's King is plainly vulnerable. Try not to move your King early on, and prepare to castle rapidly; then you can mount a full-scale campaign.

56

PROMOTION

King's Gambit Accepted

1. e4   e5
2. f4   exf4
3. b3   Qh4 +
4. g3?   fxg3
5. h3

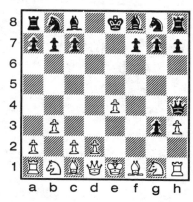

BLACK TO MOVE

Scenario: Black has several crushing wins. Surely 5. . . .Qxe4 + puts him way ahead, as does 5. . . .g2 +, which is discovered check. After the forced 6. Ke2 Qxe4 +   7. Kf2, Black could breezily win a Rook and make a new Queen, 7. . . .gxh1/Q. But better than that is 7. . . .gxh1/N!, where Black mates by underpromoting to a Knight.

Interpretation: White makes a couple of airy pawn moves, and they cost him the game. How does 3. b2-b3 concern the King's Gambit? Does White really want to flank his Queen-Bishop instead of developing it through the center after moving the d-pawn? Moreover, White's poor push, 3. b2-b3, does nothing to guard h4, the touchstone for Black Queen attacks in the King's Gambit, especially when Black has a pawn sitting on f4, guarding g3. This placement prevents White from safely blocking an h4-Queen check with his g-pawn. After the subsequent blunder 4. g3?, Black takes the g-pawn, 4. . . .fxg3, menacing a discovery along the e1-h4 diagonal. White plays the final blunder, 5. h2-h3, to avoid 5. . . .gxh2 + discovered check, but he overlooks the more serious discovery, 5. . . .g2 +, assailing the cornered Rook. The final position reveals the value of underpromotions. Here is a case where a Knight is actually stronger than a Queen.

57

KING HUNT

King's Gambit Accepted

1. e4   e5
2. f4   exf4
3. Bc4   g5
4. h4   f6?

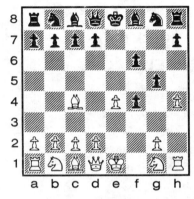

WHITE TO MOVE

Scenario: Black's last move is designed to keep his pawns connected in a chain, but Black is actually chained in after 5. **Qh5 +** **Ke7**   6. **Qf7 + Kd6**   7. **e5 + ! fxe5** (on 7. . . .Kxe5, White has 8. Qd5 mate, while 7. . . .Kc6   8. Qd5 + Kb6   9. Qb5 is also mate)   8. **Qd5 + Ke7**   9. **Qxe5** mate.

Interpretation: You can't win many games if in the first eight moves you play only your King and pawns. Black moved one too many of the latter. Pushing the f-pawn was especially negative, for that opened the h5-e8 diagonal for White's Queen. With White's Bishop already posted at c4, bearing down on f7, Black was really in gruesome-land. The square f7, therefore, becomes the focal point, or the anchor for a White Queen invasion. In the King's Gambit, f7 is often White's main target, his weapons being a c4-Bishop, a Knight on e5 or g5, a castled f1-Rook, and a Queen from h5 or f3 if the f-file is open. If Black plays to retain the f4-pawn, undoubtedly a useful idea, keeping the f-file closed, he must be careful not to overextend himself. No pawn is worth it. "Penny wise, pound foolish"—Robert Burton.

58

MATING ATTACK

King's Gambit Accepted

1. e4   e5
2. f4   exf4
3. Bc4   Bc5
4. d4   Qh4 +
5. Kf1   Bb6
6. Nf3   Qd8
7. Bxf4   Ne7
8. Ng5   0-0

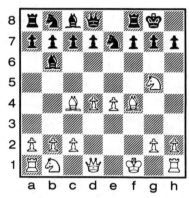

WHITE TO MOVE

Scenario: Black is in trouble after 9. **Qh5**, threatening mate at h7. After 9. . . .**h6**, White crashes through with 10. **Bxf7 +**, when Black must surrender his f8-Rook for White's checking Bishop. If he doesn't and Black decrees his King to the corner instead, 10. . . .**Kh8**, then he is blasted out of the chess world by 11. **Qxh6 +** ! gxh6   12. Be5 mate.

Interpretation: Black's third move, 3. . . .Bf8-c5, is an error. Why put your Bishop on c5 if White can gain an advantage by attacking it with a strong d-pawn thrust, as in 4. d2-d4? Black follows with the pesky Queen check, 4. . . .Qh4, forcing White's King to move, 5. Ke1-f1. The early King movement doesn't really hurt White, however, for he gains an important tempo on Black's Queen when he develops his Knight to f3. Black's final blunder is 8. . . .0-0? a move pundits call "castling into it." Instead of castling, Black should have struck back in the center with 8. . . .d7-d5, clearing the road for his c8-Bishop and neutralizing White's c4-Bishop. After 9. Qh5, Black clearly cannot guard both h7 and f7 with one move. A further sign of Black's inadequate development in that position is the Queenside. All of Black's eight Queenside units are on their original squares. Also, Black's dark-square Bishop and e7-Knight can't really contribute to the defense of the Kingside either. Black's King is truly alone against a rampaging army. Avoid castling into your opponent's attack. In this case, contrary to Ibsen's Dr. Stockmann, the strongest man in the world is not he who stands most alone.

59

KING HUNT

King's Gambit Accepted

1. e4	e5
2. f4	exf4
3. Nf3	Be7
4. Bc4	Nf6
5. Nc3	Nxe4
6. Bxf7 +	Kxf7
7. Ne5 +	Ke6?
8. Qg4 +	Kxe5
9. d4 +	Kxd4

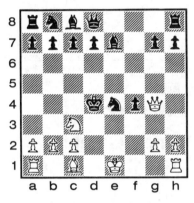

WHITE TO MOVE

Scenario: White wins in this complex position with 10. **Be3 +!**. Black can choose his own poison. He could take the Bishop with his King, which ends in mate after 10. . . .Kxe3   11. Qe2 + Kd4   12. Qxe4 + Kc5   13. Qd5 + Kb6   14. Qb5. Or, he could take the Bishop with his f-pawn, though that terminates in disaster too, via 10. . . .fxe3   11. Qxe4 + Kc5   12. Qd5 + Kb6   13. Qb5. Or instead he could get mated on the Queenside, 10. . . .Kc4   11. Qe2 + Kb4   12. Qb5. Probably his best defense is 10. . . .**Ke5**   11. **Bxf4 + Kf6**   12. **0-0**, though he faces a blistering mating attack. White's immediate threat is 13. Bg3 mate. If Black tries 12. . . .Bc5 +, White unhinges him with 13. Be3 +, with an additional attack to the e4-Knight. Black can't run away either, for 12. . . .Kf7   13. Bxc7 + glops his Queen, for starters, or White could elect to continue the mating attack by 13. Bh6 +. Black loses, loses, loses. That's the point.

Interpretation: Black takes chances playing for the fork trick with 5. . . .Nxe4, figuring 6. Nxe4 could be answered by 6. . . .d5, forking the c4-Bishop and e4-Knight. But White had the in-between desperado 6. Bxf7 +. Since the Bishop was going to be one of the forked pieces, White gives it up in a way that is more convenient for him, checking Black and forcing the King to move. A further mistake was 7. . . .Ke6, which unnecessarily exposed Black's King, for the threat to the e5-Knight is frivolous. It's safer to retreat to g8, a better shelter for Black's King. Extra material does you little good if you can't use it.

60

DISCOVERY

King's Gambit Accepted

1. ef	e5
2. f4	exf4
3. Nf3	d5
4. Nc3	dxe4
5. Nxe4	Bg4
6. Qe2	Bxf3

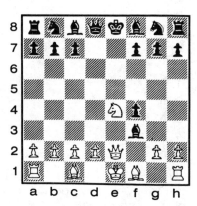

WHITE TO MOVE

Scenario: Black should look before he leaps. Here he didn't, so White mates on the move by 7. Nf6. Both White's Queen and f6-Knight are individually capturable, yet neither one can be taken because both check simultaneously. Together they give double-check, so if one is removed, the other still nails Black's King.

Interpretation: After accepting the gambit pawn, rather than keep the advantage, Black decides to return a pawn for an even game and central development by 3. . . .d7-d5. That's a good start, but then Black goes astray with a premature development of the Queen-

Bishop, 5. . . .Bc8-g4. It's a pin, but not very effective. Besides, Black should be mobilizing his Kingside and castling quickly. In the position just before the diagram, there is no need to exchange g4-Bishop for f3. Rather, Black should be concerned with safeguarding his King from a discovery along the e-file, which can be done by putting either his King-Bishop or his Queen at e7. The counter 6. . . .Qd8-e7, potentially pinning White's e4-Knight, is probably best. Black's strong opening did not carry him through. "A good breakfast is no substitute for a large dinner"—Chinese proverb.

61

FORK

King's Gambit Accepted

1. e4	e5
2. f4	exf4
3. Nf3	Nf6
4. e5	Nh5
5. Nc3	d6
6. Bc4	dxe5
7. Nxe5	Qh4 +
8. Kf1	Be6
9. Bxe6	Ng3 +
10. Kg1	

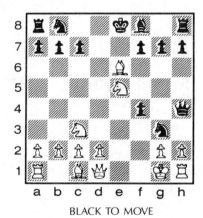

BLACK TO MOVE

Scenario: White didn't capture Black's g3-Knight on the previous move for fear of the line 10. hxg3 Qxh1 + 11. Ke2 Qxd1 12. Kxd1 fxe6, putting Black the exchange ahead. Now he pays, pays, pays, for Black zaps him with 10. . . . Bc5 +!, when White must respond 12. d4. The "sockdalager," an expression popular with Al Horowitz, is 11. . . . Bxd4 +!. After 12. Qxd4, Black wins White's Queen on the Knight-fork 12. . . . Ne2 +. White can't take the Knight, for Black's Queen then mates at e1.

Interpretation: In this example White fails to move out his d-pawn so that his Queenside pieces can make an entrance. When the d-pawn finally moves, it's too late. We see also how the black f-pawn, if maintained, can sometimes be very annoying. It, along with Black's h5-Knight and invading Queen, make for a desperate force, all converging on the square g3. One typical threat in similar situations is to move the Knight from h5 to g3. With Black's Queen at h4, White's h-pawn is unable to capture without allowing Black's Queen freely to take the h1-Rook. Whenever White's f-pawn moves early in the game, remember the potential weak points: the g3 square, the e1-h4 diagonal, and the a7-g1 diagonal.

62

KING HUNT

King's Gambit Accepted

1. e4	e5
2. f4	exf4
3. Nf3	g5
4. Bc4	Bg7
5. d4	g4
6. Bxf4	gxf3
7. 0-0	fxg2
8. Bxf7 +	Kxf7

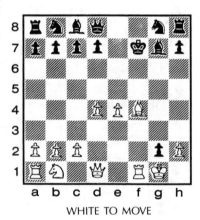

WHITE TO MOVE

Scenario: Black is a Bishop and Knight ahead, but his material superiority sits on the back rank, idle, His own exposed King reduces White's so-called weaker forces. White's attack juggernauts with 9. **Qh5 +**. If 9. . . .Ke6, then 10. Qf5 + Ke7 11. Bd6 + transposes into the main line. That continuation goes 9. . . .Ke7 10. **Bd6 +!** Kxd6 (10. . . .cxd6 allows 11. Qf7 mate) 11. **Qc5 + Ke6** 12. **d5 + Ke5** 13. **d6 + Kxe4** (or 13. . . .Ke6 14. Qd5 mate) 14. **Nd2** mate.

Interpretation: A glance at the diagram suggests that Black is playing with a paltry less than half his army. His entire Queenside force rests on original squares. Combine that with no pawn cover for his King, throw in White's pack of Queen, f1-Rook, and f4-Bishop, and the outcome could hardly be prosperous. Black kept gorging on White pieces and pawns to the point of indigestion. Certainly he should have stopped after 8. Bxf7 +, and would lasted longer by turning down this unwholesome morsel, 8. . . .Ke8-f8. Surely there was no need for 7. . . .fxg2 on the previous move, for that opens the f-file for the f1-Rook. A plausible counter for Black on move 7 is d7-d5, offering a pawn back to expedite development and to take some of the sting out of White's onslaught. All captures and no development or attack makes Jack a dull, lost boy. "Despair in vain sits brooding over the putrid eggs of hope"—John Hoakham Frere.

63

KING HUNT

King's Gambit Accepted

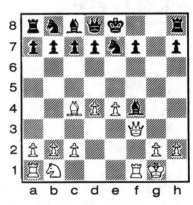

WHITE TO MOVE

1. e4	e5
2. f4	exf4
3. Nf3	g5
4. Bc4	g4
5. d4	gxf3
6. Qxf3	Bh6
7. 0-0	Ne7
8. Bxf4	Bxf4

Scenario: If White routinely recaptures on f4, Black can castle, offering some resistance to White's assault. But by interposing the riposte 9. **Bxf7 +!**, whether Black takes the Bishop or not, castling is impossible. After 9. . . . **Kxf7** 10. **Qxf4 + Kg6** (10. . . . Kg8 allows 11. Qf7 mate, and 10. . . . Ke6 is refuted by 11. Qe5 mate)   11.

Qf6 + Kh5   12. g4 + Kxg4   13. Rf4 + Kh5 (or 13. . . . Kh3   14. Qh4 mate), Black is mated by 14. Rh4.

Interpretation: Even when there is a possible variation—where Black wangles his way through the opening, withstanding a furious attack, and survives—developing players ought not to proceed this way. Black's first five moves in this game are pawn moves, yet the d-pawn never budges. What a way to facilitate development! You won't be mated in the opening if you bring out your center pawns and minor pieces expeditously. Get sidetracked by the lure of snaring inconsequential pawns, however, and watch your King topple.

64

KING HUNT

King's Gambit Accepted

1. e4	e5
2. f4	exf4
3. Nf3	g5
4. Bc4	g4
5. Nc3	gxf3
6. 0-0	fxg2
7. Rxf4	f6

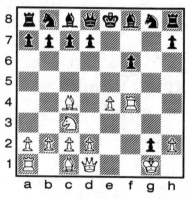

WHITE TO MOVE

Scenario: Here we go again. Black is ahead by a piece but gets mated anyway. The execution is as follows: 8. Qh5 + Ke7   9. Qf7 + Kd6   10. e5 + ! Kxe5 (10. . . . fxe5 falls flat after 11. Qd5 + Ke7   12. Qxe5 mate, while 10. . . . Kc6   11. Qd5 + Kb6   12. Qb5 is not a bad mate, either)   11. Re4 + Kd6 (or 11. . . . Kf5   12. Qh5 mate)   12. Qd5 mate.

Interpretation: Correct me if I'm wrong, but in the diagram, with White to play his eighth move, is it true that Black has not yet moved a single piece? All eight Black pieces still occupy the back rank, and except for the King, none of them moves by the variations that conclude on move 12. This is not a chess game, it's a funeral. By moving only pawns, by blindly taking all material offerings, by overextending yourself trying to hold on to useless gains, by neglecting development and King safety, you board the disaster train. Actually, I'm surprised Black lasts twelve moves. Maybe White wasn't playing too well, either. "The one-eyed man is king in the kingdom of the blind"—an old saying.

65

MATING ATTACK

King's Gambit Accepted

1. e4	e5
2. f4	exf4
3. Nf3	g5
4. Nc3	g4
5. Ne5	Qh4 +
6. g3	fxg3
7. Qxg4	g2 +
8. Qxh4	gxh1/Q
9. Nd5	Na6
10. d4	Be7?

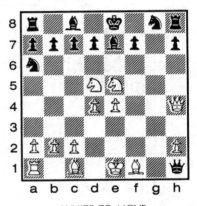

WHITE TO MOVE

Scenario: Black has an extra Rook, but that's little consolation if he's mated. After the stellar 11. **Qxe7 +!! Nxe7** 12. **Nf6 +**, mate thunders in on the next move. If Black's King goes Kingside, 12. . . . Kf8, then 13. Bh6 does it. And if Black instead moves Queenside, 12. . . . Kd8, then 13. Nxf7 ends his torment.

Interpretation: Black goes cute on move 7, momentarily abandoning his Queen with a discovered check only to regain it a move later by capturing the h1-Rook and promoting to a new Queen. That put

Black a Rook ahead, but he had no development except for a displaced Queen. Instead of immediately losing with 10. . . . Be7, Black might have tried to re-work his new Queen by 10. . . . Qg1. He also could try 10. . . . d7-d6, to develop his Queenside while assailing the e5-Knight. Many players err by gaining material and then sitting back on their laurels. That doesn't win the game, especially when the other side has enormous compensation for the sacrificed pieces. As former World Champion Emanuel Lasker (1868–1941) commented, chess more than anything else is a struggle, and the only time you can rest is between games, if even then.

66

MATING ATTACK

King's Gambit Accepted

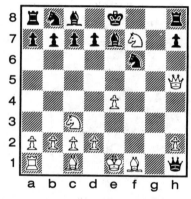

WHITE TO MOVE

1. e4	e5
2. f4	exf4
3. Nf3	g5
4. Nc3	g4
5. Ne5	Qh4 +
6. g3	fxg3
7. Qxg4	g2 +
8. Qxh4	gxh1/Q
9. Qh5	Be7
10. Nxf7	Nf6

Scenario: Black will get mated, all right—by force: **11. Nd6 + Kd8** (or 11. . . . Kf8 is mated by 12. Qf7) **12. Qe8 + ! Rxe8 13. Nf7**, a smothered mate. Note: it doesn't help Black to take White's Queen on e8 with his f6-Knight, 12. . . . Nxe8, for 13. Nf7 is still smothered mate.

Interpretation: Black's tenth move is an outright error. With 10. . . . Bh4 + , he could have given White some problems. If White's

Queen then takes the Bishop, Black's King can capture White's f7-Knight. If White answers the h4-Bishop check with a King move to e2, Black's Queen could check and capture the h2-pawn. Of course, if King to d1, as a response to the h4-Bishop check, then Black's Queen takes on f1, giving mate. The essence of the smothered mate is the double-check from White's Knight and Queen. With two checks delivered, neither piece could be captured, even though both are threatened. Don't attack and defend like an automaton. Be alert to real possibilities in the position. "Oh, the wasted hours of life/That have drifted by!"—Sarah Doudney.

67

FORK

King's Gambit Accepted

1. e4	e5
2. f4	exf4
3. Nf3	g5
4. h4	g4
5. Ne5	Nf6
6. Bc4	d5
7. exd5	Bd6
8. d4	Nh5
9. Nxg4?	

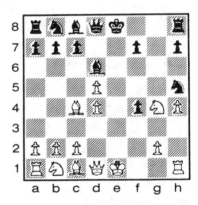

BLACK TO MOVE

Scenario: Black has a winning continuation in 9. . . .Ng3 10. **Rh2** (else h4 hangs) **Qe7 +** 11. **Kf2 h5** 12. **Ne5 Bxe5** 13. **dxe5 Qc5 +**, snaring the c4-Bishop because of the checking fork. White doesn't achieve enough for his lost piece.

Interpretation: One purpose of the King's Gambit is to lure Black's e-pawn out of the center, giving White a freer hand there. White, for one, many be able to build a classic pawn center, with pawns aligned on d4 and e4. He also hopes to build a strong attack. Black can choose to hold onto the gambit pawn, or, as Black does here (6. . . .d7-d5), give it back to get a share of the center and complete his development. There's no need to be greedy. As long as Black stymies White from winning back the f-pawn, he keeps the f-file somewhat closed and inhibits the development of White's c1-Bishop. To guard f4 is one reason Black plays 8. . . .Nh5. It also, however, brings the Knight into position to occupy the weakened g3 while clearing the d8-h4 diagonal for Black's Queen. White cannot afford to shift from the offensive to cede a tempo and take the g4-pawn. As a result, his pieces become jumbled, with his Rook winding up at h2, his King at f2, and his Knight constrained into an unfavorable exchange. As soon as the a7-g1 diagonal opens by the capture on e5, White's c4-Bishop falls like a dead duck.

68

MATING ATTACK

King's Gambit Declined

1. e4	e5
2. f4	Nf6
3. Nf3	Nc6
4. fxe5	Nxe4
5. d3	Nc5
6. d4	Na6
7. Bc4	Qe7
8. Nc3	h6
9. 0-0	g5

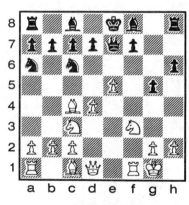

WHITE TO MOVE

Scenario: Black's Queen, holding court on e7, is about to be toppled from its perch by 10. **Nd5.** After the forced retreat 10. . . .**Qd8,** White's obvious invasion continues 11. **Nf6 +**, to which Black must respond by moving his King, 11. . . .**Ke7.** White's attentuating move is 12. **Nxg5!,** and if Black takes the Knight, 12. . . .**hxg5,** the crusher is 13. **Qh5!!,** threatening 14. Qxf7 mate and 14. Qxh8. If Black defends with the almost necessary 13. . . .**Rxh5**, the astonishing denouement is 14. **Ng8 + Ke8** 15. **Bxf7** mate.

Interpretation: Black's passive defense, surrendering the center at his own expense—notably in White having two potent center pawns—gains time for advances by attacking Black's hapless King-Knight. This poor pirouette needs four moves to reach a6, a particularly out-of-the-way square. A Knight on the edge is sludge. Another feckless placement is Black's Queen to e7, resulting in two wasted tempi once White's c3-Knight perforates the 5th rank, 10. Nd5. These time expenditures, along with severe weaknesses (notably at f6 and h5) induced by the pawn advances 8. . . .h7-h6 and 9. . . .g7-g5, were too much to overcome. In fifteen moves, Black never moved his d-pawn, which is why Black doesn't get beyond the fifteenth move. "O Jephthah, . . . what a treasure hadst thou!"—William Shakespeare, *Hamlet*.

69

FORK

King's Gambit Declined

1. **e4**	**e5**
2. **f4**	**Bc5**
3. **fxe5??**	

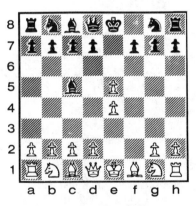

BLACK TO MOVE

Scenario: Never play White's last move. It gives Black a winning game after 3. . . . **Qh4 +**, when White has the choice of losing either of two ways. He could drop a Rook if he blocks the check, 4. **g3**, for Black follows through with 4. . . . **Qxe4 +**, forking White's King and h1-Rook. Or, better for Black, White should blunder again and play 4. **Ke2??**, which allows the deadening 4. . . . Qxe4 mate.

Interpretation: If White doesn't protect the e4 square in the King's Gambit, and if his King remains in the center, he almost never can afford to capture Black's e5-pawn with his f4-pawn. Doing so permits Black's Queen to enter at h4 with double-attack: check to the King at e1 and an attack to whatever occupies e4 (usually a pawn). And with the c5-Bishop cutting into the enemy encampment, preventing eventual escape to f2, Black actually is winning. If you want to make a capture where the f4-pawn captures the e5-pawn, prepare it by first developing your g1-Knight to f3, so that you guard h4 and prevent the intrusion of Black's Queen.

70

REMOVING THE GUARD

King's Gambit Declined

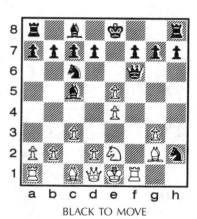

BLACK TO MOVE

1. e4	e5
2. f4	Bc5
3. Ne2	Qf6
4. c3	Nc6
5. g3	Nh6
6. Bg2	Ng4
7. Rf1	Nxh2
8. fxe5??	

Scenario: White's last move is an unfortunate gaffe. Black, with one blow, destroys Whites double protection of f3, resulting in a beautiful Bishop and Knight mate. With 8. . . . **Qxf1 + !**, Black gets rid of the Rook guarding f3. After 9. **Bxf1**, the light-square Bishop no longer controls f3 either. Black's Knight then completes the stampede: 9. . . . **Nf3 mate**.

Interpretation: In the King's Gambit Declined, it's perfectly sensible to post the g1-Knight on f3, guarding h4 and pressuring Black's center. By playing the less aggressive 3. Ne2, White transposes into Alapin's Opening, usually reached after 1. e4 e5 2. Ne2. White's problems stem from his blocked-up pieces, especially with a Knight sitting on e2, thwarting escape of the Kingside Bishop. Thus White plays 5. g3, which protects the f-pawn, gives the f1-Bishop a place to go (g2), but weakens White's light-squares, notably f3. White, throughout, can't capture safely on e5, for such a transaction clears the f-file for Black's Queen to invade at f2. With glaring weaknesses at both f2 and f3, the slightest error on White's part (7. fxe5?? is not so slight) could be fatal. In the diagrammed position, even though White has all his Kingside pieces developed, he loses. His development was simply too strained and illogical. "Be not careless in deeds, nor confused in words, nor rambling in thought"—Marcus Aurelius.

71

MATING ATTACK

King's Gambit Declined

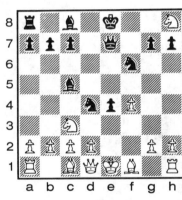

BLACK TO MOVE

1. e4	e5
2. f4	Bc5
3. Nf3	d5
4. Nxe5	dxe4
5. Nc3	Nf6
6. Qe2	Nc6
7. Nxf7?	Qe7
8. Nxh8	Nd4
9. Qd1	

Scenario: Black cruises to victory with 9. . . . Nf3 + !. If White takes the proffered Knight, 10. gxf3, then 10. . . . exf3 + 11. Be2 f2 + 12. Kf1 Bh3 is mate. So White must turn down the sacrifice and move his King, 10. Ke2; but with 10. . . . . Bg4, White loses at least his Queen. For example, 11. h3 Nd4 + 12. Ke1 Bxd1 snares it directly. And if White plays 11.gxf3, Black could shift gears and mate by 11. . . . exf3+ 12. Kd3 Qd6+ 13. Kc4 Qd4+ 14. Kb3 (or 14. Kb5) Qb4.

Interpretation: This is an irregular continuation that occurs less often than some of the other variations. With 6. Qe2, White thinks he can set a trap. He hopes to capture on f7 with his Knight, and after Black's King takes the Knight, White's Queen checks at c4, also attacking the c5-Bishop. White simply doesn't count Black, being so well-developed, as able to give up his h8-Rook for nothing. Just look at the latent power in all of Black's pieces. With the exception of the a8-Rook, all are ready for action. White has two Knights out, but the horse at h8 is not really in play. Thus White's King is a target, and the shooting can't be stopped.

72

FORK

King's Gambit Declined

1. e4	e5
2. f4	d6
3. Nf3	Bg4
4. Bc4	Be7
5. 0-0	Nc6
6. c3	Na5
7. fxe5	dxe5

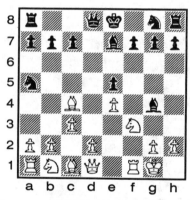

WHITE TO MOVE

Scenario: Black is banking on the g4-Bishop's pin of the f3-Knight to White's Queen, but that pin can be broken with a gain of time. The winning breakthrough is 8. **Bxf7+!**. If Black's King takes back, 8. . . .**Kxf7**, it is then on a attackable square (f7) for the f3-Knight. After 9. **Nxe5+**, White regains his sacrificed piece and is two pawns ahead. If Black aggresses in turn, 9. . . .**Ke6**, then 10. **Qxg4+ Kxe5** 11. **Qf5+Kd6** 12. **Qd5** is mate.

Interpretation: Black's choice of 2. . . .d7-d6 is quite passive, though it does defend the e-pawn. His early light-square Bishop jaunt, 3. . . .Bg4, however, is a risky follow-up. Better to mobilize Kingside pieces with rapid castling. Black's sixth move, Nc6-a5, is a mistake. It merely wastes a move and puts the Knight out of play (a Knight on the rim is dim). It weakens the e5-square and draws Black's King to f7, where it can be checked from e5 by the f3-Knight, forking King and g4-Bishop. If Black's Knight had remained on c6, this tactic would fail, for when White's Knight takes on e5, Black's c6-Knight would take back, protecting the g4-Bishop. In such situations, get the Kingside pieces out quickly and castle. Then you can fool around. "Let us therefore brace ourselves to our duties"— Winston Churchill.

73

REMOVING THE GUARD

King's Gambit Declined

1. e4	e5
2. f4	Bc5
3. Nf3	Nc6
4. c3	d5
5. d4	exd4
6. cxd4	Bb4 +
7. Nc3	dxe4
8. d5	

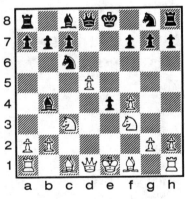

BLACK TO MOVE

Scenario: Two pieces are attacked by pawns: one of White's—the f3 Knight by the e4-pawn; and one of Black's—the c6-Knight by the d5-pawn. But Black goes first in this sequence, which means that White may come out short, which he does after 8. . . .exf3 9. dxc6 Bxc3 + 10. bxc3 f2 +. White loses his Queen if he takes the f-pawn, 11. Kxf2 Qxd1, or if he moves his King, 11. Ke2 Bg4 +.

Interpretation: Black's win hinges on removing the defender of White's Queen, the c3-Knight. So after the Knights on f3 and c6 are captured by pawns, Black interpolates a Bishop-for-Knight exchange on c3, which he does with check, forcing White to take back without the chance to play an in-between capture of Queen for Queen. When Black's pawn checks on f2, White's King can't take it, for that would leave the Queen hanging at d1, unprotected yet attacked by the opposite lady. This is how a simple exchange, though in itself winning nothing, might lead to the gain of something else. What this example clarifies also is that, in a sequence of related captures and threats, the player who goes second is at a disadvantage. Usually, whoever begins such a series controls it, and the last does not become the first.

74

DESPERADO

King's Gambit Declined

1. e4	e5
2. f4	Bc5
3. Nf3	Nc6
4. Bc4	d6
5. c3	Bg4
6. Bxf7 +	Kxf7
7. Ng5 +	

BLACK TO MOVE

Scenario: Add it all up, and White is a piece short, but Black's King is in check and his g4-Bishop is hanging. White plans to capture it in next move with his Queen. But wait; if Black were not in check he could capture White's Queen with his g4-Bishop. Black's counter, therefore, is 7. . . .**Qxg5!**, for the capture of Black's Queen, 8. **fxg5**, permits the immediate loss of White's own Queen, 8. . . .**Bxd1**. White will remain a piece behind with no compensation. So White must immerse himself in 9. **Qb3 +** **Be6** 10. **Qxb7 Qxg2** 11. **Qxa8**, but that ends in mate after 11. . . . **Qxe4 +!** 12. **Kd1** (or 12. Kf1 Bh3 mate) **Bg4**.

Interpretation: White's sixth move combination, Bxf7 +, is unsound; Black's temporary Queen sacrifice, 6. . . . Qxg5, effectively squelches it. This tactic, by which a piece sells itself for less than it's worth, is called a desperado. Black can afford to sacrifice his Queen for White's g5-Knight because Black realizes that on the next move he will be able to capture his opponent's Queen, offsetting his own Queen sacrifice. Following the ousting of the Queens would be that of a Black Bishop and a White Knight. Since Black was up a piece before these transactions, the exchanges actually serve to enhance Black's advantage. The fewer pieces on the board, the more important an extra one. "Size is not grandeur, and territory does not make a nation"—Thomas Henry Huxley.

75

TRAPPED PIECE

Falkbeer Counter-Gambit

1. **e4**	**e5**
2. **f4**	**d5**
3. **Nf3**	**dxe4**
4. **Nxe5**	**Nc6**
5. **Bb5**	**Nf6**
6. **Nxc6**	**bxc6**
7. **Bxc6 +**	**Bd7**
8. **Bxa8?**	

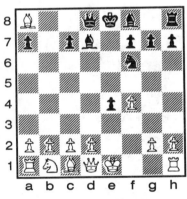

BLACK TO MOVE

Scenario: Does it matter if you're up material but badly developed, so that your advantage is worthless? White learns what it means to have garbage material after 8. . . . **Bg4**, usurping White's Queen.

White can insert the spite check, 9. **Bc6+**, but Black happily moves his King, forfeiting the opportunity to castle by 9. . . .**Ke7**, because White's Queen is then lost.

Interpretation: Black willingly sacrifices material for an edge in development, not just because he gets significant pressure against White's position but also because the slightest error by White could lead to immediate disaster. After Black blocks the check from White's light-square Bishop, 8. . . .**Bd7**, White should content himself with being up a pawn, and trade Bishops, 9. Bxd7+ Qxd7. He should then castle and play carefully, hoping to ward off the attack Black will launch because of his superiority in development. But filching the Rook in the corner—true greed—is a blunder that loses the Queen. As a further tip on how badly White does in this example, merely examine the diagram. White's entire Queenside force sits on its original squares. "They also serve who only stand and wait"—John Milton.

76

TRAPPED PIECE

Falkbeer Counter-Gambit

1. e4	e5
2. f4	d5
3. Nc3	d4
4. Nd5?	

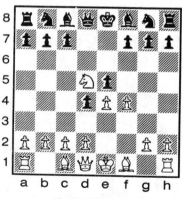

BLACK TO MOVE

Scenario: Be aggressive in the opening, but not rash. White's Knight enters the valley of death when both ends close off. Black pilfers the hapless rough-rider by 4. . . .**c6**, when it hasn't a safe retreat square, so Black gains a Knight.

Interpretation: White has to play carefully against the Falkbeer Counter-Gambit, for Black is generally better developed in that he moves both center-pawns two squares in the first two moves. The example shows a common mistake among newcomers: positioning a Knight behind enemy lines without adequate support or safe retreat. What happens if an enemy pawn attacks it? It dies for nothing. Before entering the lion's den, make sure he's out to lunch.

77

PIN

Falkbeer Counter-Gambit

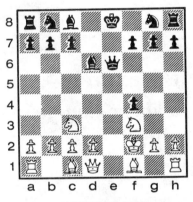

WHITE TO MOVE

1. e4	e5
2. f4	d5
3. exd5	Qxd5
4. Nc3	Qe6
5. Nf3	exf4 +
6. Kf2	Bd6?

Scenario: Black has an extra pawn and White has moved his King, but White wins with 7. **Bb5 +**. What does Black do? If he blocks the b5-Bishop check, 7. . . . .c6, then 8. Re1 pins the Black Queen to its King. Any other block of the Bishop's check, such as with the b8-Knight or the c8-Bishop, still results in the same Rook pin of the Queen. Black's King could flee instead, 7. . . . .Kd8 (or 7. . . . .Kf8), but White's trusty Rook move to e1 nets the Queen anyway; if it moved to safety off the e-file, White's Rook can shift gears to the 8th rank, protected by the b5-Bishop, and Black would be mated.

Interpretation: Black violates the spirit of this opening. Rather than bringing his Queen out early with the recapture on d5, he should push his e-pawn to e4, trying to restrain White's development. After

3. . . .e5-e4, for example, White cannot safely bring his g1-Knight to f3. With the improper 3. . . .Qxd5, however, White immediately gains a tempo by 4. Nc3, developing a Knight toward the center at Black's expense, for he must waste a turn getting his Queen to safety. No points are won by Black's Queen retreat to e6, even though it results in check, for that only forces White's King off the e-file so that his Rook is then free to go there with a deadly pin. Don't give a check solely because you can. Check only if the move relates to development or useful tactics, relying on the same criteria used in determining ordinary, nonchecking moves. And shoo away the habit of recruiting the Queen in the opening. You have other pieces; use them. The lady works better later.

78

TRAPPED PIECE

Falkbeer Counter-Gambit

BLACK TO MOVE

1. e4	e5
2. f4	d5
3. exd5	Qxd5
4. Nc3	Qd8
5. Qe2	c6
6. Qxe5 +	Be7
7. Qxg7?	

Scenario: White may think he has all bases covered, but the only thing covered is his face—with egg. His Queen plummets after 7. . . .Bf6 8. Qg3 Bh4, when it is pinned against its own King and lost.

Interpretation: White had good potential in this opening. Black brought his Queen out early, and White attacked it with his Queen-Knight, 4. Nc3, gaining a tempo. Though his fifth move, Qd1-e2, is quite playable, it hints that White is starting to think incorrectly. He unnecessarily captures the e-pawn with his Queen, albeit giving check. Several alternative moves, including 6. Ng1-f3, would give him a splendid game. After all, Black's e5-pawn is pinned and can't run away. Instead, he falls for a simple trap, blindly capturing Black's g-pawn and not realizing that the only way Black can save his threatened h8-Rook also wins White's Queen. This is not surprising. Make four moves with any piece so early in the game, and you'll buttonhole trouble. Don't "pawn grab" with the Queen, and especially be leery of pursuing Knight-pawns. These stinking varmints are typically referred to as "poison pawns." "I counted two-and-seventy stenches,/All well defined . . ."—Samuel Taylor Coleridge.

79

PIN

Falkbeer Counter-Gambit

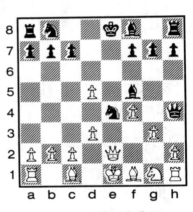

BLACK TO MOVE

1. e4	e5
2. f4	d5
3. exd5	e4
4. Nc3	Nf6
5. Qe2	Bf5
6. Nxe4	Nxe4
7. d3	Qh4 + !
8. g3?	

Scenario: Black has one more minor piece than White, but his e4-Knight is pinned and attacked by the d3-pawn at the same time as his Queen is accosted by the g3-pawn. Does White get his piece back? Not if Black plays 8. . . .Qe7!, breaking the pin. White could then capture the e4-Knight, 9. dxe4, but he has a problem after Black recaptures on e4 with his Bishop, 9. . . .Bxe4. How can he save the h1-Rook from seizure? If White blocks the diagonal by 10. Nf3 (or 10. Bg2 Bxg2 also wins), then the mere 10. . . .Bxf3 gains the

Knight, for White's Queen is unable to take back, being pinned along the e-file by Black's Queen.

Interpretation: After 7. . . .Qh4+, White had to move his King to d1, forfeiting castling rights but avoiding weaknesses. With 8. g2-g3?, however, White unwittingly weakens the e4-h1 diagonal. Black's natural Queen retreat, 8. . . .Qe7, ensured the gain of material, for there is no satisfactory way for White to save his cornered h1-Rook. White's automatic pawn block has to be a loser. Curiously, here was a case of pin/counter-pin along the same line—the e-file. First White's Queen pinned Black's e4-Knight, then Black's Queen pinned White's Queen. That's a fair turnaround, subjecting an opponent to his own tricks. "For 'tis the sport to have the engineer hoist with his petar"—William Shakespeare, *Hamlet.*

80

PIN

Falkbeer Counter-Gambit

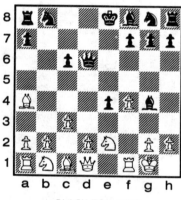

BLACK TO MOVE

1. e4	e5
2. f4	d5
3. exd5	e4
4. Bb5+	c6
5. dxc6	bxc6
6. Ba4	Qd4
7. c3	Qd6
8. Ne2	Bg4
9. 0-0	

Scenario: Black exploits the pin on White's e2-Knight by 9. . . .Qd3. After 10. **Re1** (10. Rf2 is met by another pin, 10. . . .Bc5) 10. . . .Bc5+ 11. Kh1 Bf3 12. Bc2 (please go away, Queen), Black forces mate by 12. . . .Bxg2+ 13. Kxg2 Qf3.

Interpretation: White seems to look more developed than Black at times, but his developmental lead turns out to be meaningless because his pieces coordinate poorly. His lack of Queenside development, with his d-pawn eventually blocked by Black's Queen, is critical. It means that White's c1-Bishop can't participate when needed. Note that if White defends by moving his Rook to f2 on move 10, Black pins it, shifting the f8-Bishop to c5. And if White's King ambles to the center, 11. Kf1 instead of 11. Kh1, Black mates beautifully by 11. . . .Qf3 + gxf3 12. Bh3—a criss-cross. Once White's Rook leaves the f-file, his f-pawn having moved becomes a real liability, for Black is able to control the a7-g1 diagonal. In the end, Black's force of Queen, two Bishops, and e-pawn is just too much.

4

Unusual Openings

Damiano Defense
Latvian Counter-Gambit
Queen-Pawn Counter-Gambit
Alapin Opening
Ponziani Opening

This chapter contains an assortment of unusual double King-pawn openings. Though somewhat off the beaten path, these openings occur on occasion and you should be familiar with them.

Damiano Defense (1. ef e5   2. Nf3 f6) has been discredited for centuries. It is a classic example of how *not* to play the opening. The pawn advance on Black's second move, f7 to f6, usurps the best square for the development of the g8-Knight. It critically weakens the e8·h5 diagonal. White's Queen reaching h5 would thereby check Black's King at e8. Black's 2. . . . f7-f6 doesn't even achieve satisfactorily its main objective: the defense of the e5-pawn. White can simply rip off the pawn with his f3-Knight. If Black then takes White's Knight, 3. . . . f6xe5, he falls into a withering attack beginning with White's Queen entering at h5. Poor Damiano. Back in 1512 he analyzed the move 2. . . . f7-f6. He found it wanting and condemned it. But in one of those strange quirks of history, his name has been attached to it ever since. He should have run when he could.

The *Latvian Counter-Gambit* (1. **e4 e5**   2. **Nf3 f5**) requires a two-square advance for Black's f-pawn. Like
Damiano Defense, the e8-h5 diagonal is open and a matter
of concern, but White's life is far more complicated since
his e4-pawn is under fire. Formerly known as Greco's
Counter Attack, the second move pawn advance from f7 to
f5 has been the subject of deep analytical investigation by
Latvian players in this century, which has led the gambit to
achieve a cult status. Latvian specialists regularly promote
their gambit with thematic correspondence tournaments
and a publication devoted solely to their brainchild. An
inverted brother of the King's Gambit, the Latvian has
twice the risks and can be recommended only for the most
adventurous spirits.

The *Queen-Pawn Counter-Gambit* (1. **e4 e5**   2. **Nf3 d4**)
is still another attempt by Black to tackle White's central
bastion, his e4-pawn. Whereas in the Latvian Black hits
from the flank, here Black comes straight up the middle,
opening lines of development for his pieces in the process. While Black's vigor and directness are commendable,
analytically the Queen-Pawn Counter-Gambit just doesn't
hold up. Unhappy for Black, White is in the position of
being able to capture either of Black's center-pawns with
advantage. That's life on the chessboard.

Alapin Opening (1. **e4 e5**   2. **Ne2**) is named for its most
famous practitioner, Semyon Alapin (1856–1923), an original analyst who liked to go his own way in the openings.
To the trained eye, the Alapin is weird, with the e2-Knight
blocking the development of the f1-Bishop, while exerting
only a fraction of the strength it would have were it on f3.
Nevertheless, there is method in Alapin's madness. White
plans advancing his f-pawn two squares, assailing the e5-
pawn without incurring the risks of the King's Gambit.
Naturally, Black has several ways to get a good game
against the slow-motion tactics of the Alapin. Black's main
danger is a psychological underestimation of White's
Knight to e2. That's when the Alapin shows its teeth.

In *Ponziani Opening* (1. **e4 e5**   2. **Nf3 Nc6**   3. **c3**),
named after an Italian master from Modena, Domenico

Ponziani (1719–96), White tries to build a broad pawn center with the follow-up fourth-move push, d2 to d4. In addition, White opens a path for the development of his Queen by moving it from d1 to a4, which can often be effective in this opening. Black, for his part, tries to counter White's plan by turning his attention to White's e4-pawn. Moves such as 3. . . . Nf6, 3. . . . d5, and 3. . . . f5—the latter being Ponziani's own choice—are all motivated by this same idea, pressuring e4. Curiously, every great teacher of openings who has investigated the Ponziani has concluded that it leads to interesting play and deserves to be played more often. Yet it has never captured the fancy of chessplayers in general, and it remains to be seen whether the Ponziani is an opening of the past or the future.

81

FORK

Damiano Defense

1. e4   e5
2. Nf3   f6
3. Nxe5   Qe7
4. Qh5 +

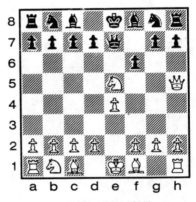

BLACK TO MOVE

Scenario: White has checked with his Queen, assuming that blocking by 4. . . . **g6** could be answered by 5. **Nxg6** hxg6   6. Qxh8 and winning the exchange—a Rook for a Knight. But if Black interpolates 5. . . . **Qxe4 +**—possible because White's e5-Knight has moved to g6—he stands tall after 6. **Kd1** (or 6. Kf1) **Qxg6** garnering the sitting-duck Knight on g6.

Interpretation: Damiano is not the best defense. But if Black must play it, he should follow White's e5-Knight's capture with Qd8-e7. Any other move essentially loses. White's early Queen jaunt was an error, as it usually is. Correct instead was 4. Nf3, and whether the game continues 4. . . . Qxe4 + 5. Be2 or 4. . . . d5 5. d3 dxe4 6. dxe4 Qxe4 + 7. Be2, White's developmental lead ensures his maintaining a solid advantage. "Development is everything—or almost," says my Washington Square adviser.

82

OVERLOAD

Damiano Defense

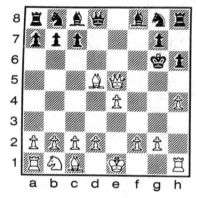

1. e4	e5
2. Nf3	f6
3. Nxe5	fxe5
4. Qh5+	Ke7
5. Qxe5+	Kf7
6. Bc4+	d5
7. Bxd5+	Kg6
8. h4	h6

WHITE TO MOVE

Scenario: White has gotten three pawns for his sacrificed Knight. He also has a blistering attack against Black's gaping King. White cashes in with 9. **Bxb7!**, switching to Black's Queenside. Black's c8-Bishop is overworked. If it captures on b7, it leaves f5 unguarded, and White's Queen can give mate. So Black tries 9. . . . **Bd6**, to drive White's Queen from the 5th rank. Correct is 10. **Qa5**, but not 10. Qd5 or 10. Qb5, when 10. . . . c6 enables Black to capture White's b7-Bishop on the next move. After 10. Qa5, Black has merely a paltry 10. . . . **Nc6 11. Bxc6 Rb8.** If White's Queen then takes Black's a-pawn, White is five pawns ahead (Black's play is sometimes described as "the five pawns gambit").

Interpretation: Few openings have as little going for them as Damiano's Defense, characterized by Black's 2. . . . f6. Damiano himself, in 1512, condemned this opener. Why place the f-pawn on the g8-Knight's best square? Why open, and therefore weaken, two diagonals—a2-g8 and h5-e8—easing White's attack on Black's King? Why defend the e-pawn with the inadequate f-pawn? Good chess demands logic, and the logic behind Damiano's Defense is shaky. The wrong opening "Dies at the opening day"—Isaac Watts.

83

TRAPPED PIECE

Damiano Defense

1. **e4**	**e5**
2. **Nf3**	**f6**
3. **Nxe5**	**fxe5**
4. **Qh5 +**	**Ke7**
5. **Qxe5 +**	**Kf7**
6. **Bc4 +**	**d5**
7. **Bxd5**	**Kg6**
8. **d4**	

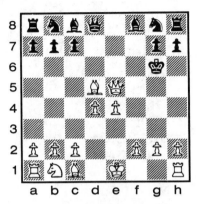

BLACK TO MOVE

Scenario: White's last move, usually a natural line-opener, is here a blunder that leads to entrapment of White's own Queen. After 8. . . . **Bd6**, madame is caught right in the middle of the board, all alone. To extricate her, White must sacrifice a piece, 9. **Bxf7 + Kxf7**. Afterward, he moves his Queen to safety. He has sacrificed a Bishop and Knight for only three pawns in exchange. That's not enough.

Interpretation: Damiano's Defense, 1. e4 e5 2. Nf3 f6, has such ill repute that it could lull White into false security. The previous example shows that White must play precisely if he is to defeat this system. Second-rate attacks will not necessarily beat a second-rate defense. They may even lose. Try not to bring out your Queen early. But if you do, for some tactical purpose, don't forget it's out there and needs help. "Oh, what can ail thee, lady, Alone and palely loitering?" (with apologies to Keats).

84

FORK

Latvian Counter-Gambit

1. **e4**   **e5**
2. **Nf3**   **f5**
3. **Nxe5**   **Qf6**
4. **Nc4**   **fxe4**
5. **Nc3**   **Qf7**
6. **Nxe4**

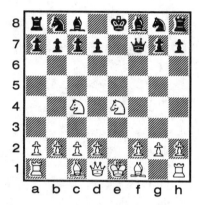

BLACK TO MOVE

Scenario: White has two Knights out there, but they are forkable, which is evident after 6. . . . **d5**. The best White can do is annoy Black a bit, starting with 7. **Ne5** (7. Ng5 is dealt with by 7. . . . Qe7 +). A strong move for Black is 7. . . . **Qe6**, skewering both undefended Knights, while the e4-Knight remains attacked by the d5-pawn. White can try 8. **Qh5 +** , which can be conquered by 8. . . . **g6**. If White continues 9. **Nxg6**, Black grabs the e4-Knight with check, 9. . . . **Qxe4 +** . After White's obvious block, 10. **Be2**, the variation concludes 10. . . . **Nf6**   11.**Qe5 + Qxe5**   12. **Nxe5,** leaving White with only two pawns for his missing minor piece.

Interpretation: It's easy to fool yourself that your opponent must automatically have a bad game, if his King is somewhat exposed and the only developed piece is his Queen. White has out two Knights to Black's none. Surely White has the edge, but that doesn't entitle him to switch gears and play recklessly with his possible advantage. Taking the pawn at e4, walking into the d-pawn fork, is a boldfaced error. Don't take your opponent lightly if he gets off to a suspicious start. He might be wily enough to steal your shirt.

85

PIN

Latvian Counter-Gambit

1. e4	e5
2. Nf3	f5
3. Nxe5	Qf6
4. Nc4	fxe4
5. Nc3	Qf7
6. d4	d5
7. Ne5	Qe6
8. Qh5 +	g6

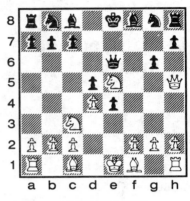

WHITE TO MOVE

Scenario: Black's nemesis in the Latvian is the e8-h5 diagonal. This conduit to Black's King becomes immediately exposed after his second move. White inflicts conflagration on Black with 9. **Nxg6**, when 9. . . .hxg6 allows White to capture the h8-Rook, while 9. . . .Qxg6 is met by 10. Qe5 +. After 10. . . .Be7, White uproots 11. **Nxd5**, threatening two Rooks: the a8-Rook by Nxc7 + and the h8-Rook by a timely capture by the Queen.

Interpretation: Black doesn't fare too well here because he doesn't really develop his game, relying instead on his Queen and questionable tactics. If White uses his obvious developmental advantage, he must triumph, if there is such a thing as justice. The final trick he must evade occurs after Black's dark-square Bishop blocks the e5-Queen check by interposing at e7. If White rapaciously gobbles the h8-Rook, 11. Qxh8, he drops his Queen to 11. . . .Bf6.

86

PIN

Latvian Counter-Gambit

1. e4   e5
2. Nf3   f5
3. Nxe5   Qf6
4. d4   d6
5. Nc4   fxe4
6. Be2   Qg6??

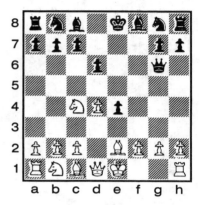

WHITE TO MOVE

Scenario: Black's last move is a blunder, on both tactical and conceptual levels: tactically, because White pins the Queen handily with 7. **Bh5**; conceptually, in that Black should be very sensitive to errors like this because of his chosen defense. He should realize that in the Latvian Counter-Gambit, White's main devastations occur along the e8-h5 diagonal, which is weakened after Black's second move.

Interpretation: Black blunders with 6. . . .Qg6, trying to take advantage of White's undefended g2-pawn, gone weak after White develops his f1-Bishop to e2. Black hopes that White will disturb his Kingside pawn cover, advancing his King-Knight pawn to g3 and weakening the light squares, permitting Black's c8-Bishop invasion at h3. Or perhaps he wishes White will castle Kingside, 7. 0-0, which he thinks will drop the exchange to 7. . . .Bh3. But all these ideas fail to the more obvious h5-Bishop pin, of which Black should be aware, having played the Latvian Counter-Gambit. If you're going to play an opening, try to familiarize yourself with its general strengths, weaknesses, do's and don'ts prior to playing it. Otherwise you will have to do it while playing, which can be costly. "Imagination is as good as many voyages—and how much cheaper"—George William Curtis.

87

DOUBLE-ATTACK

Queen's Pawn Counter-Gambit

1. e4   e5
2. Nf3   d5
3. Bd3   dxe4
4. Bxe4   f5
5. Nxe5

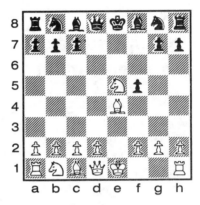

BLACK TO MOVE

Scenario: White hopes for 5. . . .fxe4, when 6. Qh5+ cuts his eye again in the e8-h5 diagonal. And if Black answers White's h5-Queen check with 6. . . .g7-g6, White cuts again with 7. Nxg6, which can't be conveniently captured because the Queen pins the h-pawn to the h8-Rook. But Black has an unforeseen winner, 5. . . .Qf6! (also strong is 5. . . .Qd4, forking two pieces and defending h8 along the diagonal d4-h8 after moving his King-Knight pawn from g7-g6). If 6. Qh5+, then 6. . . .g6 works, for 7. Nxg6 can safely be responded to by 7. . . .hxg6 because of the guarded h8-Rook. Black wins at least a minor piece.

Interpretation: Just because your opponent is a risk-taker doesn't mean you should be one, too. This defense naturally carries a few question marks, but that doesn't justify blatant violations of principles, such as, on move 3 when White develops his King-Bishop to d3, blocking the advance of his d-pawn. But even worse than the positional liability incurred by hampering central advances needed for development is White's failure to see what happens if Black merely answers 3. Bd3 by 3. . . .fxe4. White's Bishop and Knight are forked after 4. Bxe4 f5   5. Bd3 e4. Little things like position play the window when a line loses as easily and immediately as this one does.

88

PIN

Queen's Pawn Counter-Gambit

1. e4	e5
2. Nf3	d5
3. Nxe5	dxe4
4. Bc4	Qg5
5. Bxf7 +	Ke7
6. d4	Qxg2
7. Rf1	Bh3
8. Bc4	Qxh2?

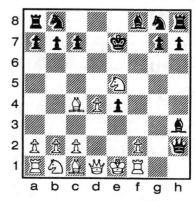

WHITE TO MOVE

Scenario: Black has gotten a little too greedy. White counters first by 9. **Qh5**, pinning the h3-Bishop to Black's Queen, so that it can't capture White's f1-Rook. If Black tries the likely 9. . . .**g6**, to drive away White's Queen and breaking the h-file pin, White polishes the win with 10. **Qh4 + Nf6** 11. **Ng4**, when Black will have to abandon his h3-Bishop to salvage his more important Queen.

Interpretation: This is a variation with burrs. Complications develop from black's fourth move, when he abandons his f-pawn with check and counterattacks with his Queen, Qd8-g5, forking White's e5-Knight and g2-Pawn. White is able to take the pawn with check and then protect his Knight, further gaining time by discovering an attack to Black's Queen, 6. d2-d4. Black compensates after capturing on g2 and then invades on h3 with his c8-Bishop. In this materially even game after White's eighth move, Black should insert the natural developer, 8. . . .Ng8-f6, getting out the King-Knight and taking away the h5-square from White's Queen. Black would thus gain invasion possibilities on g4 when it became timely. But instead greed claimed another victim.

89

OVERLOAD

Queen's Pawn Counter-Gambit

1. e4	e5
2. Nf3	d5
3. Nxe5	dxe4
4. Bc4	Qg5
5. Bxf7 +	Ke7
6. d4	Qxg2
7. Rf1	Bh3
8. Bc4	Nf6
9. Nf7?	

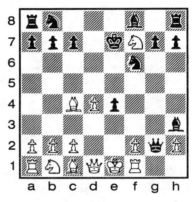

BLACK TO MOVE

Scenario: This and the previous example are the same through the first seven moves. Black got greedy in the first case, and now it's White's turn to try gobbling. With 9. . . . **b5!**, Black flashes light on how much hinges on placement of White's c4-Bishop. It becomes a yeoman, protecting the f7-Knight as well as the f1-Rook. The two threats are overwhelming, and he will wind up losing a piece. After 10. Nxh8 bxc4   11. Qe2 Qxf1 +   12. Qxf1 Bxf1   13. Kxf1, White must face that his h8-Knight is trapped and eventually lost.

Interpretation: Much stronger than the overly materialistic Knight invasion on f7 is 9. Nc3, developing a new piece toward the center and creating the possibility of a d5-Knight check at some timely occasion. Whether attacking or defending, your best is when your forces are mobilized. Try not to move your pieces in order to win material, even if sometimes you do win a lot of material, as with the h8-Rook here. As Fred Reinfeld used to say, "Development is better than riches."

90

MATING ATTACK

Queen's Pawn Counter-Gambit

1. **e4**	**e5**
2. **Nf3**	**d5**
3. **Nxe5**	**dxe4**
4. **Bc4**	**Qg5**
5. **Bxf7 +**	**Ke7**
6. **Qh5**	**Qxg2**
7. **Bxg8**	**Qxh1 +**
8. **Ke2**	**Rxg8**
9. **Qf7 +**	**Kd6**
10. **Qxg8**	**Kxe5**
11. **Qxf8?**	

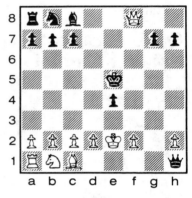

BLACK TO MOVE

Scenario: This is bad news for White. After 11. . . . . **Bg4 +**, White must lose at least his Queen after 12. f3 Bxf3 + 13. Qxf3 Qxf3 + 14. Ke1 Nc6, when there is no satisfactory answer to the threatened a8-Rook move to f8, backing up Black's Queen. The most painless conclusion occurred in a game of David Bronstein's. The Russian great finished off a frustrated opponent by 12. **Ke3** 12. . . . **Qe1** mate.

Interpretation: Another wild and woolly example. On the sixth move, White offers a Queen trade and Black turns him down. What follows is a seemingly endless series of checks and captures, with Black's King going from an exposed liability to a fierce attacking weapon, guarding key squares in the very center of the board! Rather than capture Black's f8-Bishop on move 11, White should at least throw out his d-pawn, moving it two squares and giving check. He has no choice, for he must activate his remaining pieces. But the urge to take sets in once again, and Black gets the last cackle. The final position, in which the two Kings confront each other in the center, with White mated, is somewhat droll, like the Marx Brothers' mirror scene in their famous movie *Duck Soup*.

91

REMOVING THE GUARD

Alapin Opening

1. e4	e5
2. Ne2	d5
3. exd5	Qxd5
4. Nbc3	Qa5
5. d4	Nc6
6. d5	Nb4
7. Bd2	Bf5
8. Rc1	

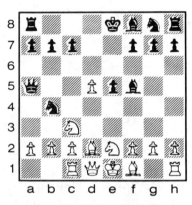

BLACK TO MOVE

Scenario: White thinks he's covered by guarding c2 with his Queen-Rook. The unveiling takes place with 8. . . . **Bxc2!**, garnering White's Queen, for if White captures the Bishop with his Rook, 9. **Rxc2**, Black buries White six feet under with 9. . . . **Nd3**—smothered mate!

Interpretation: This shouldn't happen to a dog. Black brings his Queen out early and White kicks it around by the good development, 4. Nbc3. White then plays for quick advance of his d-pawn, strong and sharp. A safer plan is to shift his e2-Knight to g3, then posting the King-Bishop and later castling Kingside. White is now prepared for hand-to-hand combat. After the game continuation 5. d4 Nc6   6. d5 Nb4, White should proceed with 7. Ng3 and in the next move develop his King-Bishop. He would still retain the edge. You can't waste time in the Alapin, for with a Knight already occupying e2, it takes several moves just to reposition it to get out the King-Bishop.

92

MULTIPLE ATTACK

Alapin Opening

1. e4	e5
2. Ne2	Bc5
3. c3	Nc6
4. d4	Bb6
5. f4	Nf6
6. fxe5	Nxe4
7. Nd2	Qh4 +
8. g3	Nxe5

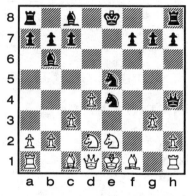

WHITE TO MOVE

Scenario: White is in boiling water. Four Black pieces are swarming around White's King, three of them themselves under attack, though none can be taken yet. For example, if 9. gxh4, then 9. . . .Nd3 mate; or if 9. dxe5, then 9. . . .Bf2 mate; or if 9. Nxe4, then 9. . . .Qxe4 10. Rg1 Nf3 +, followed next move by 11. . . .Nxg1. White blares through with 9. **Qc2!**. This stops the most potent threat, Ne5-d3 mate, and leaves Black's pieces still seizable. No matter how Black retorts, White gains at least a piece.

Interpretation: The rarely played Alapin Opening, 1. e4 e5 2. Ne2, is designed to enable White to build a broad pawn center by not blocking White's f-pawn, as the normal Ng1-f3 does. Black's second move, Bf8-c5, therefore is inaccurate, for it encourages White to timely advance the d-pawn to attack the c5-Bishop. More appropriate for Black's second move are Nb8-c6 or Ng8-f6. Rather than the audacious 7. . . .Qh4 +, which works only if White defends poorly, Black should have cut his losses with 7. . . .Nxd2, reaching a position only slightly inferior to White's. If you see your chosen path is ending in a blind alley, try a detour.

93

MATING ATTACK

Alapin Opening

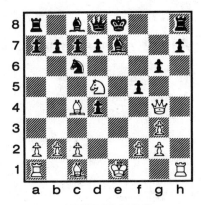

1. e4   e5
2. Ne2   Nf6
3. d4   Nxe4
4. Ng3   Nxg3
5. hxg3   Nc6
6. Nc3   exd4
7. Nd5   Be7
8. Qg4   g6
9. Bc4   f5

WHITE TO MOVE

Scenario: White is already down two pawns, and his Queen is threatened by Black's f5-pawn. Ignoring the threat, White barrels forward with 10. **Rxh7!**, offering Black a capture of either the Rook or the Queen. Plucking the Rook leads to trouble: 10. . . . Rxh7 11. Qxg6+ Kf8 (or 11. . . . Rf7 12. Nf6+ and 13. Qxf7 mate) 12. Nf6 Rg7 (else 13. Qg8 mate) 13. Nh7+ Rxh7 14. Qg8 mate. So Black grabs the Queen, 10. . . . **fxg4.** But here also White has enough ammunition to create a mating net. White clears the decks for the c4-Bishop to enter with 11. **Nxc7+**, forcing 11. . . . **Qxc7** (if 11. . . . Kf8, then 12. Bh6 mate). Now comes 12. **Bf7+ Kd8** (again, if 12. . . . Kf8, then 13. Bh6 mate). Only now does White capture the loose Rook, 13. **Rxh8+**, and the finish is 13. . . . **Bf8** 14. **Bg5+ Ne7** 15. **Rxf8** mate.

Interpretation: White's opening play deserves no academy award. It is designed to bamboozle an unsuspecting opponent, and here succeeds brilliantly. Most likely Black is all right up to the second he plays 9. . . . f5. Instead 9. . . . d6 is a perfectly healthy defense. But once he moves his f-pawn, weakening his King's position, White zooms in on Black like a hawk. He will devour his prey, and both his Queen and his d5-Knight are expendable.

94

UNPIN

Alapin Opening

1. e4   e5
2. Ne2   Nf6
3. d3   Bc5
4. Bg5?

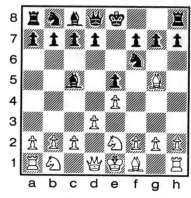

BLACK TO MOVE

Scenario: Development, in terms of numbers, is even, both sides having out a Bishop and Knight. But it's Black's turn, and even though his f6-Knight is pinned, Black zaps White with 4. . . . **Nxe4!.** If White takes Black's Knight, 4. **dxe4**, then White loses his g5-Bishop, 4. . . . **Qxg5.** Black's Queen, however, is hanging. If White gloms it, 4. **Bxd8**, he gets mated by 4. . . . **Bxf2.**

Interpretation: Mindless, automatic pins may get by in very casual chess, but against a real opponent they must lead to nothing. It's bad enough that White develops his King-Knight only to the second rank, but to follow by activating the Queen-Bishop (Knights before Bishops) and set up an ineffectual pin is folly's height. Once White's f2-square comes under fire, White must get ready for potential reinforcements zeroing in on that square, especially the f6-Knight shifting to g4. White plays 4. Bg5 to stop the incursion of Black's Knight, but, as we can see, it doesn't work.

95

OVERLOAD

Alapin Opening

1. e4   e5
2. Ne2   Nf6
3. f4   exf4
4. Nxf4   Nxe4
5. Qe2   Qe7
6. Nd5   Qe5
7. Nbc3   c6

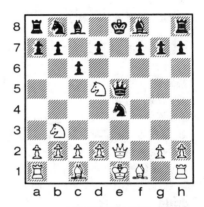

WHITE TO MOVE

Scenario: Black's e4-Knight is a pinned target for White's pieces, so Black attacks one of White's Knights in turn. But White bursts through the door with 8. **d4!**, trying to drive Black's Queen off the defense of either the e-file or the c7-pawn. If Black captures White's Queen-pawn, 8. . . .**Qxd4**, then 9. **Nxe4 cxd5**   10. **Nd6+ Kd8**   11. **Nxf7+** (or 11. Qe8+ Kc7 12. Nb5+ Kb6 13. Qd8+ Kc5 14. Qc7+ gains the Queen) clearly wins. And if Black answers 8. d4 instead by 8. . . .**Qf5**, then 9. **Nxe4 cxd5**   10. **Nd6+** also nets Black's Queen.

Interpretation: Black's ailment is overuse of the Queen. It can't guard, attack, or be everywhere at once. In trying to be omnipresent, it steps on its own toes and trips. It doesn't help Black that his Queen-Bishop is ineptly blocked on the back rank, either. Black winds up not only moving his Queen too much but also not getting anything else out. In the opening, develop the Bishops and Knights so the Queen won't be Coleridge's Ancient Mariner, "Alone, alone . . . on a wide, wide sea."

96

DISCOVERY

Ponziani Opening

1. e4   e5
2. Nf3   Nc6
3. c3   d5
4. Qa4   Nf6
5. Nxe5   Bd6
6. Nxc6   bxc6
7. d3   0-0
8. Be2   Ng4?

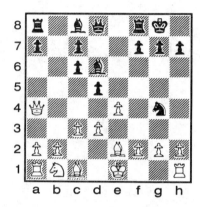

WHITE TO MOVE

Scenario: Black moves his Knight off the d8-h4 diagonal, clearing the way for entrance of his Queen. He overlooks the Queen on the other side of the board, also getting ready. With 9. **Bxg4 Bxg4** 10. **e5!**, white attacks two Bishops. The d6-Bishop is menaced by White's e5-pawn, while the g4-Bishop is targeted by White's Queen from the other side of the 4th rank. Black can choose which of his Bishops to jettison.

Interpretation: White wisely eschews taking the doubled c-pawn with his Queen on move 7 in favor of the quietly solid line-opener, 7. d2-d3. He wants to nurse home his extra pawn, until the game ends. Black needs brisk counterplay to compensate for the pawn minus, and so goes in for 8. . . .Ng4?, blundering away a piece. Instead, he should exert more pressure on White's center, and 7. . . .Re8 is a good way to start. If you are behind in material, you ought to try utilizing the open lines available to your pieces. It will be a fight, with one player's developmental advantage weighed against his opponent's material superiority.

97

PIN

Ponziani Opening

1. e4	e5
2. Nf3	Nc6
3. c3	d5
4. Qa4	dxe4
5. Nxe5	Qd5
6. Bb5	Qxe5

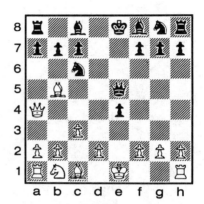

WHITE TO MOVE

Scenario: Black was a piece ahead, but it's not all roses. After 7. **Bxc6+**, he cannot afford to recapture on c6, for 7. . . .bxc6 8. Qxc6+ forks King and a8-Rook. So Black must settle for moving his King, 7. . . .Kd8, but with 8. **Qxe4**, he suddenly finds himself short one very useful pawn.

Interpretation: White's basic play revolves around the pin on Black's c6-Knight. His Queen buys a condo at a4, pinning the Knight in question and also observing e4. White's Bishop travels to b5, reinforcing the pin and assault on the c6-Knight. And his f3-Knight comes into e5, piling up on the same hapless horseman. It's no wonder that unless Black defends against this or develops meaningful counterplay, he's going to be in trouble. He's lucky he lost only a pawn, albeit a worthy one.

98

MATING ATTACK

Ponziani Opening

1. e4	e5
2. Nf3	Nc6
3. c3	d5
4. Qa4	dxe4
5. Nxe5	Qd5
6. Bb5	Ne7
7. f4	Bd7
8. Nxd7	Kxd7
9. 0-0	Nf5
10. b3	Bc5+
11. Kh1	

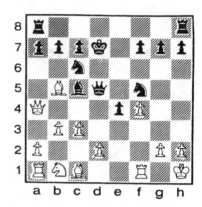

BLACK TO MOVE

Scenario: How did this happen? Black was forced into all sorts of ballet to safeguard c6, including a move of his King, and now his pieces are laden with potential. They actually mate after 11. . . . .Ng3+! 12. hxg3 Qh5.

Interpretation: Black is better able to secure c6 in this variation, developing his g8-Knight to e7 and breaking the a4-e8 pin by interceding his Bishop at d7. Surprisingly, capturing with his King on move 8 strengthened rather than weakened his game. Black's King is really quite safe at d7—it augments c6 and it clears the back rank to connect the Rooks. In the diagram, Black has a terrific position. His Queen is safely centralized. He has three nicely developed minor pieces and a debilitating King-pawn that controls vital squares in White's half of the board. And whenever desired, his Rooks are clear to come to the center. On the other side is a displaced White Queen, unable to get back to defend the Kingside. Joining her are three Queenside pieces sitting on their original squares. White is undeveloped; Black is practically all developed. The outcome cannot be in doubt. "Have a case where there is more sail than ballast"—William Penn.

99

MATING ATTACK

Ponzani Opening

1. e4	e5
2. Nf3	Nc6
3. c3	Nf6
4. d4	d5
5. Bb5	Nxe4
6. Nxe5	Bd7
7. Qb3	Qe7
8. Qxd5	Nxe5
9. Qxb7	Nf3 +
10. Kf1	

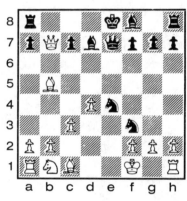

BLACK TO MOVE

Scenario: On the previous move, Black had three pieces hanging, two attacked by White's Queen: the a8-Rook and the e4-Knight. The other, the e5-Knight, was pestered by White's d4-pawn. But none of that matters anymore, for Black now wins with 10. . . .Ng3 + !. Whether the g3-Knight is captured by White's f-pawn or h-pawn, Black's Queen invades to e1, protected by the f3-Knight, giving mate.

Interpretation: Let's analyze a bit. If White had taken Black's f3-Knight on move 10—gxf3—he loses his Queen to the discoveries 10. . . .Nc5 + or 10. . . .Nd6 + . White's problem is that his Queen is out of play at b7, unable to help defend its King. In fact, White has no protection up the middle, where Black, especially from move 7 on, is ominously strong. White could opt for simplification by 7. Bxc6 bxc6   8. Nxd7, trading a couple of minor pieces and relieving the tension. The three moves his Queen winds up making, however, are too sapping. Want to avoid all these headaches? Then be W. S. Gilbert's "very model of a modern Major-General." Castle early, and move those minor pieces, please.

100

DISCOVERY

Ponziani Opening

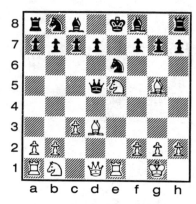

1. e4	e5
2. Nf3	Nc6
3. c3	Nf6
4. d4	Nxe4
5. d5	Nb8
6. Bd3	Nc5
7. Nxe5	Qe7?
8. 0-0	Qd6
9. Bg5	Qxd5
10. Re1	Ne6

WHITE TO MOVE

Scenario: White's army is poised for plunder, carried out by 11. **Bg6!**. Black must submit to one of two deadly threats—one to his Queen, the other to his King. If he saves his Queen, then 12. Bxf7 is mate. The Queen, therefore, goes away to visit her sister in never-never land.

Interpretation: Black seems to be in a fog. He allows his Knight to be driven back to b8, ceding time and space to White's advancing d-pawn. He makes several feckless moves with his Queen that cost him development and position. As that's not all. He moves his King-Knight three times, so that after ten moves his Queen and King-Knight are the only units out to play. In the interim, White castles, deploys three minor pieces powerfully, places a Rook on the open e-file, and has clear sailing on the d-file for his Queen. White wins because he was right on the beam. He dressed his forces for combat, whereas in the final position, Black's army hasn't even brought its wardrobe out of the closet.

101

KING HUNT

Ponziani Opening

1. e4   e5
2. Nf3   Nc6
3. c3   Nf6
4. d4   Nxe4
5. d5   Ne7
6. Nxe5   Ng6
7. Bd3   Nxf2?

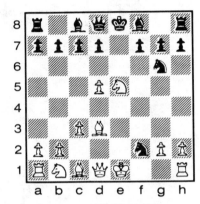

WHITE TO MOVE

Scenario: White has three pieces under attack, and Black naturally expects **8. Kxf2 Nxe5**, winning a pawn. But Black has been too clever. White crosses him with **8. Bxg6!**, which sacrifices the Queen. After **8 . . . Nxd1 9. Bxf7+ Ke7 10. Bg5+ Kd6 11. Nc4+ Kc5**, Black's King is on a high wire without a net. The King hunt terminates with **12. Nba3** (threatening 13. b4 mate) **12 . . . Nxb2 13. Be3** mate.

Interpretation: At the start, the squares f2 and f7 are quite vulnerable, being guarded solely by Kings. Both sides watch these squares keenly. Here, each side attacks the other's weak point, but White's attack is more coordinated, relying on several pieces. Black's lone invading Knight is rebuffed, while White's poised forces score with a sustained attack. Instead of 7 . . . Nxf2?, Black should have continued 7 . . . Nxe5 8. Bxe4 Bc5, furthering his development.

5

The Knight's Game

Philidor Defense
Petroff Defense
Three Knights Game
Four Knights Game

This chapter offers four separate openings. Two of them, Philidor Defense and Petroff Defense, are systems whereby Black heads White off at the pass and leads the play into lines of specialty. The other two openings, the Three Knights Game and the Four Knights Game, are instances of the sound beginning principle "Knights before Bishops." In first deploying the cavalry, each side leaves options on where to develop the Bishops.

In *Philidor Defense* (1. **e4 e5** 2. **Nf3 d6**), Black gives solid reinforcement to his e5-pawn before contemplating further action. Philidor had in mind the follow-up advance of the King-Bishop pawn, from f7 to f5, but most masters consider the loosening of the position around Black's King too precarious. Usually, the Philidor is played with the Hanham Variation (3. **d4 Nd7**). Black hunkers down to reliable defense, trusting that his strong point in the center (e5) will be sufficient to hold White at bay.

Petroff Defense (1. **e4 e5** 2. **Nf3 Nf6**), also known as the Russian Defense, is less a defense than a counterattack.

Ignoring the attack on his e5-pawn, Black focuses attention on eliminating White's e4-pawn, aiming toward later advancing his Queen-pawn from d7 to d5. This in turn leads to an opening of the center, with the minor pieces and Rooks rapidly mobilizing. Both sides display active piece play, leading to highly tactical situations. In recent years, the Petroff Defense, long forgotten, has seen a remarkable upsurge in popularity. A word of caution, however, for players of the Black side. Black initially copies White's early moves, but he must not seek safety in symmetry. White's first-move advantage must eventually lead to a check, capture, or threat that Black cannot imitate. Black therefore should break the symmetry, when desirable and in a timely way.

With the *Three Knights Game,* Black avoids maintaining symmetry. He does this by not developing his King-Knight on the third move, turning instead to his f8-Bishop. In the Russian version of the Three Knights Game (1. **e4 e5**   2. **Nf3 Nf6**   3. **Nc3**), likely to arise out of Petroff's Defense, Black continues pressuring White's e4-pawn by developing his King-Bishop to b4, assailing White's c3-Knight with clangor. In the more standard approach (1. **e4 e5**   2. **Nf3 Nc6**   3. **Nc3**), the f8-Bishop may be played on the third move to b4 or c5, and if Black chooses to flank it at g7, he could push his King-Knight pawn, 3. . . . g7-g6. Obviously, the Three Knights has enormous flexibility and transpositional possibilities.

In the *Four Knights Game,* (1. **e4 e5**   2. **Nf3 Nc6**   3. **Nc3 Nf6**), each side builds his game before deciding on a course of action. For a long time, the Four Knights was thought to be a transitional opening to disguise one's true intentions. The terminal is White's fourth move. If he advances his Queen-pawn from d2 to d4, the opening is likely to transpose into a Scotch. Instead, developing the King-Bishop from f1 to c4 generally produces an Italian Game or a Vienna Game. Finally, the aggressive posting of the f1-Bishop on b5 augurs a Ruy Lopez, also known as the Spanish Game. In selecting the Four Knights, White for the most part plans to play a quiet, maneuvering game, jockeying to gain small positional advantages. Black may agreeably pursue symmetry, developing his King-Bishop on the fourth move from f8 to b4. If Black prefers livelier combat, he could select Rubinstein's fourth-move variant, jumping his Queen-Knight from c6 to d4. The resulting play is sharp and fraught with tactics.

102

UNPIN

Philidor Defense

1. e4   e5
2. Nf3   d6
3. Bc4   Bg4
4. Nc3   h6?

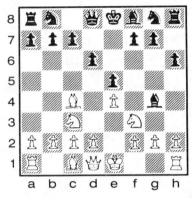

WHITE TO MOVE

Scenario: Black's last two moves are losers, as White demonstrates with 5. **Nxe5!**, introducing a version of Legal's sacrifice, where a pinned Knight departs off the diagonal line of a Bishop-pin, allowing capture of his Queen: 5. . . . **Bxd1** 6. **Bxf7+ Ke7** 7. **Nd5** mate. If Black in turn takes White's intrusive Knight, 5. . . . **dxe5**, then 6. **Qxg4** regains the piece and leaves White a pawn ahead, with a powerful position.

Interpretation: Many players who dabble in the Black side of Philidor Defense toy with the early development of the c8-Bishop. This doesn't usually turn out so well, and the principle "Knights before Bishops" reigns here. Even the pin Black strives to set up fails if he doesn't follow through correctly. The advance 4. . . . h7-h6? presumably is to stop White's f3-Knight from going to g5 to join the c4-Bishop in attacking f7. But this is a totally illogical, unnecessary defense, for Black supposedly prevents White's f3-Knight from moving by pinning it on the previous move. Black's either third or fourth move is therefore redundant. Every turn is critical in the opening phase of a chess game. Don't waste a single tempo. "Even the gods cannot strive against necessity"—Diogenes Laertius.

103

UNPIN

Philidor Defense

1. e4   e5
2. Nf3   d6
3. Bc4   Bg4
4. Nc3   Nc6
5. h3   Bh5?

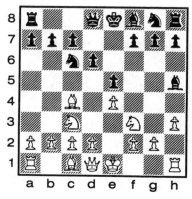

WHITE TO MOVE

Scenario: Black's poor Queen-Bishop once again is about to be exploited. The profit is a single pawn at e5, which White pockets by 6. Nxe5!. Since Black cannot capture White's Queen, 6. . . . Bxd1, because of Legal's Mate, 7. Bxf7+ Ke7 8. Nd5, Black must take something: White's Knight. The most promising way seems to be 6. . . . Nxe5, which projects an additional attack to White's c4-Bishop. But after 7. Qxh5 Nxc4, White regains the temporarily sacrificed piece by the forking Queen check, 8. Qb5+. After disposing of the check, White's Queen takes the c4-Knight, and White emerges a pawn to the good.

Interpretation: Black, in a common misdirection, has developed his Queen-Bishop very early, establishing a substandard pin on White's f3 Knight. To avoid Legal's sacrifice on e5, Black countered by developing his b8-Knight to c6, so that he could capture on e5 and also protect his g4-Bishop from White's usurping Queen. The fly in the soup was White's feeler, 5. h2-h3. Either Black must surrender a Bishop for a Knight, exchanging on f3, or he must retreat. By playing back to h5, however, Black defused the c6-Knight from stopping Legal's sacrifice, for when it captures on e5 it does not protect the h5-Bishop from capture.

104

MATING ATTACK

Philidor Defense

1. e4	e5
2. Nf3	d6
3. Bc4	f5
4. d4	Nf6
5. Nc3	exd4
6. Qxd4	Bd7
7. Ng5	Nc6

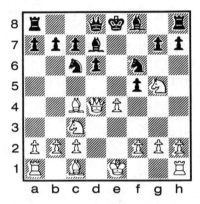

WHITE TO MOVE

Scenario: Black thinks he has the time to attack White's Queen, dislodging it from the center. But White doesn't have to move his Queen just yet; instead, he inserts an explosive check at Black's Achilles' heel, f7. With **8. Bf7+ Ke7** **9. Qxf6+ Kxf6** (9. . . . gxf6 10. Nd5 mate is conclusive) **10. Nd5+ Ke5 11. Nf3+ Kxe4** 12. Nc3 mate, White demonstrates a sense of humor, in that his Knights steadfastly do their jobs on the natural squares f3 and c3.

Interpretation: The line where Black in an early mood pushes his King-Bishop pawn to f5 is sometimes tactically rewarding, but most often the offense goes White's way, for it gives him two weakened diagonals to exploit: a2 to g8 and e8 to h5. Black is also a wastrel. He plays 6. . . . Bd7 to prevent his b8-Knight from being pinned by White's light-square Bishop once the Knight moves to c6, attacking White's Queen. This overpreparation is a total time-expender. Black ought to see that if White's light-square Bishop ever set up a pin along the a4-e8 diagonal, it would have to abandon the much more critical a2-g8 diagonal, White's main avenue of attack in this variation. So Black is on a completely illogical course. Once White's minor pieces converge on f7, Black is defenseless. White's Queen, in the end, proves to be only an aide to the light forces, not their means of sustenance.

105

REMOVING THE GUARD

Philidor Defense

1. e4   e5
2. Nf3   d6
3. Bc4   Be7
4. d4   exd4
5. Nxd4   Nd7?

WHITE TO MOVE

Scenario: It's a night without stars. Black's pieces have no coordination, with his d7-Knight blocking his c8-Bishop and his e7-Bishop impeding his d8-Queen. But after 6. **Bxf7+!** comes the dawn. Black must take the Bishop, 6. . . . **Kxf7** (6. . . . Kf8 is answered by 7. Ne6+, forking King and Queen). White then continues with the invasionary 7. **Ne6!!**, when 7. . . . Kxe6 is confuted by 8. Qd5+ Kf6 9. Qf5 mate. So Black saves his Queen, 7. . . . **Qe8**, but 8. **Nxc7 Qd8** 9. **Qd5+ Kf8** 10. **Ne6+** unsaves it.

Interpretation: When Black captures White's d-pawn on move 4 with his e-pawn, he surrenders the center to White, who still has one pawn sitting on a central square (e4). White also has great freedom of action in the middle, promising him attacking possibilities. The defense-minded 5. . . . Nb8-d7? is a further mistake, for with it Black cuts communication between his c8-Bishop and the e6-square, weakening that point and allowing White to land there safely. The sacrifice on f7 draws out Black's King and knocks out Black's pawn control of e6, which White then capitalizes on by immediately occupying e6 with a Knight. Black doesn't have the resources available to salvage himself. "For all we take we must pay, but the price is cruel high"—Rudyard Kipling, *The Courting of Dinah Shadd.*

106

MATING ATTACK

Philidor Defense

1. e4	e5
2. Nf3	d6
3. d4	Nd7
4. Bc4	c6
5. Ng5	Nh6
6. 0-0	Be7?
7. Ne6!	fxe6
8. Bxh6	gxh6

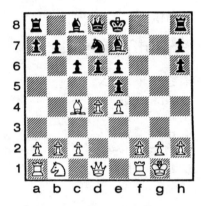

WHITE TO MOVE

Scenario: What happened to Black's pawns on the g- and f-files? Their absence exposes Black's King; and indeed, mate is forced after 9. Qh5+ Kf8 10. Bxe6 Qe8 11. Qh6—criss-cross.

Interpretation: After White castles, the pressure on Black's position, and the f7-square in particular, is great. Black must counter the control White has over the a2-f7 diagonal. One way is to move the d7-Knight possibly to b6, attacking the c4-Bishop and clearing the c8-Bishop's own diagonal. But the thoughtless development 6. . . .Be7? blocked up Black in the center, so that his pieces couldn't combine to muster a defense. White's Knight-sacrifice at e6 then drew the f-pawn out of position, while capturing the h6-Knight got rid of Black's g-pawn. Having no pawn shelter for his King, Black was unable to stop White's Queen and light-square Bishop from weaving a mating net. "I should have been a pair of ragged claws/ Scuttling across the floors of silent seas" T. S. Eliot, "The Love Song of J. Alfred Prufrock".

107

FORK

Philidor Defense

1. e4   e5
2. Nf3   d6
3. d4   Bg4
4. dxe5 Bxf3
5. Qxf3 dxe5
6. Bc4   Nf6

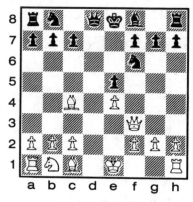

WHITE TO MOVE

Scenario: White wins at least a pawn with 7. **Qb3**, forking pawns at f7 and b7. If Black defends the more important f-pawn, 7. . . . **Qe7**, White may freely capture Black's Queen-Knight pawn with no reservations, 8. **Qxb7**. Black's best is then to simplify to a lost, pawn down endgame: 8. . . . **Qb4+**   9. **Qxb4 Bxb4+**   10. **c3**.

Interpretation: In a famous game of Paul Morphy's, the brilliant American as White chose not to take the pawn on move 8, and continued his development instead, 8. Nc3. Black could try to defend the f-pawn differently on move 7, opting instead for 7. . . . Qd7??. That, however, loses much more, for 8. Qxb7 Qc6 drops the Queen to 9. Bb5, when it is pinned to its King. Finally, if Black proposes to defend his b-pawn rather than his f-pawn by 7. . . . b6, he gets mated after 8. Bxf7+ Kd7 (or 8. . . . Ke7) 9. Qe6. Black's chief weaknesses are on light squares; his b7-pawn, his f7-pawn, and the a2-f7 long diagonal. These became weak by the premature development and subsequent disappearance of Black's light-square Bishop. There's a reason for the maxim Knights before Bishops, and unless you have a better move based on specific circumstances, be guided by this principle. "Few things are harder to put up with than the annoyance of a good example"—Mark Twain.

108

DISCOVERY

Petroff Defense

1.	e4	e5
2.	Nf3	Nf6
3.	Nxe5	Nxe4
4.	Qe2	Nf6??

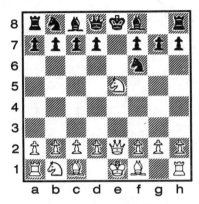

WHITE TO MOVE

Scenario: Black has walked into a crushing discovery. White gains Black's Queen with 5. **Nc6 +**, when White's c6-Knight, though in range of Black's b7 and d7 pawns, cannot be captured because of the discovered check unleashed by White's Queen. Nor can Black save his Queen by interposing it at e7, for, while blocking the check, Black's Queen is still imposed on by White's c6-Knight.

Interpretation: The second player can't play symmetrical chess forever. Sooner or later, the first player will introduce a move that cannot be duplicated, either a check or forcing capture or threat. So it is unwise to concoct one's plans on a copycat strategy. Once Black commits the error of capturing White's e4-pawn on the third move, he has to answer 4. Qe2 ironically by 4. . . .Qe7, prolonging the mimicking course for one move longer. After 5. Qxe4 d6, Black regains his piece but still comes away with an inferior position. At least, however, he doesn't lose his Queen. Best for Black after 3. Nxe5 is not to take on e4 immediately, but first to drive back White's e5-Knight with 3. . . .d6. After the Knight retreats, it is then perfectly safe for Black to take White's e-pawn. Don't copy your opponent's moves unless at that time it's best for you. Symmetry is mainly for the "Tiger! Tiger! burning bright/In the forest of the night"—William Blake.

109

UNPIN

Petroff Defense

1. e4   e5
2. Nf3   Nf6
3. Nxe5   Nc6
4. Nxc6   dxc6
5. d3   Bc5
6. Bg5?

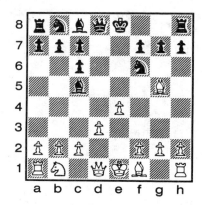

BLACK TO MOVE

Scenario: White falls victim to the disease of prematurely developing the Queen's Bishop. That Black's f6-Knight is meaninglessly pinned, as is evident by 6. . . .Nxe4!, winning back the sacrificed pawn and garnering the better of it. White should then respond 7. Qe2, for 7. dxe4 loses the Queen after 7. . . .Bxf2 + . A worse idea would be to take Black's Queen, 7. Bxd8??, for that ends in the junkyard after 7. . . .Bxf2 +   8. Ke2 Bg4 mate.

Interpretation: Black's spirited pawn sacrifice, 3. . . .Nc6, resulted in Black's seizing the initiative, ensured by White's need to expend time defending his extra footman, 5. d3. After 5. . . .Bc5, however, White can hold his own by 6. Be2, developing to prepare castling, defending his Queen and guarding g4 against invasion. The onus is then on Black to manufacture sufficient play for the pawn. Facilitating Black's developmental edge is the capture on c6 with his d-pawn, moving it away from the center but opening up the c8-Bishop's diagonal. Usually one takes back toward the center (b7xc6) to gain greater control of the middle. But having gambited a pawn, Black needs to increase his attacking possibilities, which is accomplished by capturing away from the central files.

110

SKEWER

Petroff Defense

1. e4   e5
2. Nf3   Nf6
3. Nxe5   Nc6
4. Nxc6   dxc6
5. e5   Ne4
6. d3   Bc5
7. dxe4?

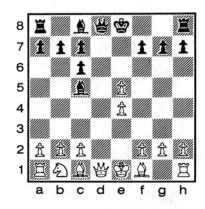

BLACK TO MOVE

Scenario: White's King defends two things: the Queen at d1 and the f2-pawn. Black exploits this by 7. . . . **Bxf2 +!**, when capturing the invader, 8. Kxf2, drops the Queen straightaway to 8. . . . **Qxd1**. But hardly better is 8. **Ke2**, for 8. . . . **Bg4 +** skewers White's King and Queen. White's Queen goes next move.

Interpretation: White is already lost by his seventh move. A wiser play is 6. d2-d4 rather than 6. d2-d3, for the former at least prevents Black's deadly dark-square Bishop from assuming the dangerous a7-f2 diagonal. White's downfall is precipitated by his lack of development (no pieces out at all after 6. d3?). The key in the opening is to rapidly develop the pieces. Get out the Knights and Bishops, castle quickly; don't grab pawns or waste time. Otherwise, it's pointless even to play. "If you do not think about the future, you cannot have one"—John Galsworthy.

111

DISCOVERY

Petroff Defense

1. e4	e5
2. Nf3	Nf6
3. Nxe5	d6
4. Nf3	Nxe4
5. d4	Bg4
6. h3	Bh5
7. Qd3	Qe7!
8. Qb5 +	c6
9. Qxh5?	

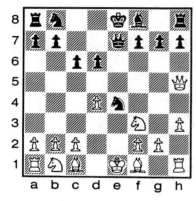

BLACK TO MOVE

Scenario: White's greedy Queen has just pilfered Black's apparently hapless Bishop. Now its Black's move, and he resurrects his game with 9. . . . Nf6 +, uncovering a check to White's King from Black's Queen, while Black's f6-Knight cheeringly assaults White's ravenous Queen. The Queen gets swallowed.

Interpretation: White's Queen needn't go in for this rampaging journey. Instead of 8. Qb5+, he could develop his Queen-Bishop to e3, closing off the e-file from discovered attack. That allows Black to disrupt his Kingside pawn cover by capturing White's f3-Knight. But White's game, especially with the two Bishops at his side, is not all that bad. Of course it makes even more sense not to develop the Queen to d3 in the first place, and instead simply activating his light-square Bishop to e2, readying the Kingside for castling. Once again, rely on forces other than the Queen in the opening. The lady can always be brought into play after the minor pieces are deployed, when she really amounts to something. Until then, treat her like "Mommie Dearest."

112

UNPIN

Petroff Defense

1. e4   e5
2. Nf3   Nf6
3. Bc4   Nxe4
4. Nc3   Nxc3
5. dxc3   d6
6. 0-0   Bg4?

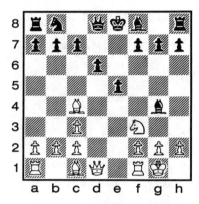

WHITE TO MOVE

Scenario: This example is a mirror-image of Black's attack in example #109. White disposes of Black's pointless Bishop-pin by 7. **Nxe5!.** Black must lose a lot of material, for instance 7 . . . . Be6 8. Bxe6 9. Qh5 + g6 10. Nxg6. If Black takes White's Queen, however, 7. . . . **Bxd1,** he then gets mated by 8. **Bxf7 + Ke7 9. Bg5.**

Interpretation: What good is an extra pawn if you lose your Queen or get mated because of inadequate development? Instead of the erroneous 6. . . . Bg4?, bringing out one of the worst units to develop immediately, Black should expedite Kingside castling with 6. . . . Be7, which also guards against a possible invasion on g5. White would then have to play energetically to muster enough counterplay for the gambited pawn. If you want to accept a gambit—and that's often the best way to handle it—you must make sure to play exactly afterward. Your opponent will have the initiative, and you'd better take steps to thwart his attack before it's too late. "Why should the Devil have all the good tunes?"—Rowland Hill.

113

DOUBLE ATTACK

Petroff Defense

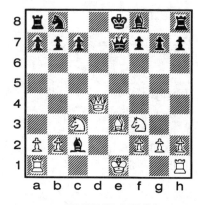

WHITE TO MOVE

1. e4	e5
2. Nf3	Nf6
3. d4	exd4
4. e5	Ne4
5. Qxd4	d5
6. exd6	Nxd6
7. Bd3	Qe7 +
8. Be3	Nf5
9. Bxf5	Bxf5
10. Nc3	Bxc2

Scenario: White wins material, not by taking but simply by continuing his development with a gain of time. He plays 11. **Rc1**, assailing Black's light-square Bishop. After the Bishop retreats to safety, 11. . . . **Bf5**, White's Knight springs into action with 12. **Nd5**. Black must save his Queen and then White's Knight captures on c7 with check, gaining the a8-Rook.

Interpretation: As the pawns disappear in the center, White's pieces take up fine central posts. Black's idea of gaining a Bishop for Knight by first pinning White's e3-Bishop and then forking it and Queen with 8. . . . Nf5 is simply a waste of time, in that Black moves the Knight four times to get it to f5. Even if Black's light-square Bishop could not be immediately attacked by a developing Rook, Black cannot afford to go pawn-hunting when he is so far behind in development. Wouldn't it have been wiser to develop the b8-Knight to c6, attacking White's Queen with a gain of time and clearing the way for the a8-Rook to reach the d-file? Don't let your pieces nap on the back rank. Like Endymion, they may slumber forever under the moon.

114

DISCOVERY

Three Knights Game

1. e4   e5
2. Nf3   Nc6
3. Nc3   Bc5
4. Nxe5   Nxe5
5. d4   Bxd4
6. Qxd4   Qf6?
7. Nd5?

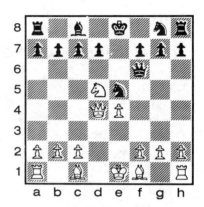

BLACK TO MOVE

Scenario: It looks good for White. His d5-Knight forks Black's Queen and c7-pawn, while his Queen on d4 menaces Black's e5-Knight. Should Black play an obstructive Queen-move to d6, to block the advance of the d-pawn? No, he can do better, in the guise of 7. . . . Nf3+, which is a discovered attack. Though White takes away Black's Knight, Black's Queen captures the unprotected White Queen on d4.

Interpretation: White's fork-trick of temporarily sacrificing a Knight to destroy Black's e-pawn, and regaining a minor piece by following with a d4-pawn fork, is reasonable. It advertises a free hand for White in the center. But 7. Nd5? is a blunder that loses the Queen. Better is to move his c3-Knight to b5 instead of d5. Then the Knight can hit c7 as well as it could from d5, but it can also protect the Queen on d4, avoiding Black's deadly discovery. One is reminded of Emanuel Lasker's maxim: "If you see a good move, look for a better one." Your first impressions may be dead wrong.

115

DOUBLE-ATTACK

Three Knights Game

1. e4	e5
2. Nf3	Nc6
3. Nc3	Bc5
4. Nxe5	Nxe5
5. d4	Bxd4
6. Qxd4	Qf6
7. Nb5	Kd8

WHITE TO MOVE

Scenario: Black has already made a concession: he had to move his King to d8 to guard c7, for his Queen was leashed to the defense of the e5-Knight. He now pays an exorbitance, however, for White's 8. **Qc5** threatens two-way disaster. He menaces capture on c7 and mate at f8. Black is lost.

Interpretation: This line is obviously bleak for Black. For the novice player, I recommend sacrificing a pawn and continuing to develop with 4. . . .Nf6, bringing another minor piece to the center. If White's e5-Knight then captures Black's c6-Knight, then take back away from the center, 5. . . .dxc6, to facilitate development. If you must get your pawn back, however, it's wiser to retreat the Bishop to d6 and to capture on e5 after the Knight is taken. You could also sacrifice your Bishop on f2, drawing out White's King. White gets the center and advantage, but you get practice attacking the enemy King—though White has adequate defenses. If you've never sacrificed pieces before, you can overcome your reluctance by doing so every opportunity. You might even get to like it, especially after the first couple of mating attacks roll off your fingers. "Perhaps the most valuable result of all education is the ability to make yourself do the thing you have to do . . . whether you like it or not"—Thomas Henry Huxley.

116

MATING ATTACK

Three Knights Game

1. e4	e5
2. Nf3	Nc6
3. Nc3	f5
4. d4	fxe4
5. Nxe5	Nf6
6. Bc4	d5
7. Nxd5!	Nxd5
8. Qh5+	g6
9. Nxg6	Nf6

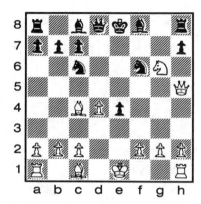

WHITE TO MOVE

Scenario: Black's h8-Rook and White's h5-Queen are attacked, but White gets in a vicious check, followed by a shattering discovery, a winning double check, if Black takes White's invading Bishop: 10. **Bf7+! Kd7** (if 10. . . .Kxf7, then 11. Ne5+ Ke7 12. Qf7+ Kd6 13. Nc4 is mate) **11. Qf5+ Kd6 12. Bf4+ Ne5 13. Bxe5+ Kc6 14. Qxf6+,** when White wins sizable material, for the h8-Rook is a goner no matter what.

Interpretation: Black's early 3. . . .f7-f5 thrust is a radical attempt to seize the initiative. With proper follow-up, it makes an interesting, if risky game. But Black must remain aware of the weakness attending by this advance. When Black's Knight on move 7 captures on d5, it abandons control of h5, so that White's Queen can enter on that square, exploiting the e8-h5 diagonal to Black's King. As a final tactical point, if Black answers 10. Bf7+! with 10. . . .Kxf7, and after 11. Ne5+ Ke6 12. Qf7+ tries 12. . . .Kf5, that loses at once to 13. g4 mate.

117

UNPIN

Four Knights Game

1. e4   e5
2. Nf3   Nc6
3. Nc3   Nf6
4. Bc4   Bb4
5. 0-0   d6
6. Nd5   Bg4
7. c3   Bc5
8. d3   Ne7?

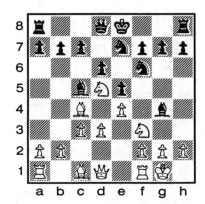

WHITE TO MOVE

Scenario: The center is all blocked up, but White has clear sailing with 9. **Nxe5!**, exposing his Queen to capture because of a Legal's unpin/combination. If Black captures White's Queen, 9. . . .**Bxd1**, then 10. **Nxf6+ gxf6**   11. **Bxf7+ Kf8**   12. **Bh6** is indubitably mate. Best for Black is to settle for the loss of a pawn by 9. . . .dxe5   10. Nxf6+ gxf6   11. Qxg4.

Interpretation: Black could try to save himself in other ways, but they don't really help him, either. After 9. Nxe5, he could also explore 9. . . .Nexd5, but 10. Nxg4 is satisfactory for White. Also worth considering is taking the Queen, 9. . . .Bxd1, and then answering 10. Nxf6+ with 10. . . .Kf8, though White then wins back the Queen with 11. Ned7+ Qxd7   12. Nxd7+. White then follows 12. . . .Ke8 with 13.Nxc5 dxc5   14. Rxd1; and he comes out on top. One thing for sure, 8. . . .Nc6-e7 is an error, for it weakens e5 and permits the combination 9. Nxe5.

118

MATING ATTACK

Four Knights Game

1. e4	e5
2. Nf3	Nc6
3. Nc3	Nf6
4. Bb5	Bb4
5. 0-0	Nd4
6. Nxd4	exd4
7. e5	dxc3
8. dxc3	Be7
9. exf6	Bxf6
10. Re1 +	Be7

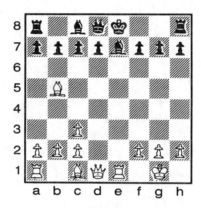

WHITE TO MOVE

Scenario: White begins his offensive with 10. **Bg5**. After the forced response 10. . . .**f6**, blocking the diagonal leading to his e7-Bishop, White sacrifices his g5-Bishop to destroy Black's Kingside pawn cover, 11. **Bxf6! gxf6**. There follows 12. **Qh5 + Kf8** 13. **Bc4**, threatening mate at f7. If 13. . . .**d5**, then White maintains the same threat after 14. Bxd5. So Black guards f7 by 13. . . .**Qe8**, but White double-crosses him with 14. **Qh6** mate.

Interpretation: To avoid all this trouble, Black has to answer 10. Re1 + with the King move 10. . . .Kf8. He still has problems because of his undeveloped state and potentially attackable King, but White doesn't show a burning threat yet. After 10. . . .Be7, however, the full power of White's position, with all his forces ready to steamroll the fray through the open center, becomes evident. Try not to allow the center to be opened with your King still in it and your opponent castled, with a Rook prepared to shift into action. You could be hurt in a lot of ways, such as losing the chance to castle, getting pinned, or simply being forced to play passive defense. "The wrong way always seems the most reasonable"—George Moore.

119

MATING ATTACK

Four Knights Game

1. e4   e5
2. Nf3   Nc6
3. Nc3   Nf6
4. Bb5   Bb4
5. 0-0   0-0
6. d3   d6
7. Bg5   Bg4
8. Nd5   Nd4
9. Bc4   Qd7
10. Nxb4

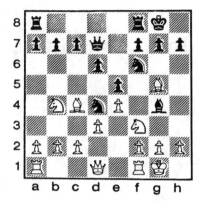

BLACK TO MOVE

Scenario: White's gotten greedy. The tax must be paid after 10. . . .**Bxf3**, when 11. **gxf3**, weakening White's castled position, is taken advantage of by 11. . . .**Qh3**. Black threatens to capture on f3 with his d4-Knight which, to stop mate, will force White to surrender his Queen.

Interpretation: The first eight moves of this game are the same for both sides. Usually the trick to getting an advantage in symmetrical positions is to find a way to break the symmetry, whereby the second player cannot copy the symmetry because he must respond to a serious threat, such as a check or capture, or because continued duplication results in some problem. With the voracious 10. Nxb4?, White overlooks the point of Qd7: to enter the Queen on h3 after the exchange of minor pieces on f3. A better try for White was 9. c3, strengthening his position in the center and forcing Black to commit himself. The same rule holds for art, holds for chess. In symmetrical positions, play for assymetry.

120

MATING ATTACK

Four Knights Game

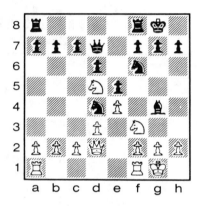

WHITE TO MOVE

1. **e4**	**e5**
2. **Nf3**	**Nc6**
3. **Nc3**	**Nf6**
4. **Bb5**	**Bb4**
5. **0-0**	**0-0**
6. **d3**	**d6**
7. **Bg5**	**Bg4**
8. **Nd5**	**Nd4**
9. **Nxb4**	**Nxb5**
10. **Nd5**	**Nd4**
11. **Qd2**	**Qd7**

Scenario: This is another symmetrical position, but here it's White trying to instill assymetry, with 12. **Bxf6**. Of course, 12. . . .gxf6 loses to 13. Nxf6+, forking King and Queen. So Black must continue 12. . . .**Bxf3**, when 13. **Ne7+ Kh8** 14. **Bxg7+ Kxg7** 15. **Qg5+ Kh8** 16. **Qf6** is mate.

Interpretation: Black has a few ways to improve his overall play. On move 5, he could break the symmetry with . . . Bxc3, followed by . . . d7-d6, fortifying his center and continuing his development. And on move 7, instead of riskily transferring his Bishop to g4, he could guard the center with 7. . . .Bc8-e6. If White's Knight then enters on d5, it could be taken by the light-square Bishop. In the Four Knights' Game, one could play to lull the opponent to sleep, as if nothing eventful is happening. For the player handling Black, who merely copies White's moves, this holds practically until he's shaken awake just before he gets mated. Don't play copycat chess. Think for yourself. "There can be no progress . . . except by the individual himself"—Charles Baudelaire.

6

The Italian Complex

Hungarian Defense
Paris Defense
Giuoco Piano
Evans Gambit
Two Knights Defense

The Italian Complex (1. **e4 e5**   2. **Nf3 Nc6**   3. **Bc4**) is a major branch of the double King-pawn openings, and its popularity among amateurs and professionals alike has never wavered in over five hundred years.

In the *Hungarian* (1. **e4 e5**   2. **Nf3 Nc6**   3. **Bc4 Be7**) and *Paris* (1. **e4 e5**   2. **Nf3 Nc6**   3. **Bc4 d6**) *Defenses*, Black veers off the main highway and accepts a restricted role for his dark-square Bishop. Black thereby manages to sidestep many of the trappy and zappy variations, but his position is passive and offers few chances of winning. The defender conducts his game along the same lines as in Philidor's Defense from the previous chapter. Black reinforces his e5-pawn, trusting that White's opening advantage—having the first-move initiative—will eventually wither away, reaching a position of tranquil equality.

The *Giuoco Piano* (1. **e4 e5**   2. **Nf3 Nc6**   3. **Bc4 Bc5**) is by far the biggest tree in this Italian forest. Black plays his Bishop from f8 to c5, confidently believing that sound, active development will secure him against any surprises White may be secreting. In the Italian Four Knights Game

(1. e4 e5   2. Nf3 Nc6   3. Bc4 Bc5   4. d3 Nf6   5. Nc3 d6), both players continue symmetry. This is the "quiet game," a literal translation of *"Giuoco Piano."* Here the center cannot easily be opened and the emphasis is on deployment of the minor pieces. At the opposite pole is the Greco Variation (1. e4 e5   2. Nf3 Nc6   3. Bc4 Bc5   4. c3 Nf6   5. d4), named after Gioacchino Greco (1600–1634), a master from Celico, Italy. This variation leads to wild and intricate complications. White's aggressive play collapses the Black center and obliges Black to play most energetically and accurately to avoid being overrun. Between these two extremes is the Giuoco Pianissimo (1. e4 e5   2. Nf3 Nc6   3. Bc4 Bc5   4. c3 Nf6   5. d3), where White serenely stabilizes his e4-pawn while retaining the option for later activity in the center with the advance d3 to d4. In the 1980s, the Pianissimo Variation of the Giuoco has attracted the greatest of grandmaster attention. Twice it was adopted by then World Champion Anatoly Karpov in his 1981 title defense in Merano, Italy, against challenger Victor Korchnoi.

The *Evans Gambit* (1. **e4 e5**   2. **Nf3 Nc6**   3. **Bc4 Bc5**   4. **b4**) is the most exciting offshoot of the Giuoco. It was invented by English sea captain William Davies Evans (1790–1872). Sacrificing a relatively unimportant flank pawn in the opening (the b-pawn), White gains time to build a broad pawn center after 4. . . .Bxb4   5. c3 Bc5   6. d4. This center in turn hinders Black's development while promoting White's attacking chances. For over sixty years (1834–1895), the Evans Gambit enjoyed widespread popularity, with both club players and those of world class. Then, in the St. Petersburg Tournament of 1895–96, the new champion, Emanuel Lasker, demonstrated a defensive setup that rocked the Evans on its heels. Offering to return the gambit pawn, Lasker was able to break the White attack and continue with his development. To the chagrin of Evans lovers everywhere, Lasker's Defense took all the fun out of the gambit, and it has never regained its former popularity.

The *Two Knights Defense* (1. **e4 e5**   2. **Nf3 Nc6**   3. **Bc4**

Nf6) is Black's most aggressive attempt to evade the Giuoco proper. In the early stages of the Two Knights evolution, Black tries to meet White's fourth-move Knight invasion from f3 to g5 by striking back with a central push, advancing his Queen-pawn from d7 to d5. After White takes Black's d-pawn with his e4-pawn and Black recaptures on d5 with his f6-Knight, White knocks Black off the high wire, sacrificing his Knight on f7 and exposing Black's King to a sustained attack. This line is often referred to as the Fried Liver Attack, because it was supposedly first played by an Italian master while eating fried liver.

Subsequent investigations into the variations stemming from 1. e4 e5 2. Nf3 Nc6 3. Bc4 Nf6 4. Ng5 d5 5. exd5, however, have shown that instead of 5. . . .Nxd5 allowing the Fried Liver, Black could profitably gambit a pawn with 5. . . .Na5 (Chigorin's move), or 5. . . .Nd4 (Fritz's move), or 5. . . .b5 (Ulvestad's move). In this century, some attention has focused on the extraordinarily violent Wilkes Barre Variation (1. e4 e5 2. Nf3 Nc6 3. Bc4 Nf6 4. Ng5 Bc5 5. Nxf7 Bxf2+), which leads to unfathomable complications. But the Two Knights is a gambit by invitation only, for White doesn't have to enter its unknown waters with 4. Ng5. He can further his own aggressive aims with 4. d4; and after the forced response 4. . . .exd4, he can reach a murky place where the Two Knights (5. 0-0 Nxe4) merges with the Max Lange Attack (5. 0-0 Bc5) and the Scotch Gambit (5. e5 d5). In each of these three branches, the play is highly tactical, with enough intricacies to satisfy most mortal chessplayers. Finally, White can decline Black's overture with 4. Nc3 or 4. d3, guarding his e4-pawn. In this case, play tends to move along the relatively quiet channels of the Italian Four Knights or Pianissimo variants.

121

PIN

Hungarian Defense

1. e4	e5
2. Nf3	Nc6
3. Bc4	Be7
4. d4	exd4
5. Nxd4	Nxd4
6. Qxd4	Nf6
7. e5	c5

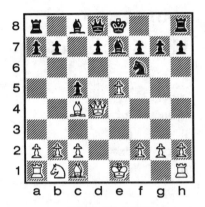

WHITE TO MOVE

Scenario: White's Queen is attacked and must seek shelter. Combining defense and attack in one motion, White essays 8. **Qf4**, saving the Queen, eyeing f7, and holding the f6-Knight under attack. The Knight in fact is pinned to the square f7. Should it move away, say 8. . . . Ng8, then White returns 9. **Qxf7 mate**. And if Black tries to end his dilemma with 8. . . . **d5**, then 9. **exf6 dxc4** 10. **fxe7** leaves him minus a piece.

Interpretation: Black cannot get by in the Hungarian without playing. . . d7-d6. He has no other way to control the e5-square to stop pawn advances. He could have played his Queen-pawn from d7 to d6 at move 4 or 5. His actual fifth move, Knight takes on d4, was very weak, helping White to centralize his Queen. Even then, Black might have tried to scramble with 6. . . . Bf6 (instead of 6. . . . Nf6), since the consequences of 7. e5 Qe7 8. f4 are not clear. And one move later 7. . . . d5 (instead of 7. . . . c5?) was worth trying: 8. exf6 dxc4, etc. His actual seventh move was a superficial one-move threat to White's Queen, which completely failed to address the needs of the position. "The Queen is quaint, and quick conceit"—Nicholas Breton.

122

MATING ATTACK

Hungarian Defense

1. **e4**   **e5**
2. **Nf3**   **Nc6**
3. **Bc4**   **Be7**
4. **d4**   **exd4**
5. **c3**   **dxc3**
6. **Qd5**   **d6**

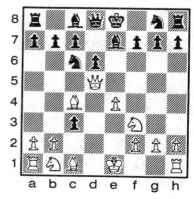

WHITE TO MOVE

Scenario: White has built up overwhelming pressure on Black's traditional weak spot, the f7-square. With two attacking units, Queen and Bishop, versus Black's lone defender, his King, White is able to conquer f7 with 1. **Qxf7 +**, driving Black's King into a mating net after 1. . . . **Kd7**   2. **Be6** mate.

Interpretation: Black's fifth move, d-pawn takes on c3, is too greedy and opens the way for White's Queen to reach d5. Instead, he could have eliminated all danger on the a2-g8 diagonal by 5. . . . Na5 attacking the c4-Bishop. After 6. Qxd4 Nxc4   7. Qxc4 Nf6, Black has everything in order. Even one move later, Black could have offered a much stiffer defense with 6. . . . Nh6 (instead of the erroneous 6. . . . d6??). Black might reject this move because White's dark-square Bishop could then remove the h6-Knight, renewing the mate f7-threat, but Black doesn't have to recapture on h6. He could simply castle. That would avert the f7-mate and threaten to regain the lost piece, while retaining the possibility of taking on b2. After 7. Bxh6 0-0, White does best to stay clear of 8. Bc1 Nb4! and play directly 8. Bxg7 Kxg7 9. Nxc3, with an advantage in position since Black's King is exposed.

123

REMOVING THE GUARD

Hungarian Defense

1. e4	e5
2. Nf3	Nc6
3. Bc4	Be7
4. Nc3	Nf6
5. d4	exd4
6. Nxd4	d6
7. 0-0	0-0
8. h3	Re8
9. Re1	Nd7

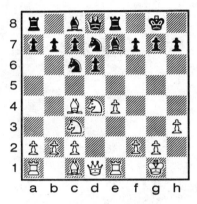

WHITE TO MOVE

Scenario: In a cramped position, Black has devised a regrouping maneuver for his pieces. The idea is to focus his forces over the e5-square: Bishop to f6 and Knight on d7 to e5. Except that the first move of the plan, 9. . . . Nd7, cramps his position even more, sealing in his light-square Bishop and his Queen, standing on her home square, entirely surrounded by friends. White cashes in with 10. **Bxf7+**, when 10. . . . Kxf7 is countered by 11. **Ne6! Kxe6** 12. **Qd5+ Kf6** 13. **Qf5** mate.

Interpretation: Black's idea of regrouping his forces over the central e5 is sound enough in principle, but the execution was faulty. Instead of the deadly 9. . . . Nd7, Black could have played 9. . . . Bf8, allowing his e8-Rook to observe not only e5 but the White e4-pawn as well. A plausible sequence of moves might be 9. . . . Bf8 10. Bg5 h6 11. Bh4 Ne5 12. Bf1 Ng6. White truly controls more space and stands slightly better, but Black's position is quite playable. Avoid blocking lines of development. Try not to put pieces in each other's way. If you want to win, remember Siegbert Tarrasch's maxim: "It is not enough to be a good player; you must also play well."

124

MATING ATTACK

Paris Defense

1. **e4**	**e5**
2. **Nf3**	**Nc6**
3. **Bc4**	**d6**
4. **0-0**	**Nge7**
5. **Ng5**	**f6**
6. **Bf7 +**	**Kd7**
7. **Qg4 +**	**f5**
8. **exf5**	**h5**

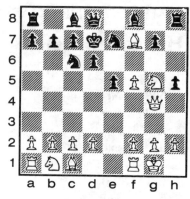

WHITE TO MOVE

Scenario: Faced with the murderous discovered check f5 to f6, Black tries to scare off White by attacking his Queen. He did not realize that 8. . . . h5 was just the move White was banking on. There's still some kill in 9. **f6 +**. After Black takes the Queen, 9. . . . **hxg4**, White concludes with 10. **Be6 + Ke8** and the clever pawn mate, 11. **f7**.

Interpretation: Black plays the opening with heedless disregard for the sensitive f7-square. His fourth move, Knight on g8 to e7, is an open invitation for White to pounce with his Knight on f3 to g5. Much better was 5. . . . Be7 and then Knight to f6. His fifth move, f7 to f6, saved the pawn but not the square. White could have wrapped things up with 6. Nf7 or 7.Ne6, but he went for the quick finish by 7. Qg4 +. The odds of Black's finding his best defense, 8. . . . Nd4, are minimal; and it turns out that Black plays right into White's hands with 8. . . . h7-h5?. One nagging question remains. After 5. Ng5, could Black have saved himself by 5. . . . d5   6. exd5 Nxd5? No, because White inaugurates the Fried Liver Attack, 7. Nxf7 Kxf7   8. Qf3 + Ke6   9. Nc3, with an extra tempo. Conclusion: After 4. . . . Nge7, Black is done for. Don't weaken your King's position. Try to develop your pieces to their most aggressive squares.

125

IN-BETWEEN MOVE

Paris Defense

1. e4   e5
2. Nf3   Nc6
3. Bc4   d6
4. d4   Bg4
5. Bxf7 +

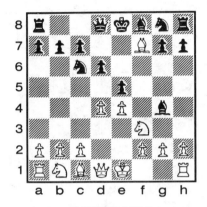

BLACK TO MOVE

Scenario: Black's Bishop is dangling at g4 and White's last play (5. Bxf7 +) is the start of a combination to pick off the apparently unprotected prelate, displacing Black's King in the process. But the Bishop is defended, albeit indirectly. Black takes at f7, 5. . . . Kxf7 and awaits the g5-Knight check. White continues as programmed, 6. Ng5 +, and Black inserts his *zwischenzug*, an in-between move that escaped White's attention, 6. . . . Qxg5!, which sacrifices the Queen. The g4-Bishop is now defended, White's Queen is assailed, and with two pieces in his pocket, Black can afford to return one of them: 7. **Bxg5 Bxd1**   8. **Kxd1** still leaves Black one piece ahead.

Interpretation: The tactical implications of 4. . . . Bg4, while important, should not be allowed to obscure the strategic objectives of this move. Pinning the f3-Knight, Black increases the pressure on d4, hoping to induce on move 5 either the advance d4 to d5 or the exchange of d-pawn for e-pawn. Both moves release the tension in the center and further Black's aims. Probably best for White (after 4. . . . Bg4) is 5. c3, keeping up the center tension. True, after the fifth-move advance c2 to c3, his b1-Knight can no longer reach its ideal square (c3) and his development is slowed up. But in maintaining the integrity of his center-pawns, White still retains his opening-move initiative. Don't be afraid to sacrifice your Queen if your opponent's own Queen is also lost. If both Queens must go, try to get something for yours that outweighs what your opponent gets for his.

126

FORK

Paris Defense

1.	e4	e5
2.	Nf3	Nc6
3.	Bc4	d6
4.	c3	Bg4
5.	Qb3	Qd7
6.	Ng5	Nh6
7.	Bxf7 +	

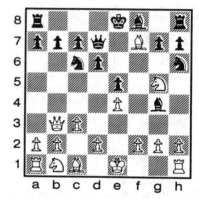

BLACK TO MOVE

Scenario: White has begun a faulty combination and Black can well afford to gather in the offering: 7. . . . **Nxf7** 8. **Nxf7** and then 8. . . . **Be6!**, forking White's Queen and Knight. The best that White can do is get three pawns for his piece by 9. **Qxb7 Rb8** 10. **Nd6 +**, but after 10. . . . **Bxd6**, Black's advantage is clear. His pieces are all developed, his center is secure, and after he castles the next move, his Rooks will be connected and his King safe.

Interpretation: White's Queen excursion to b3 and b7 is a dangerous proposition since he may easily find it out of town. This is well illustrated by the game Rodzinski-Alekhine, Paris 1913, which gave the Paris Defense its name. Here, White played 7. Nxf7 (instead of 7. Bxf7 +) and the continuation was 7. . . . Nxf7 8. Bxf7 + Qxf7 9. Qxb7 Kd7! 10. Qxa8 Qc4 11. f3 Bxf3! 12. gxf3 Nd4! 13. d3 Qxd3 14. cxd4 Be7 15. Qxh8 Bh4 mate. This miniature by the future World Champion Alekhine highlights the risks of early sorties with the Queen. After capturing the Rook at a8, it had nothing further to say; and at the end, White's King and Queen both became targets of the attack. Use your Queen early in the game, lose your Queen early in the game.

127

MATING ATTACK

Giuoco Piano

1. e4	e5
2. Nf3	Nc6
3. Bc4	Bc5
4. d3	d6
5. 0-0	Bg4
6. Nc3	Nd4
7. Be3	

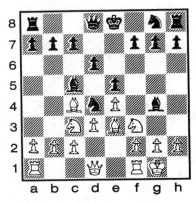

BLACK TO MOVE

Scenario: A pure count of the forces deployed would imply that White has the advantage: no less than four minor pieces out to Black's three, with castling thrown in. But Black's army is more purposefully employed and White's King, far from being safe, is the object of Black's attention. His 7. . . . Nxf3+ 8. gxf3 forces a decisive weakening around the castled position, and Black enters with 8. . . . Bh3. Relatively best for White now is 9. Kh1, letting Black win the exchange with 9. . . . Bxf1. If instead White tries to keep his Rook, 9. Re1, he comes under a mating attack after 9. . . . Bxe3 10. fxe3 (or 10. Rxe3) Qg5+ 11. Kf2 Qg2 mate.

Interpretation: White's lead in development is deceptive since he has not the means to capitalize on this advantage by opening up the center. Black sits in firm control of the d4 square, and his centralized d4-Knight, coupled with the pin of White's f3-Knight, is really the most important feature of the position. Had White truly appreciated the significance of controlling d4, he would hardly have selected 6. Nc3. More appropriate was 6. Be3, or even better, 6. c3, keeping d4 firmly in hand. Fight to control the key central squares, especially with pawns. Squares guarded by pawns are generally inaccessible to enemy pieces.

128

TRAPPED PIECE

Giuoco Piano

1. e4	e5
2. Nf3	Nc6
3. Bc4	Bc5
4. d3	d6
5. 0-0	Nf6
6. Be3	Bb6
7. Bxb6	axb6
8. Nbd2	0-0
9. Re1	Nh5
10. Nxe5	

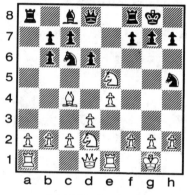

BLACK TO MOVE

Scenario: Black's h5-Knight appears out on a shaky limb. White is all set to gather in the errant steed after 10. . . . dxe5 11. Qxh5, winning a pawn. What White has overlooked is the significance of the recapture 10. . . . Nxe5!. Now after 11. **Qxh5 Bg4**, it is White's Queen that is trapped at the end on a limb with no way back.

Interpretation: Through the ninth move, the position offers approximately even chances to both sides, and Black's ninth (9. . . . Nh5) represents an interesting train of thought. Superficially, with knowledge of the consequences of 10. Nxe5?, it seems to be merely a clever trap. But it is more than that. Black's idea is to bring his Knight to the strong square f4; or failing that, to provoke a weakening in White's castled position with g2-g3. In addition, Black is also considering moving his King to h8, followed by advancing his King-Bishop pawn from f7 to f5, taking on White's e4-pawn. That 9. . . . Nh5 also sets White a little pitfall is a plus, but its true objectives are strate-gical. This is the way it should be when setting snares for the opponent to fall into. "Look before you ere you leap; for as you sow, ye are like to reap"—Samuel Butler, *Hudibras*.

129

MATING ATTACK

Giuoco Piano

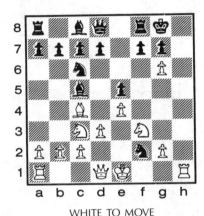

WHITE TO MOVE

1. e4	e5
2. Nf3	Nc6
3. Bc4	Bc5
4. Nc3	Nf6
5. d3	0-0
6. Bg5	h6
7. h4	hxg5
8. hxg5	Ng4
9. g6	Nxf2

Scenario: White is a piece down and appears about to self-destruct. But his concentration of attacking units in the vicinity of Black's King more than offsets these losses. Then 10. Nxe5! opens the line of White's Queen to h5 and paves the way for the possible finish 11. Rh8+ Kxh8 12. Qh5+ Kg8 13. Qh7 mate. And if 10. . . .Nxh1, there follows 11. Qh5 Re8 12. gxf7+ Kf8 13. Ng6 mate. Black therefore has nothing better than to remove White's Queen from the board: 10. . . .Nxd1. But White no longer needs his Queen. His advanced g6-pawn, his minor pieces, and his Rook are quite suffi-cient to hound Black's King to oblivion: 11. gxf7+ Rxf7 12. Bxf7+ Kf8 13. Rh8+ Ke7 14. Nd5+ Kd6 15. Nc4 mate.

Interpretation: The purpose of castling is to remove the King from the danger zone in the center and tuck him at the board's edge. When Black played the greedy 7. . . .hxg5, he negated the whole object of castling. By allowing White to open the h-file, Black participated in his own destruction. He should simply have left the g5-Bishop alone. Breaking the pin with 7. . . .Be7 was a good continuation, followed eventually by advancing the Queen-pawn to d6 and developing the light-square Bishop to e6. Don't allow your opponent to exchange wing pawns that open files leading to your castled King. "Nothing so easily ruins a position as pawn moves"— Siegbert Tarrasch.

130

TRAPPED PIECE

Giuoco Piano

1. e4	e5
2. Nf3	Nc6
3. Bc4	Bc5
4. Nc3	Nf6
5. d3	d6
6. Ng5	0-0
7. f4	Bg4
8. Qd2	Nb4
9. f5	

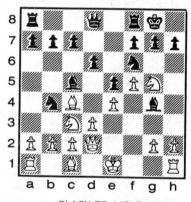

BLACK TO MOVE

Scenario: With his last move, 9. f5, White cuts off the radius of the Black g4-Bishop. Given another few moves, White will close the circle by h3, when Bh5, is met by g4. Is this the reason for calling this "Trapped Piece"? Not quite. It is the White Queen that is restricted in its movements and in danger of being caught. Black demonstrates the technique with 9. . . .Be3! 10. Qxe3 Nxc2+ and 11. . . .Nxe3, winning the White Queen.

Interpretation: White's problem is that he got so wrapped up with his own plans he failed to consider his opponent's. Always bear in mind that sitting opposite is your opponent. Just as you are looking to gain something from him, he wishes to gain something from you. Had White stopped to ask himself "What's he up to?" he would have noticed the threat on c2 and defended himself with 9. Bb3. When uncertain how to proceed, ask yourself leading questions to elicit information about the position. Asking the right probing questions is more than half the battle. "A good question is never answered. It is not a bolt to be tightened into place but a seed to be planted . . ."—John Ciardi.

131

MATING ATTACK

Giuoco Piano

1. e4	e5
2. Nf3	Nc6
3. Bc4	Bc5
4. Nc3	Nf6
5. d3	d6
6. 0-0	Bg4
7. h3	h5
8. hxg4	hxg4
9. Ng5	g3
10. Nxf7	

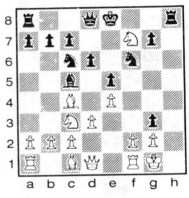

BLACK TO MOVE

Scenario: Black has let his light-square Bishop go astray in order to obtain an attacking line, the h-file, against White's castled King position. What's needed is a little more fuel on the fire. The bit of kerosene that Black requires is 10. . . .Nxe4. The immediate threat is mate down the h-file, 11. . . .Rh1+ 12. Kxh1 Qh4+ 13. Kg1 Qh2 mate. White might as well take the Queen, 11. Nxd8. But Black still has enough to finish the job: 11. . . .gxf2+ 12. Rxf2 Bxf2+ 13. Kf1 Rh1+ 14. Ke2 Nd4 mate.

Interpretation: Three unmoved pawns in front of his King plus a Knight at f3 were all that White needed to keep his castled position safe. White's problems began when he forgot that pawns do not move backward. After touching his h-pawn there was no place to go but forward. First the h-pawn went to h3 and then one move later, now totally out of control, it took the White Bishop at g4. That brought Black's h-pawn to g4, drove off White's Knight from f3, and opened the h-file for Black's Rook. Two of White's castled defenders were no longer in place. A bit later, Black worked his pawn to g3 and White's f2-pawn disappeared. Only the g2-pawn remained and that was not enough to save White's beleaguered King.

132

MATING ATTACK

Giuoco Piano

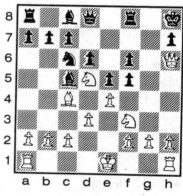

WHITE TO MOVE

1. e4	e5
2. Nf3	Nc6
3. Bc4	Bc5
4. Nc3	Nf6
5. d3	d6
6. Bg5	0-0
7. Nd5	Kh8
8. Bxf6	gxf6
9. Qd2	f5
10. Qh6	f6

Scenario: Black's castled position has been ripped apart and White's pieces are entering through the open doors. White brings yet another piece into the fray with 11. **Nh4** threatening 12. Ng6+. Black tries to cover with 11. . . . **Rf7**, but 12. **Ng6+** forces 12. . . . **Kg8**, when Black's King comes into line with the White Bishop on c4. The capture 13. **Nxf6+**, putting the c4-Bishop immediately to work, pins Black's f7-Rook. The forced response is 13. . . . **Qxf6**, and White finishes off with 14. **Qf8**, a pin mate.

Interpretation: Black's difficulties arise because he fails to take measures against the pin of his f6-Knight. White is allowed to pile on pressure (7. Nd5) and break up the protective pawn skeleton around Black's King. To start with, Black would have done better to postpone castling and develop his light-square Bishop (5. . . . d6 and 6. . . . Be6). Failing that, he might at least have broken the pin: 6. . . . Be7, instead of 6. . . . d6. Later, when Black was already in the soup, 9. . . . Rg8 or perhaps 9. . . . Be6 (instead of 9. . . . f5) would still have offered some resistance.

133

OVERLOAD

Giuoco Piano

1. e4	e5
2. Nf3	Nc6
3. Bc4	Bc5
4. c3	d6
5. d4	Bb6

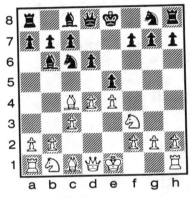

WHITE TO MOVE

Scenario: White's aggressive play with his center-pawns has put him in position where he can dictate the course of events. Here the simple exchange 6. **dxe5** leads by force to White's gaining an extra pawn. No matter how Black decides to recapture he will find that one of his units becomes overburdened with too many chores to perform. Here are the variations: **(A)** 6. . . .Nxe5 7. **Nxe5 dxe5** 8. **Bxf7+** (of course 8. Qxd8+ Kxd8 9. Bxf7 is also good enough) 8. . . .Ke7 (the Bishop is invulnerable: 8. . . .Kxf7?? 9. Qxd8) 9. **Qxd8+ Kxd8** and White has won a pawn; **(B)** 6. . . .dxe5 7. **Qxd8+ Kxd8** (or 7. . . .Nxd8 8. Nxe5) 8. **Bxf7** and again Black is a pawn minus.

Interpretation: White's fifth move (5. d4) is a two-pronged assault on Black's c5-Bishop and his e5-pawn. The Bishop's retreat from c5 to b6 deals only with the safety of the Bishop, not with the threat to the e-pawn. Naturally, Black is reluctant to play 5. . . .exd4 since the recapture 6. cxd4 gives White what he wants, a powerful double-pawn center. Yet this was relatively Black's best. When the position becomes difficult, sometimes one must choose the lesser evil. "To win you have to risk loss"—Jean-Claude Killy.

134

FORK

Giuoco Piano

1. e4   e5
2. Nf3   Nc6
3. Bc4   Bc5
4. c3   d6
5. d4   exd4
6. cxd4   Bb4 +
7. Kf1   Nf6

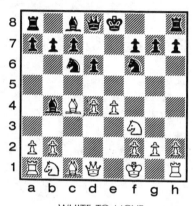

WHITE TO MOVE

Scenario: White's center pawns are powerful weapons. They are put to good use by 8. **d5**, attacking the c6-Knight and forcing it to move to safety. If Black retreats it, 8. . . .**Ne7**, for example, then the b4-Bishop is lost to a double attack, 9. **Qa4 +**, followed by 10. **Qxb4**.

Interpretation: Black's b4-Bishop check was too optimistic. He should have retreated the Bishop to b6. White's 7th move, Kf1, was rather astute. If White instead blocks the check at d2 with his c1-Bishop, then Black can trade Bishops, getting equal value for a piece that otherwise might be lost for nothing. The key is White's willingness to sacrifice the ability to castle. Usually, moving the King early leads to trouble, but here it was the only way to show the weakness inherent in Black's incorrect check. Don't give pointless checks. They could waste time. They might cost material. They may even lose the game.

135

UNPIN

Giuoco Piano

1. e4   e5
2. Nf3   Nc6
3. Bc4   Bc5
4. c3   Qe7
5. d4   Bb6
6. b4   a6
7. dxe5   Nxe5
8. Bg5   Nf6
9. Be2

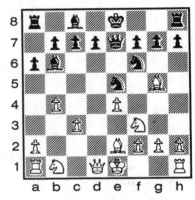

BLACK TO MOVE

Scenario: The object of pinning an enemy piece is to restrict its movement. Here the g5-Bishop pins the f6-Knight. If the f6-Knight moves, then Black loses his Queen. But what if Black seriously considers moving his Knight? The tables are turned and a White pin becomes a Black fork: 9. . . . **Bxf2 +**   10. **Kxf2 Nxe4 +** followed by 11. . . . **Nxg5**, gaining two White pawns.

Interpretation: Black's opening play is on a much higher level than in the examples where 4. . . . d6 is played. Keeping firm control over e5, he places a serious obstacle in White's path. White may not understand how to continue. First he flails away on the Queenside (6. b4), then comes an exchange in the center (7. dxe5), and finally he posts his dark-square Bishop on the Kingside (8. Bg5). All this is in the short space of three moves. Such disjointed play in every sector of the board must bring weaknesses in its wake and ultimately retribution. That's what finally happens here. His c4-Bishop is driven from its post, his center-pawn falls and his Bishop on the Kingside is lost. "Chess, . . . if it is anything, it is a struggle"— Marcel Duchamp.

136

MATING ATTACK

Giuoco Piano

1. e4	e5
2. Nf3	Nc6
3. Bc4	Bc5
4. c3	Nf6
5. d4	exd4
6. cxd4	Bb6
7. Ng5	0-0
8. e5	Ne8

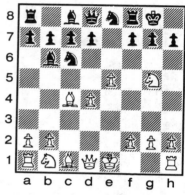

WHITE TO MOVE

Scenario: A Knight on f6 is an important element in the defense of a castled position. The f6-Knight keeps watch on the h7-square while preventing the enemy Queen from approaching via h5. Here the Knight has been driven from f6 so White's Queen approaches, 9. **Qh5**, threatening nothing less than 10. Qxh7 mate, only to be stopped by 9. . . . **h6**. But now White breaks through with 10. **Nxf7**. Black's defenses are shattered. If he saves his Queen, 10. . . . **Qe7**, he is soon mated: 11. **Nxh6 + Kh8** 12. **Nf7 + Kg8** 13. **Qh8** mate. And if he tries to placate White with 10. . . . **Rxf7** he is still mated after 11. **Qxf7 + Kh7** 12. **Bd3 + Kh8** 13. **Qf8**.

Interpretation: Black's opening play reveals that he did not understand the importance of controlling the center. His exchange on move five (5. . . . exd4) gave White two powerful center-pawns. Left unchecked, the e-pawn pushed on to e5, driving Black's Knight to e8, after which it was all over. For Black it was vital to make some stand in the center. His last chance was move 8, when he could have played d7-d5! "In chess—as in any conflict—success lies in attack"—Max Euwe.

137

TRAPPED PIECE

Giuoco Piano

1. e4	e5
2. Nf3	Nc6
3. Bc4	Bc5
4. c3	Nf6
5. d4	exd4
6. cxd4	Bb6
7. e5	Ng4
8. h3	Nh6
9. d5	Ne7
10. d6	Ng6

WHITE TO MOVE

Scenario: The White center-pawn roller has practically pushed the Black cavalry off the board. Turning his attention now to Black's Queen, which is also restricted in its movement, White sallies forth with 11. **Bg5**, a direct attack which can only be answered by 11. . . .**f6**. The move 12. **exf6** sets up the threat 13. f7+ and Black's response is the forced 12. . . .**gxf6**. White could already gather in the unprotected h6-Knight, but he looks for more and plays 13. **Qe2+**. Black cannot avoid heavy loses. Mate is 13. . . .Kf8 14. Bxh6, and if 13. . . .**Ne5**, then 14. **Nxe5 fxg5** 15. **Ng6+** is murderous.

Interpretation: Black's fourth move, Ng8-f6, was made in the spirit of counterattack and should have been followed on move 6 with Bb4+, intending to answer 7. Nc3 by 7. . . .Nxe4 and 7. Bd2 with 7. . . .Bxd2+ 8. Nxd2 d5. After the erroneous 6. . . .Bb6, the proper way for White to advance his center-pawns was 7. d5 Ne7 8. e5. His actual choice, 7. e5, could have been met by the counter advance 7. . . .d5. This was Black's last chance to stay in the game. Stay alert to resources. Even after getting a bad game, opportunities may arise that require total concentration to detect. "The good player is always lucky"—Jose Raoul Capablanca.

138

DISCOVERY

Giuoco Piano

1. e4	e5
2. Nf3	Nc6
3. Bc4	Bc5
4. Bxf7 +	Kxf7
5. Nxe5 +	Nxe5
6. Qh5 +	g6
7. Qxe5	d6
8. Qxh8	Qh4
9. d4	Nf6
10. dxc5	Qxe4 +
11. Be3	Qxg2
12. Rf1	

BLACK TO MOVE

Scenario: Don't be misled by White's extra Rook. It's a meaningless ornament. White is in serious trouble. His King is exposed and his cornered Queen is in danger of being trapped. The cruncher is 12. . . . **Bh3**, which wins White's Queen by discovery from the a8-Rook. If White tries to save the Queen by capturing the Rook, 13. **Qxa8**, then 13. . . . **Qxf1 +** 14. **Kd2 Ne4** is mate.

Interpretation: White began with a very aggressive, sacrificial line of play which, because of Black's cavalier pawn move (6. . . .g6), led to the gain of material. The price White had to pay was the removal of his Queen from the center of the board. Without his Queen being available for defense, White has to play carefully, and every move becomes critical. Instead of saving his h1-Rook, he should be more concerned with the potential trap of his Queen. The correct response to 11. . . . Qxg2 is 12. Nc3, which later prevents Black's Knight from moving to e4 and giving mate. After 12. . . . Qxh1 + 13. Kd2 Qxa1? (13. . . . Qxh2 keeps Black's Queen in play), White turns the tables with 14. Bd4!. Black's extra Rook then means little in the face of White's strong counterattack.

139

MATING ATTACK

Evans Gambit

1. e4   e5
2. Nf3   Nc6
3. Bc4   Bc5
4. b4   Bxb4
5. c3   Bc5
6. 0-0   d6
7. Bb2   Bg4
8. h3   h5
9. hxg4   hxg4
10. Nh2

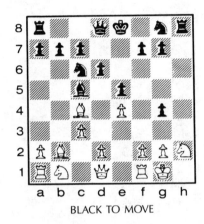

BLACK TO MOVE

Scenario: It's a rare day when Black gets a chance to attack in the early stages of the Evans Gambit. Usually he's defending. After investing a piece, Black has such an opportunity, and seizing the moment, he issues 10. . . .Qh4, threatening nothing less than 11. . . .Qxh2 mate. White gives his King an escape hatch with 11. **Re1**, but it's purely temporary, as Black quickly demonstrates: 11. . . .Qxf2+ 12. **Kh1 Rxh2+** 13. **Kxh2 Qh4** mate.

Interpretation: The Evans Gambit calls for White to take the initiative in the center with the advance d2 to d4. White could have played this move anywhere from move 6 on, but didn't. Further, he committed the serious error of opening an attacking line, the h-file against his own castled King's position. This was too much. Appropriately Black, led by his Queen, concluded the punishment by mating on the h-file. "Therewith Fortune seyde 'Chek her!'/And 'Mat' in myd poynt of the chekker"—Geoffrey Chaucer.

140

FORK

Evans Gambit

1. e4	e5
2. Nf3	Nc6
3. Bc4	Bc5
4. b4	Bxb4
5. c3	Bc5
6. 0-0	Nf6
7. d4	Bb6
8. dxe5	Nxe4

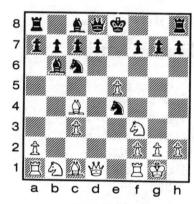

WHITE TO MOVE

Scenario: A piece placed in the center without any support is a natural object of attack; so is an uncastled King. Combining these two elements together into one unified theme, White zooms in with 9. **Qd5.** The mate threat at f7 is the top priority and must be attended to. But after 9. . . .0-0 White wins a piece for nothing, 10. **Qxe4.**

Interpretation: In the Evan's Gambit, White strikes hard and fast in the center, before Black can get his act together. It is not enough for Black to rely on a natural developing move like 6. . . .Nf6; he must also ensure that a White pawn, suddenly arriving at e5, will not push the Knight out of position. Lasker's handling of Black's game at move six is more sensible. Lasker played 6. . . .d6, and after 7. d4 Bb6 offered the return of the gambit pawn by 8. dxe5 dxe5 9. Qxd8+ Nxd8 10. Nxe5 Nf6. White's attack is broken, and Black will be able to develop his game with . . . Be6, etc. Moreover, in the coming endgame, White's split pawns on the Queenside give cause for concern. "It is always better to sacrifice your opponent's men"— Savielly Tartakover.

141

PROMOTION

Evans Gambit

1. e4	e5
2. Nf3	Nc6
3. Bc4	Bc5
4. b4	Bxb4
5. c3	Ba5
6. d4	Nf6
7. dxe5	Ng4
8. Bg5	f6
9. exf6	Nxf6
10. e5	h6

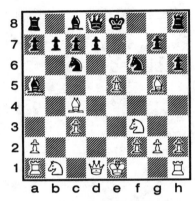

WHITE TO MOVE

Scenario: White is trying to parlay his pin of the f6-Knight into winning a piece. Black's counter is to place the pinning Bishop under fire. The two threats are not equal. White follows through with 11. **exf6** and Black has no choice but to carry on by 11. . . .**hxg5.** But now White's former e-pawn runs rampant with 12. **fxg7,** threatening to Queen at either h8 or g8. Black tries to catch up with the pawn 12. . . .**Qe7 +**, but the pinning counter 13. **Qe2** holds Black's Queen firmly on the e-file, and his g7-pawn must promote. At the very least Black loses a Rook.

Interpretation: Black's problems began with the premature developing move 6. . . .Nf6. Better was 6. . . .d6 or else 6. . . .exd4. White's d-pawn came to e5 (7. dxe5) and forced the Knight away. A bit later the Knight was able to return to f6, but White's original e-pawn was still on the board and this pawn too came marching into e5. The poor Knight has nowhere to go and had to stay his ground. And the White e-pawn, now running at full throttle, cleared a path for devastation. The moral: two White e-pawns are stronger than one Black f6-Knight.

142

DISCOVERY

Evans Gambit Declined

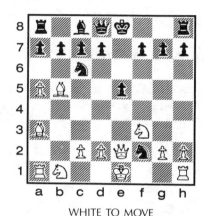

WHITE TO MOVE

1. e4	e5
2. Nf3	Nc6
3. Bc4	Bc5
4. b4	Bb6
5. a4	a6
6. a5	Ba7
7. b5	axb5
8. Bxb5	Nf6
9. Ba3	Nxe4
10. Qe2	Nxf2

Scenario: Black's Knight has ventured deep into White's territory, and he's all set to win a Rook. But 11. **Nxe5!** threatening a killing discovered check gives him no time to take the h1-Rook. His only chance is 11. . . . **Nd4** to eliminate White's Queen. Unfortunately for Black, there is more than one discovery in the air, and 12. **Nxd7 +** creates the preconditions by letting the b5-Bishop join in. Black must remove White's checking Queen, 12. . . . **Nxe2**, but now White concludes with the most powerful of all discoveries, 13. **Nf6**, double-check and mate.

Interpretation: Declining the Evans with 4. . . . Bb6 is obviously not the way to refute gambit, but it is a safe-and-sound method of defense. Of course, even the Evans Declined has its share of pitfalls as Black discovered (pun intended) here. Actually, Black was doing quite well up to the point where he lets his greed get the better of his judgment, 10. . . . Nxf2??. Had he played instead 10. . . . Nd6, cutting the diagonal of White's a3-Bishop and preparing to castle, there was nothing seriously amiss with his game. By not castling, Black allowed his King to come under the crossfire of White's minor piece, and this is always fatal in an Evans. "The move is time's, the loss is ours"—Louis MacNeice.

143

MATING ATTACK

Two Knights Defense

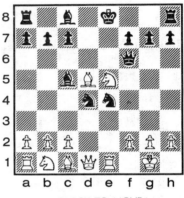

BLACK TO MOVE

1. e4	e5
2. Nf3	Nc6
3. Bc4	Nf6
4. 0-0	Nxe4
5. Re1	d5
6. Bb3	Bc5
7. d4	Nxd4
8. Nxe5	Qf6
9. Bxd5	

Scenario: Over the last several moves, White has made a determined effort to clear out Black's center-pawns. Only in this way can White hope to get at Black's e4-Knight, and through the Knight, Black's King. For example: 9. . . .Qxe5? 10. Rxe4, pinning and winning Black's Queen. The catch is that it is Black's turn to move, and he can get at White's King starting with 9. . . .Qxf2+, forcing White into the corner, 10. Kh1. Now comes a lovely Queen sacrifice, 10. . . .Qg1+, which lines White up for a discovery: 11. Kxg1 (11. Rxg1 Nf2 mate) 11. . . .Ne2+! 12. Kf1 (again 12. Kh1 Nf2 mate), and a minor piece mating finish: 12. . . .N2g3+! 13. hxg3 Nxg3 mate.

Interpretation: In this game, Black's g8-Knight played a hero. His first move off the back rank was a threat to the e4-pawn, which promptly was snapped up. This was followed by central expansion 5. . . .d5, securing the Knight at e4 and in turn shielding Black's King at the opposite end of the e-file from White's Rook. Later, with the c5-Bishop, and the Queen at f6, the Knight turned his attention to the weak f2-square and just missed with a smothered mate. Still, the Knight was not to be denied and at the very end administered checkmate at g3. "The Knight is knowledge how to fight against his prince's enemies"—Nicholas Breton.

144

IN-BETWEEN MOVE

Two Knights Defense

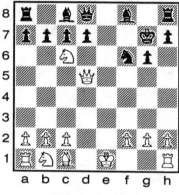

WHITE TO MOVE

1. e4	e5
2. Nf3	Nc6
3. Bc4	Nf6
4. d4	exd4
5. Nxd4	Nxe4
6. Bxf7 +	Kxf7
7. Qh5 +	g6
8. Qd5 +	Kg7
9. Nxc6	Nf6

Scenario: Black's last is a clever in-between move that attempts to get more out of the position than the straightforward recapture, 9. . . .bxc6. After 10. Nxd8 Nxd4, White's d8-Knight will be trapped and ultimately lost. But Black has outsmarted himself, failing to consider an in-between check on White's part. This is 10. **Bh6 + !**, which after the forced sequence 10. . . .Kxh6 11. Qd2 +, leads to Black losing his Queen by 12. **Nxd8 +**.

Interpretation: Starting with White's fourth move (4. d4) the center of the board lights up in a series of captures and counter-captures. This chain reaction spreads to Black's King, displacing him from his home square. The normal process of development has been suspended as a mere handful of pieces seize the stage and perform a dance whereby each move must be a capture or a check. A moment of relative quiet occurs when Black plays 9. . . .Nf6. This position, frozen in the diagram, shows both Queens hanging in the balance. Suddenly a new piece, the c1-Bishop, enters the proceedings and tips the scales in White's favor. "Don't make a strong move too soon"—James Mason.

145

MATING ATTACK

Two Knights Defense

1. e4	e5
2. Nf3	Nc6
3. Bc4	Nf6
4. d4	exd4
5. e5	Ng4
6. Bxf7 +	Kxf7
7. Ng5 +	Kg8
8. Qxg4	d6

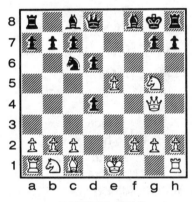

WHITE TO MOVE

Scenario: It is well documented that the weak link in Black's armor is the f7-square, defended only by Black's King. If White can manage to bring superior numbers to bear on this point, Black's survival chances are practically nil. The first wave of White's assault ended with the disappearance of White's light-square Bishop from the board. But the second wave, beginning with 9. **Qf3**, is not so easy to meet. This is a two-pronged attack on f7, since White's Queen can approach directly over the f-file or indirectly over the d5-square. Black cannot deal with both approaches and his relatively best defense, 9. . . .**Qe8** 10. **Qd5 + Be6** 11. **Qxe6 +**, leaves him one piece short.

Interpretation: After capturing White's Bishop (6. . . .Kxf7), Black seems to have relaxed his guard, thinking the worst was over. This attitude was totally unjustified, for immediately after the Bishop capture, a White Knight appeared on g5, bearing down on f7. It was essential then for Black to drive the Knight away with 8. . . .h6, before it could link up with White's Queen in a concerted attack on f7. Don't let enemy invaders, especially Knights, linger in your half of the board. Try to drive them into retreat.

146

FORK

Two Knights Defense

1. e4	e5
2. Nf3	Nc6
3. Bc4	Nf6
4. d4	exd4
5. e5	Ng4
6. Bxf7 +	Kxf7
7. Ng5	Kg8
8. Qf3	Bb4 +
9. c3	Ncxe5

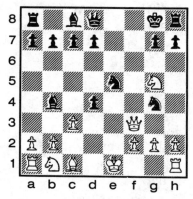

WHITE TO MOVE

Scenario: Black has covered the mate threat at f7, and his e5-Knight is attacking White's Queen. He's all set to answer 10. **Qd5+** with 10. . . .**Kf8**, the square that Black has cleared for himself with his Bishop check at b4. But he's overlooked something rather important in his calculations: 11. **Ne6!**, forking King and Queen. True, Black can capture the Knight, 11. . . .**dxe6**, but he still drops the Queen after 12. **Qxd8**.

Interpretation: Black was on the right track when he checked at b4 with his Bishop, but he chose the wrong Knight to capture on e5. Had he played instead 9. . . .Ngxe5, he would have stopped White dead in his tracks, since 10. Qd5+ Kf8 11. Ne6+ can be met with 11. . . .dxe6, thanks to the c6-Knight defending the Queen at d8. White's attack, conducted with only two pieces, should not succeed. But saying this and proving it are two different things. What was required from Black was precision defense, which is what was lacking.

147

FORK

Two Knights Defense *(Max Lange Attack)*

1. e4	e5
2. Nf3	Nc6
3. Bc4	Nf6
4. d4	exd4
5. 0-0	Bc5
6. e5	d5
7. exf6	dxc4
8. Re1+	Be6
9. Ng5	Qxf6

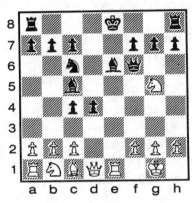

WHITE TO MOVE

Scenario: Black appears to be doing all right for himself. He's two pawns ahead and has developed four pieces to White's two. The problem is that his King is still in the center. This is noticed by White, who continues 10. **Nxe6 fxe6**, creating a new weakness in Black's position, the diagonal e8-h5. The stage is set for exploitation: 11. **Qh5+** attacks the Black King, and after Black gets out of check, 12. **Qxc5** confiscates the unprotected Bishop.

Interpretation: Since Black's King proved so vulnerable in the center, there is a strong temptation to substitute 9. . . .0-0 for the faulty 9. . . .Qxf6. However, 9. . . .0-0 still leaves Black's King in the danger zone: 10. Rxe6! fxe6 11. f7+ Kh8 (11. . . .Rxf7 12. Nxf7 Kxf7 13. Qh5+ and 14. Qxc5) 12. Qh5 h6 13. Qg6 hxg5 14. Qh5 mate. The correct ninth move for Black is 9. . . .Qd5!, centralizing Black's Queen and preparing for Queenside castling. It is only on the Queenside that Black's King can find security. "Was of a Fers so Fortunat/Into a corner dryve and maat"—John Lydgate.

148

MATING ATTACK

Two Knights Defense

1. e4	e5
2. Nf3	Nc6
3. Bc4	Nf6
4. Ng5	Bc5
5. Nxf7	Bxf2+
6. Kxf2	Nxe4+
7. Kg1	Qh4
8. g3	Nxg3
9. Nxh8	Nxh1
10. Qf1	d6

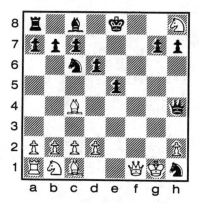

WHITE TO MOVE

Scenario: The opening is the insane Wilkes Barre Variation of the Two Knights Defense, where each side has removed its safety belt. Giving no thought to defense, both parties pursue their own aggressive objectives. Here, White on move, pursues Black's King to mate: 11. Qf7+ Kd8 12. Qf8+ Kd7 13. Be6+! Kxe6 14. Qf7 mate.

Interpretation: In the violent positions characteristic of the Wilkes Barre, both players go all out for the attack. Checks and captures are the order of the day, and the value of being on move cannot be overemphasized. In the hand-to-hand fighting, the process of development is pushed into the background. Only when there is a momentary lull is there time for a new piece to come into play. Black's error here occurred on move ten (d7 to d6) when he wrongly thought such a lull existed. Instead, he had to keep up the pressure with 10. . . .Qg4+ 11. Kxh1 Qe4+, which leads to a draw.

7

The Ruy Lopez

The Ruy Lopez (1. **e4 e5**   2. **Nf3 Nc6**   3. **Bb5**) derives its strength from the logic of White's second and third moves. His second move, Knight on g1 to f3, attacks the enemy e-pawn. His third move, Bishop on f1 to b5, also attacks the e-pawn in that, at a timely moment, White hopes to exchange b5-Bishop for c6-Knight, removing the e-pawn's protector.

From this slender beginning, White builds formidable pressure against Black's center, a pressure so long lasting that the Lopez has been nicknamed the Spanish Torture. It should come as no surprise, therefore, to learn that of all the double King-pawn openings, the Lopez is the one most frequently played and also the one that has accumulated the greatest body of theory.

Fortunately for Black, the threat to his e5-pawn takes several moves to materialize, so he has time to plot his defense. He can, for example, insert the move 3. . . .a6, since 4. Bxc6 dxc6   5. Nxe5 Qd4 offers White nothing. And if White, instead of playing 4. Bxc6, retreats his Bishop on move 4 to a4, Black can opt later to driving the a4-Bishop away with 4. . . .b7-b5. He thereby avoids a pin on his c6-Knight when he advances his d-pawn, something he must do eventually.

Yet in essence, Black's defensive scheme must fall into one of two categories: active or passive defense. Active defense is characterized by counterattack on White's e4-

pawn. The Berlin Defense (3. . . .Nf6   4. 0-0 Nxe4), the Tarrasch Defense (3. . . .a6   4. Ba4 Nf6   5. 0-0 Nxe4), and the Schliemann Defense (3. . . .f5) are typical methods. In these instances, Black relies on his increased piece-mobility to carry him over the badlands. The passive or strong point defense is marked by Black's strengthening his e5-pawn.The Steinitz Defense (3. . . .d6), Steinitz Defense Deferred (3. . . .a6 4. Ba4 d6), and the Closed Defense (3. . . .a6   4. Ba4 Nf6   5. 0-0 Be7   6. Re1 b5   7. Bb3 d6) are the most reliable of the fortress defenses. Here, Black hangs on to e5 with might and main. It remains to be seen if White can translate his slight space advantage into something more tangible.

For the student who wishes to incorporate the Ruy Lopez into his opening armory, take a bit of care. The data masses systematized under the Ruy Lopez heading exceed the total of all double King-pawn openings combined. Main-line variations commonly extend well beyond move 20, often running out to move 30 and even further.

To expect someone in one session to comprehend the intricate twists and turns in the vast structure of the Lopez, to memorize or otherwise acquire the mountain of variations, is to expect the impossible. I therefore recommend that you go slowly at first, gradually orienting yourself in the different phases of the Lopez.

The Exchange Variation (3. . . .a6   4. Bxc6), the Center Attack (3. . . .a6 4. Ba4 Nf6   5. d4), and direct defense of the e4-pawn (3. . .Nf6 4. Nc3 or 4. d3) are all excellent starts. In this manner, you will garner a solid body of Lopez experience, enabling you to tackle the more difficult main lines of the Spanish Game. Good hunting in the Lopez!

149

DISCOVERY

Ruy Lopez

1. e4   e5
2. Nf3   Nc6
3. Bb5   d6
4. 0-0   Nf6
5. d4   Nxe4

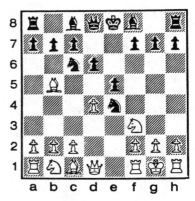

WHITE TO MOVE

Scenario: The full refutation of Black's last move employs pins, forks, and mainly a discovery. White starts by ganging up on the pinned c6-Knight: 6. **d5.** Black's only recourse to save his piece is to counterattack White's Bishop, 6. . . .**a6.** Now 7. **Bd3** puts both Black Knights under fire, so Black must answer 7. . . .**Nf6,** when after 8. **dxc6,** Black tries to regain his piece with the forking advance, 8. . . .**e4.** White's bag of tricks then offers 9. **Re1,** pinning the e-pawn to its King. Black can protect his e-pawn, 9. . . .**d5,** but that gives White the time to move one of his menaced pieces away without fear of the other's capture, 10. **Be2!.** Does this last move lose a piece to 10. . . .**exf3?** No, for 11. **cxb7** wins by either 11. . . .**fxe2** 12. **bxa8/Q** or 11. . . .**Bxb7** 12. **Bb5** double-check and mate.

Interpretation: Several things should have discouraged Black from capturing White's e-pawn, 5. . . .**Nxe4:** (a) his c6-Knight was pinned and helpless, (b) his King would be subject to White's Rook attack along the unveiling e-file, (c) the position would generally open up, favoring the better developed side, White. Black should have kept the position closed until his King was safely castled and his game was more consolidated.

150

PIN

Ruy Lopez

1. e4   e5
2. Nf3   Nc6
3. Bb5   d6
4. 0-0   Bg4
5. d4   a6
6. Ba4

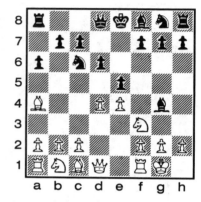

BLACK TO MOVE

Scenario: Both sides exercise pins. White's a4-Bishop hinges Black's c6-Knight to its King, and Black's g4-Bishop adheres White's f3-Knight to its Queen. Yet it's Black's turn and he can break the pin with his b-pawn. After White's Bishop hies to safety at b3, Black's c6-Knight takes White's d-pawn for nothing. A pawn down, White can play riskily and get mated: 6. . . . b5 7. **Bb3 Nxd4** 8. **c3 Nxf3+** 9. **gxf3 Bh3** 10. **Qd5 Qf6!** 11. **Qxa8+ Ke7**, when White is hard pressured to deter a check from Black's Queen at g6 and a swoop to g2 for mate.

Interpretation: The Ruy Lopez is characterized by the moves 1. e4 e5 2. Nf3 Nc6 3. Bb5. Black, in many variations, attacks White's bishop by playing a7-a6. This is putting the question to the Bishop: either back off or take my Knight. Taking on c6 is almost always good, but sometimes it's stronger to retreat to a4, maintaining pressure on the Knight. White has no choice but to exchange Bishop for Knight on move 6. After 6. Bxc6 bxc6 7. dxe5 Bxf3 8. Qxf3 dxe5, White has an excellent game. Eschew mechanical play. A reputable move may not always be the best one.

151

PIN

Ruy Lopez

1. e4	e5
2. Nf3	Nc6
3. Bb5	d6
4. d4	Bd7
5. Nc3	Nf6
6. Bxc6	Bxc6
7. Qd3	exd4
8. Nxd4	g6
9. Bg5	Bg7
10. 0-0-0	0-0

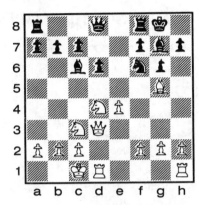

WHITE TO MOVE

Scenario: Black's last move, castling Kingside, seemed a natural, but look again: it loses material. It didn't address the problem of Black's pinned f6-Knight. White strikes by 11. **Nxc6**, clearing the d-file for operations. After 11. . . . **bxc6**, White pierces the f6-Knight with 12. **e5**. Since the counterattack 12. . . . h6 drops a piece to 13. exf6 hxg5 14. fxg7, Black has to remove White's e5-pawn, 12. . . . **dxe5**. White then exchanges a few heavy pieces, 13. **Qxd8 Raxd8** 14. **Rxd8 Rxd8**. The f6-Knight is still pinned, and White gangs up on it by entering e4 with his c3-Knight. Black has nothing better than to take the e4-Knight but loses his remaining Rook.

Interpretation: The opening variation selected by Black is difficult, fraught with tactics favoring White. Black must handle it with finesse. Instead of 10. . . . 0-0, Black at very least should have shifted his Queen off the d8-f6 diagonal, perhaps to c8. That would have avoided the loss of material. White began his winning transaction by first trading Knights on c6. Whenever there are exchanges in the position, evaluate them carefully. Afterward, winning threats may suddenly emerge not evident before the trade.

152

REMOVING THE GUARD

Ruy Lopez

WHITE TO MOVE

1. e4	e5
2. Nf3	Nc6
3. Bb5	d6
4. d4	Bd7
5. Nc3	Nge7
6. Bc4	exd4
7. Nxd4	g6
8. Bg5	Bg7
9. Nd5	Bxd4

Scenario: Black fianchettoed his King-Bishop—that is, he developed it to the flank, where it attacks the center without actually being in it. At g7, the dark-square Bishop exerts pressure along the b2-h8 diagonal. If the Bishop disappears, the diagonal is weakened. With **10. Qxd4!**, White exposes the vulnerability of Black's dark squares. After 10. . . . **Nxd4** 11. **Nf6+ Kh8** 12. **Bh6**, White can declare mate. If Black saves his hanging h8-Rook by castling, 10. . . . **0-0**, White finishes him by 11. **Nf6+ Kh8** (or 11. . . . **Kg7** allowing 12. Nh5 double-check, and mate next move) 12. **Ng4+ Nxd4** 13. **Bf6+ Kg8** 14. **Nh6** mate.

Interpretation: Black mixed up ideas. He tried too much in a conservative opening, flanking his King-Bishop. This developed real dark-square weaknesses, and Black's game collapsed. The square f6, in particular, was vulernable because neither Black's e-pawn or g-pawn were positioned to guard it. Had Black grasped the spirit of his third, fourth, and fifth moves, he would have continued with the line 7. . . . Nxd4 8. Qxd4 Nc6, following with 9. . . . Be7 and 10. . . . 0-0. If you begin the game with your e-pawn, you needn't also move the g-pawn to develop your King-Bishop. In such cases this move is generally unnecessary and weakening.

153

PIN

Ruy Lopez

1. e4   e5
2. Nf3   Nc6
3. Bb5   d6
4. Bxc6 +   bxc6
5. d4   Bg4
6. dxe5   dxe5
7. Qxd8 +   Rxd8
8. Nxe5??

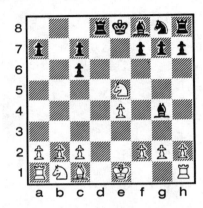

BLACK TO MOVE

Scenario: White's last move is a losing blunder. Capturing a pawn on e5 loses the game to 8. . . .**Rd1** mate. White failed to digest that the Knight, when at f3, was pinned to d1 by the g4-Bishop.

Interpretation: Indirect defense, whereby something is secured because of circumstances or consequences rather than actual protection, is a vital tactic in the opening. Black understood that his e5-pawn did not have to be guarded, for if White had captured it, the price would be a mating intrusion at d1. White succumbed to a deadly sin in the opening—pawn-grabbing. He emphasized winning material, disregarding more important aspects of his position. Win a pawn if you can, but don't overlook possible enemy counterattacks and indirect defenses, such as pins.

154

MATING ATTACK

Ruy Lopez

1. e4   e5
2. Nf3   Nc6
3. Bb5   d6
4. d3   Bd7
5. Nc3   f6?
6. h3   a6
7. Bc4   Nh6?

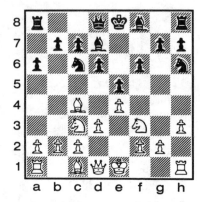

WHITE TO MOVE

Scenario: Black's last move invites White to capture the Knight and bust up the enemy Kingside, 8. **Bxh6 gxh6.** The diagonal e8-h5 is ripe for a Queen check, for Black no longer has a g-pawn to block it. So White clears the Queen's path with 9. **Ng5!**, where the Knight is immune to capture, for 9. . . .hxg5 (or 9. . . .fxg5)   10. Qh5 + Ke7 11. Of7 is mate. If Black plays 9. . . .Qe7, dealing with the threatened Knight-fork at f7, White runs with 10. **Qh5 + Kd8** 11. **Nf7 +**, picking off the Rook at h8 on the next move.

Interpretation: Black lost because he disregarded his King's safety. The hobbling 5. . . .f6 exposed the h5-e8 diagonal and weakened the a2-g8 diagonal as well. The inept 7. . . .Nh6 that allowed for annihilation of his Kingside pawn cover compounded the disaster. In the opening, be on the alert for enemy attacking lanes that lead to your King. If you find one, ready your game to cope with assaults.

155

FORK

Ruy Lopez

1. e4   e5
2. Nf3   Nc6
3. Bb5   Nf6
4. d3   Ne7
5. Nxe5?

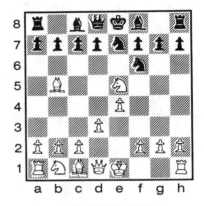

BLACK TO MOVE

Scenario: Black has deliberately hung out his e-pawn as bait, and White has bitten. After 5. . . .c6, White must withdraw his Bishop to either a4 or c4, permitting Black to fork White's King and e5-Knight by 6. . . .Qa5 +. White could try his own sucker punch, answering with 6. Nc4, so that if Black blindly takes White's b5-Bishop, White has 7. Nd6, a smothered mate. But Black still wins a piece by 6. . . .Ng6, which enables his dark-square Bishop to guard d6 against invasion. After White saves his Bishop, 7. Ba4, Black pawn-forks two pieces with 7. . . .b5.

Interpretation: This ruse is known as Mortimer's Trap, playing on a basic human weakness: greed. Rather than take the fifth-move plunge of capturing Black's unprotected e-pawn, White should be pondering Black's apparent generosity. By pausing to reflect on the position, White might espy the trick and castle, or develop his Queen-Knight instead. If he still doesn't see the point of Black's sacrifice and loses a piece in the trap at least he'll more likely understand his error afterwards. And his past experiences may enable him to avoid similar lapses in the future. "Those who forget the past are condemned to repeat it"—George Santayana.

156

REMOVING THE GUARD

Ruy Lopez

1. e4   e5
2. Nf3   Nc6
3. Bb5   Nf6
4. d3   a6

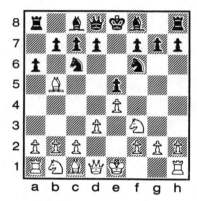

WHITE TO MOVE

Scenario: In the early stages of the Ruy Lopez, White aims at Black's e5-pawn. White's second move, Ng1-f3, attacks Black's e5-pawn directly, and White's third move, Bf1-b5, makes possible exchanging away the e5-pawn's c6-defender. If Black overlooks White's inherent threats, he gives up the e-pawn for nothing: 5. **Bxc6 dxc6**   6. **Nxe5**.

Interpretation: In many of the fashionable lines of the Ruy Lopez, or Spanish Game, Black has a built-in defense to e5. After White gives up the b5-Bishop for the c6-Knight, instead of taking back with a pawn toward the center, b7xc6, Black takes back away from the center, d7xc6. This opens the d-file for Black's Queen. If White then obtains the e5-pawn with his f3-Knight, Black's Queen might be able to transfer to d4, delivering a double-attack: to the e5-Knight and the e4-pawn. White will save his Knight but relinquish the pawn he had just won, and the game evens up materially again. This tactic fails to work, however, if White has first protected e4—say, by d2-d3. Then, when Black's Queen shifts to d4, it does not initiate a true double-attack, for the e4-pawn is guarded. Since only White's e5-Knight is at bay, White need only move it to safety, usually back to f3, counterattacking Black's Queen. The end result: White has gained a pawn.

157

PIN

Ruy Lopez

1. e4	e5
2. Nf3	Nc6
3. Bb5	Nf6
4. 0-0	Nxe4
5. d4	f6
6. Re1	Nd6
7. Bxc6	dxc6
8. dxe5	fxe5
9. Nxe5	Be7

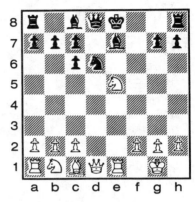

WHITE TO MOVE

Scenario: White bears down on the exposed Black King with 10. Qh5 + . Should Black block the check with a pawn move to g6, White's e5-Knight takes it for nothing, since White's Queen pins the h-pawn to the Rook at h8. Fleeing with the King to f8 is no better, for White's Knight still plays to g6, this time checking, and Black's pinned h-pawn still cannot capture it. Should Black should take White's Knight, White's Queen grabs Black's Rook at h8.

Interpretation: When Black captures White's pawn on the fourth move, he is really interested in lessening the pressure on his center and thereby getting a freer game. Black ought to give the pawn back by allowing White's d-pawn to capture on e5. Once the e-file again closes, White's Rook cannot harass Black's King. Thus, on move 5, Black should have retreated his Knight to d6 or developed his Bishop to e7. By placing his pawn on f6 to protect his e-pawn, he exposed his King to attack along the h5-e8 diagonal.

158

REMOVING THE GUARD

Ruy Lopez

1. e4   e5
2. Nf3   Nc6
3. Bb5   Nf6
4. 0-0   Nxe4
5. d4   a6
6. Bd3   d5
7. c4   exd4?

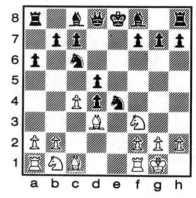

WHITE TO MOVE

Scenario: Black's last move was a clodish error. Using the open e-file and exploiting Black's loose e4-Knight, White pinches a piece. The capture 8. **cxd5** knocks away the underpinnings from Black's advanced Knight while combining with an attack against the other steed at c6. After Black's forced capture, 8. . . .**Qxd5**, White wins a Knight for nothing with 9. **Bxe4**. Black is unable to recapture on e4 with his Queen for fear of being pinned to Black's King by 10. **Re1**.

Interpretation: If White had retreated his Bishop (6. Ba4) after 5. . . .a6, then by transposition the players would find themselves in Tarrasch Defense of the Ruy Lopez, usually reached after the moves 1. e4 e5 2. Nf3 Nc6 3. Bb5 a6 4. Ba4 Nf6 5. 0-0 Nxe4. White's 7. c4 in the actual variation is a gamble. It becomes justified only after Black errs with 7. . . .exd4? If Black instead plays 7. . . .Nxd4!, then he may even get the better of it after 8. Nxd4 exd4 9. cxd5 Nf6. If you have a number of possible captures in a given situation, think about the ramifications of each.

159

TRAPPED PIECE

Ruy Lopez

1. e4   e5
2. Nf3   Nc6
3. Bb5   Nf6
4. 0-0   Nxe4
5. d4   exd4
6. Re1   f5
7. Nxd4   Ne7

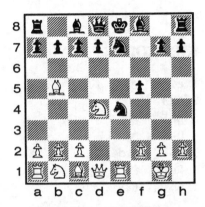

WHITE TO MOVE

Scenario: Black's last Knight move accomplished two things: it (A) protected the f-pawn, attacked by White's d4-Knight; and it (B) blocked the e-file, unpinning Black's e4-Knight. A drawback is the smothering of Black's Queen, with no place to go. White's 8. **Ne6,** exploiting the pinned d-pawn, snares Black's most powerful weapon.

Interpretation: The theme is the "trapped piece," but the pin tactic—by which a friendly Queen, Rook, or Bishop prevents an enemy unit from moving off the line of the piece's power—played a major role in Black's defeat. The Rook pin of the e4-Knight led Black to interpose his Knight at e7, and the b5-Bishop pinning on the d-pawn allowed White's Knight to enter on e6 without capture. Pin, if you can, your opponent's pieces and pawns. Avoid getting pinned yourself.

160

FORK

Ruy Lopez

1. e4	e5
2. Nf3	Nc6
3. Bb5	Nf6
4. 0-0	Nxe4
5. d4	exd4?
6. Re1	f5
7. Nxd4	Bc5

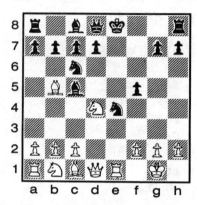

WHITE TO MOVE

Scenario: White had hoped to win Black's pinned e4-Knight by a pawn attack from f3, but clearly 8. f3 drops the Knight at d4 with check. Nevertheless, Black's Bishop at c5 is very vulnerable. After 8. **Rxe4 + fxe4**, the 5th rank is suddenly unveiled and White's Queen propels to h5, forking Black's King and Bishop. White wins two minor pieces (a Bishop and Knight) for a Rook.

Interpretation: Black's pawn capture on move 5 harmed his position. It opened the e-file for White's Rook. Black erred further by moving his f-pawn, exposing his King along the h5-e8 diagonal. Finally, an ill-considered development of his Bishop to c5 led to a deadly fork of King and Bishop. If your King is in the center, avoid perfunctory developments and pawn moves that expose your King. Keep the game closed. If you're on the offense, look for ways to pursue the enemy King that also employ threats to other enemy pieces. Look for double-attacks.

161

DISCOVERY

Ruy Lopez

1. e4	e5
2. Nf3	Nc6
3. Bb5	Nf6
4. 0-0	Nxe4
5. d4	exd4?
6. Re1	d5
7. Qxd4	a6
8. Bxc6 +	bxc6
9. Ng5	Qf6

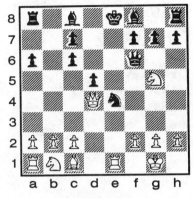

WHITE TO MOVE

Scenario: White has one less pawn than Black and his Queen at d4 hangs, unprotected and attacked. White could win back the pawn by trading Queens on f6 and then Knights on e4, but he has better than that. After 10. **Nxe4! Qxd4** 11. **Nf6 + Kd8** 12. **Re8**, Black is mated.

Interpretation: Black could have avoided being mated. Instead of taking White's Queen, he could have captured White's e4-Knight (10. Nxe4 dxe4). Even so, White could have achieved a winning game with 11. Qxe4 + . Now how would Black get out of check? If he blocks on e6 with his Queen or light-square Bishop, White's Queen captures at c6 with check. If Black instead blocks with his dark-square Bishop at e7, White deploys his Bishop to g5, diverting Black's Queen from control of c6. Black really went wrong on his fifth move. He captured White's d-pawn, making it possible for White's Rook to pin the Knight at e4. In open games, when your opponent has castled and your King remains in the center, avoid exchanging central pawns if it lets down the drawbridge to your King.

162

FORK

Ruy Lopez

1. e4   e5
2. Nf3   Nc6
3. Bb5   Nf6
4. 0-0   Nxe4
5. Re1   f5
6. d3   Nd6

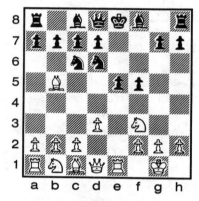

WHITE TO MOVE

Scenario: White will regain his e-pawn by first exchanging on c6, 7. **Bxc6 dxc6.** The question is, can he gain more from the position? He can, with 8. **Rxe5 +.** Now 8. . . .Be7 loses at least a Bishop to 9. Bg5, and 8. . . .Kd7 elbows the Queen back to 9. Bg5. So that leaves 8. . . .Kf7, which fails to 9. **Bg5 Qd7**   10. **Re7 +! Bxe7**   11. **Ne5 +,** forking Black's King and Queen. White gives up a Rook and minor piece to win a Queen—a net gain.

Interpretation: Black tried for too much in the opening. He need only have eliminated White's e-pawn, dropping his Knight back to d6 on move 5 instead of move 6. Playing f7-f5 unnecessarily weakened his position. White's d2-d3 forced the Knight to back anyway. The one tempo lost was enough to give White a winning initiative. "Lost time is never found again," cautioned Ben Franklin's Poor Richard.

163

DISCOVERY

Ruy Lopez

1. e4 e5
2. Nf3 Nc6
3. Bb5 Nf6
4. 0-0 Nxe4
5. Re1 Nd6
6. Nc3 Nxb5
7. Nxe5 Nxc3?

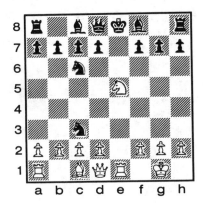

WHITE TO MOVE

Scenario: White is behind by two minor pieces and his Queen is being lashed. But it's White's turn and he has a decisive discovered attack: **8. Nxc6+!**. Black's best reply is 8. . . .**Be7**, for 8. . . .Qe7 donates the Queen to 9. Rxe7+. Now the correct move for White is 9. **Nxe7** (not 9. Rxe7+ Qxe7 10. Nxe7 Nxd1), when 9. . . .**Nxd1** 10. **Ng6+ Qe7** 11. **Nxe7** eventually puts White a piece ahead. Black's Knight is trapped and White menaces 12. Ng6+, blasting the enemy King and h8-Rook simultaneously.

Interpretation: Could Black have escaped by trying 7. . . .Nxe5 instead of 7. . . .Nxc3? No, for White would then win by 8. Rxe5+ Be7 9. Nd5! 0-0 10. Nxe7+ Kh8 11. Qh5 (which threatens 12. Qxh7+ Kxh7 13. Rh5 mate) g6 12. Qh6 d6 13. Rh5! gxh5 14. Qf6 mate. The correct plan for Black was 7. . . .Be7 followed by castling on the next move. When an enemy Rook lines up on the open e-file leading to your King, or makes noises to do so, castle quickly. Get your King away from central target practice.

164

DOUBLE ATTACK

Ruy Lopez

1. e4   e5
2. Nf3   Nc6
3. Bb5   Bc5
4. d3   Nf6
5. Bxc6   dxc6
6. Nxe5?

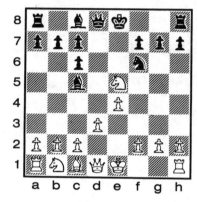

BLACK TO MOVE

Scenario: A main idea of the Ruy Lopez is to conquer Black's e5-pawn, often by removing Black's c6-Knight. But there are indirect defenses and counterattacks that White must contend with. After 6. . . .Qd4, White is faced with the Herculean task of defending both his e5-Knight and his mate at f2. White's e5-Knight suffers at his handler's greed.

Interpretation: Black realized that there was no need to actually protect his e5-pawn, for he had in reserve an indirect defense. The pawn couldn't be captured because of the changing arrangement of the pieces. The very move needed to win the pawn, Bb5xc6, created the mechanism to prevent the e5-pawn's capture, d7xc6. That recapture on c6 opened the d-file, making it possible for Black's Queen to connect at d4 with his c5-Bishop. Even before this transaction, on move 4, rather than defend his e5-pawn by d7-d6—where the d-pawn would then be out of position to capture on c6—Black developed his dark-square Bishop to c5. There it could combine with Black's Queen along the a7-f2 diagonal, if an exchange on c6 eventually took place. How should White have continued instead of 5. Nf3xe5? By either castling or positioning his c1-Bishop to e3 strengthen his game while making the threat to win the e5-pawn a reality.

165

FORK

Ruy Lopez

1. e4   e5
2. Nf3   Nc6
3. Bb5   Bc5
4. c3   Nf6
5. d4   exd4
6. 0-0   d5
7. exd5 Nxd5
8. Qa4   Bd7

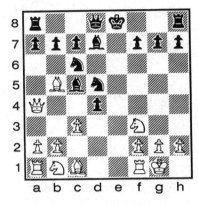

WHITE TO MOVE

Scenario: Black's last move was a reaction to the pin on his c6-Knight, but he's left himself open to another prong: 9. **Qc4!**, a winning fork of c5-Bishop and d5-Knight. Black's only choice is which piece he prefers losing. Whichever is salvaged, the other goes down.

Interpretation: After White essays 8. Qa4, Black must find a way to guard c6 without leaving the d5-Knight in the lurch. A move that copes with both targets is 8. . . .Qd6. White, with 9. cxd4 however, gets the upper hand anyway. Black would have done better to capture White's e4-pawn with his f6-Knight on the sixth move. The actual advance, d7-d5, only created the seedbed for Black's own demise: the weakening of the a4-e8 diagonal resulting from the movement of the d-pawn. After 6. . . .Nxe4, Black can then meet 7. Re1 with 7. . . .d5, supporting his e4-Knight. And if White instead plays 7. cxd4, leading to 7. . . .Bb6 8. Qc2, Black has a comfortable interchange with 8. . . .Nd6, and his game is still alive. As Bunan said, "When alive, be a dead man, and act as you will."

166

TRAPPED PIECE

Ruy Lopez

1. e4   e5
2. Nf3   Nc6
3. Bb5   Bc5
4. c3   f5
5. d4   fxe4
6. Ng5   Be7
7. dxe5 Nxe5?

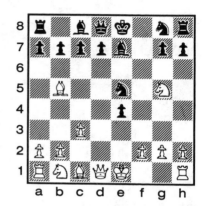

WHITE TO MOVE

Scenario: Black's last move was unwise. It exposed the d-pawn to the pinning b5-Bishop, preventing the d-pawn from moving off the a4-e8 diagonal. The pawn is not guarding e6, and White's g5-Knight enters the position on e6, smothering the ensnared Black Queen.

Interpretation: Black mistakenly sought to eliminate White's e5-pawn too soon. First he should have exchanged the e7-Bishop for the g5-Knight: 7. . . .Bxg5 8. Qh5+ g6 9. Qxg5 Qxg5 10. Bxg5. Then Black could have captured on e5 with his c6-Knight. The example shows how two apparently unrelated pieces—the g5-Knight and the b5-Bishop—can coordinate, even though they're on different sides of the board. If Black had focused on these two pieces in tandem, he could have harmonized their powers into a useful force.

167

FORK

Ruy Lopez

1. e4   e5
2. Nf3   Nc6
3. Bb5   Bc5
4. Nxe5   Bxf2+
5. Kxf2   Nxe5
6. Qh5   Qe7
7. d4   Nf6
8. Qxe5?

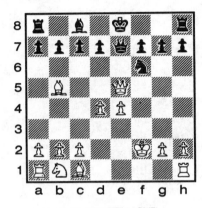

BLACK TO MOVE

Scenario: Did Black really leave his Knight on e5 inadequately protected and subject to capture? No, White was tricked, and loses his Queen to 8. . . . .Ng4+, an obvious Knight fork. White is fleeced of his Queen for two Knights.

Interpretation: White needn't blunder away his Queen. He could continue as in an actual game played by mail in 1975: 8. Bg5 Neg4+ 9. Kg1 Qxe4 10. Nc3 Qxd4+ 11. Kf1 Qf2 mate. Or he could simply withdraw his Queen to e2, losing a tempo, for stirring his Queen in the first place accomplished nothing. Instead, he should have advanced his Queen-pawn two squares, 6. d4, driving back Black's Knight and also seizing control of the center. Then he should have shifted his Rook to e1, reinforcing his central grip and clearing the back rank for his King to "castle by hand." The Queen is a powerhouse, but bringing it out too early in the game without a specific purpose—and without supporters—exposes it to attack. The enemy can then develop his game at your expense.

168

PIN

Ruy Lopez

1. e4   e5
2. Nf3   Nc6
3. Bb5   Nf6
4. 0-0   Bc5
5. c3   0-0
6. d4   Bb6
7. Bg5   Qe7

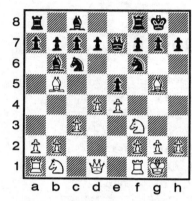

WHITE TO MOVE

Scenario: Black's f6-Knight is pinned and his e5-pawn needs solid support. White merges these two themes into a winning game with 8. **Bxc6.** No matter how Black takes back, either b7xc6 or d7xc6, White captures Black's e-pawn with his d-pawn, billeting the immobile f6-Knight. Black loses a piece.

Interpretation: While Black's f6-Knight could have captured White's e4-pawn—before it became pinned—Black didn't have to worry much about the pressure on his own e5-pawn. But White's pinning development, Bc1-g5, incapacitated Black's steed and substantiated the threat against Black's e5-pawn. Needing to secure e5, Black should have continued 7. . . .d6 rather than the flimsy 7. . . .Qe7. The Queen, which is the strongest piece, becomes as weak as the King when used merely for defense. In time of pestilence, "Queens have died young and fair"—Thomas Nash.

169

MATING ATTACK

Ruy Lopez

1. e4   e5
2. Nf3   Nc6
3. Bb5   Nf6
4. 0-0   Bc5
5. Re1   Ng4
6. d4   exd4
7. Nxd4   Qh4
8. Nf3

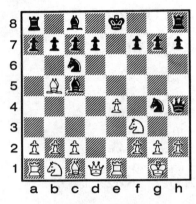

BLACK TO MOVE

Scenario: Black is clearly ascending, menacing White at f2. The most convincing method is 8. . . .Qxf2+   9. **Kh1 Qg1+!**, clearing f2 for a Knight-check. No matter how White captures on g1, with his Knight or Rook, Black's Knight deals a smothered mate from f2.

Interpretation: White's castling fourth move was fine, but his fifth move, shifting the Rook from f1 to e1, was not. The incursion Nf6-g4 exploited White's error. White could have avoided this mess if he had defended his e4-pawn by d2-d3 rather than with his f1-Rook. Another viable defense was delivering his Knight from b1 to c3. But moving the Rook weakened the f2-square, after which his game became unhinged. Don't make the mistake of automatically playing your Rook from f1 to e1. Such a move may weaken f2, and it may not even be the best way to activate the King-Rook, especially if White has a fixed pawn at e4, blocking the Rook's line.

170

DISCOVERY

Ruy Lopez

1. e4   e5
2. Nf3   Nc6
3. Bb5   Nf6
4. 0-0   Bc5
5. Bxc6   dxc6
6. Nxe5   Nxe4
7. Qe2   Nxf2

WHITE TO MOVE

Scenario: In chess, "he who laughs last" may not be the disadvantaged second mover. The opportunity may not come his way. Such is so with discovered attacks. Here, White's Queen plans one along the e-file, while Black's c5-Bishop readies fire along the a7-g1 diagonal. But White's first-move prerogative never gives Black the chance to respond with spirit: 8. **Nd3+! Ne4+** 2. **Nxc5 Qd4+** 10. **Kh1 Qxc5** 11. **Qxe4+**, and White laughs last with a full piece ahead.

Interpretation: One game in Ohio, in 1972, teed off from the diagram 8. Nxc6+ Ne4+ 9. Kh1 bxc6 10. Qxe4+ Be6 11. Qxc6+ Qd7 12. Qxa8+, and Black resigned. Yet Black could have cut his losses with 10. . . .Be7 instead of 10. . . .Be6. The real lemon in his game was capturing on f2 with his Knight. Instead, Black should have played 7. . . .Qd5, after which he would still be kicking. Instead, Black moved mechanically. He was hung up on his discovered check and forgot about White's—the one that came first. "Laughter winged his polished dart" . . ."—William Winter.

171

TRAPPED PIECE

Ruy Lopez

1. e4   e5
2. Nf3   Nc6
3. Bb5   Bc5
4. 0-0   Nge7
5. c3   f5
6. d4   Bb6
7. d5   fxe4
8. Ng5   Nb8

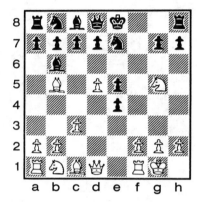

WHITE TO MOVE

Scenario: Black retreats his Knight, reasoning that White simply recaptures the e-pawn, 9. Nxe4. Comes a trade of pawns, White's superior 9. **Ne6!** wins the smothered Black Queen. Black's d-pawn cannot capture the e6-Knight because the pawn is pinned to its King by the light-square Bishop at b5.

Interpretation: Chess is a game of war, and naturally Black looks to attack as soon as possible. White, however, has the advantage of the first move, with a natural initiative and control of the flow of play. If Black counterattacks, his move must also deal with White's threats. White's initiative enables him to advance his pawns without losing tempi. Black, on the other hand, loses time. His dark-square Bishop had to be removed from attack, dropping one tempo, and his f-pawn hopped twice (f7-f5 and f5xe4) without developing his game. White's Knight thereby had time to make three moves, piercing his opponent at e6. Don't be fooled; the opening is not for wasting time or moves.

172

FORK

Ruy Lopez

1. e4   e5
2. Nf3   Nc6
3. Bb5   f5
4. Nc3   Nd4
5. Bc4   fxe4?

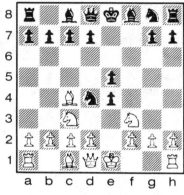

WHITE TO MOVE

Scenario: Black's last move blunders. It clears the 5th rank between h5 and e5, so White's Queen can deliver a nasty double-attack. After **6. Nxd4** (to open the d1-h5 diagonal) 6. . . . **exd4** 7. **Qh5 +**, Black must choose between allowing 7. . . . Ke7   8. Qe5 mate or 7. . . . **g6**   8. **Qe5 +**, attacking Black's King and h8-Rook. In the latter, play might go: 8. . . . **Ne7**   9. **Nd5** (threatening Knight-mate at f6) 9. . . . **Bg7** (to stop it) 10. **Qxg7 Rf8**   11. **Nf6 + Rxf6**   12. **Qxf6,** leaving White a Rook to the good.

Interpretation: Schliemann's Variation of the Ruy Lopez, 1. e4 e5   2. Nf3 Nc6   3. Bb5 f5, has strong points, especially the attack against White's e4. Its drawback is that it weakens the h5-e8 diagonal, allowing White's Queen in some situations to give a winning check at h5. True, it doesn't help to Queen-check at h5 if the attack can be blocked by the advance g7-g6 and White doesn't have a follow-up. But when the 5th rank is open, and nothing obstructs the path from h5 to e5, Black must be leery, for he could be caught in the meshes of the chessboard's illusions. "If a man look sharply and attentively, he shall see fortune"—Francis Bacon.

173

FORK

Ruy Lopez

1. e4   e5
2. Nf3   Nc6
3. Bb5   f5
4. Nc3   Nd4
5. Nxe5   Qf6
6. f4   fxe4
7. Nxe4?

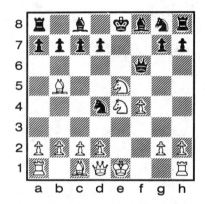

BLACK TO MOVE

Scenario: White's Knight has snatched Black's e4-pawn, endangering Black's Queen. But the Queen's table turns with 7. . . . .**Qxf4**, forking both White Knights while maintaining a Knight attack to the b5-Bishop. Thus it's a triple threat. If White strikes back with 8. **Qh5 +** , Black coolly sacrifices his Rook: 8. . . . .**g6** 9. **Nxg6 hxg6** 10. **Qxh8**. Black then scoops White's e4-Knight with a check, gaining a decisive advantage of two Knights for a Rook. Now Black mounts a gathering assault.

Interpretation: Black played the Schliemann Variation of the Ruy Lopez (3. . . .f5), following with one of its sharpest lines (4. . . .Nd4). Current trend recommends either 5. Bc4 or 5. exf5. White's actual 5. Nxe5 has less force than appears. Instead of 6. f4, White might better withdraw his Knight to f3. Of course, 7. Nxe4? loses outright; if a blunder can lose a game, so can a string of second-rate moves. "For destruction, ice is also great, and would suffice," noted Robert Frost.

174

SKEWER

Ruy Lopez

1. e4   e5
2. Nf3   Nc6
3. Bb5   f5
4. Nc3   fxe4
5. Nxe4   Nf6
6. Nf6+   gxf6
7. d4   e4
8. Ng5   fxg5

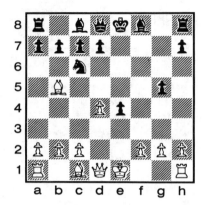

WHITE TO MOVE

Scenario: White has sacrificed a piece to get an attack against Black's King. After 9. **Qh5+ Ke7**   10. **Bxg5+**, White's Bishop skewers (or x-rays) Black's King and Queen, leading to her majesty's capture next move.

Interpretation: Before capturing 8. . . .fxg5, Black could have interposed 8. . . .Bb4+ and then taken on g5 the next move. That wouldn't have saved the game, for 8. . . .Bb4+   9. c3 fxg5   10. Qh5+ Kf8 (avoiding putting his King in a skewer line with his Queen) 11. Bxg5 wins just the same: (A) If 11. . . .Qe8, then 12. Qh6+ Kf7 13. Qf6+ Kg8 14. Bc4+ demolishes; (B) If 11. . . .Ne7, then 12. Bc4 d5 13. Bxd5! Qxd5 14. Bh6+ Kg8 15. Qe8 is mate; (C) And if 11. . . .Be7, then 12. Bh6+ Kg8 13. Bc4+ blows Black away. Black's error was his sixth-move capture, exposing the h5-e8 diagonal. He should have taken with his Queen. Do not expose your King's position by making weakening pawn moves.

175

TRAPPED PIECE

Ruy Lopez

1. e4   e5
2. Nf3   Nc6
3. Bb5   f5
4. Bxc6   dxc6
5. 0-0   fxe4
6. Nxe5   Nf6
7. Nc3?

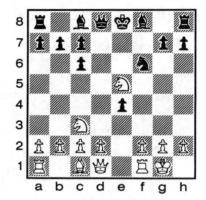

BLACK TO MOVE

Scenario: Knights are generally well placed in the center, but not so in this case. White's aggressive-looking Knight at e5 is lassoed by 7. . . .Qd4!, leaving it no safe place to move. Protection won't come from a pawn, for the f-pawn is pinned and the d-pawn is blocked.

Interpretation: The fight for central squares requires good cooperation between pieces and pawns. Invariably, both center-pawns, for each side, join the battle. Bishop-pawns often lend a hand, for though they can't occupy central squares, they can assail them. At least one pawn must help to position a Knight on a central post. White should have moved his d-pawn two squares ahead on move 7, instead of the more shortsighted 7. Nc3.

176

DOUBLE ATTACK

Ruy Lopez

1. e4	e5
2. Nf3	Nc6
3. Bb5	f5
4. Bxc6	dxc6
5. Nxe5	Qd4
6. Qh5 +	

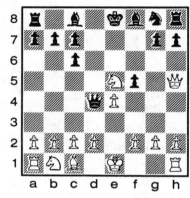

BLACK TO MOVE

Scenario: Black is in some difficulty since he cannot allow either White's Queen or e5-Knight to invade f7. The block 6. . . .g6! solves the dilemma and leaves both White soldiers under attack. Black need not fear the counter 7. **Nxg6**, for he is free to play 7. . . .**hxg6** without losing his h8-Rook. His Queen, imperious from d4, protects it. White can get a third pawn for his lost piece, 8. **Qxg6 +**, but after 8. . . .**Kd8** equilibrium swings toward Black. A correspondence game continuing from this position went: 9. **exf5 Qe4 +** 10. **Kd1 Bxf5** 11. **Qg5 + Be7** 12. **d3 Bg4 +**, and White resigned. He drops his Queen after 13. **f3 Bxf3 +** 14. **gxf3 Qxf3 +** and 15. . . .**Bxg5**.

Interpretation: On move 6 White should have retreated his e5-Knight to safety on f3. Black gets back his pawn, 6. . . .Qxe4 +, but the game equalizes after 7. Qe2 Nf6 8. Nc3 Qxe2 + 9. Nxe2 Bd6. Instead, White got carried away with attack and the possibility of checking at h5. Pointless checks should always be avoided. In some cases, a check could force your opponent to improve his position or help him exploit an unaddressed problem you created on the previous move. For example, if instead of dealing with an enemy threat you give a threat of your own, and if your opponent can answer your threat with a new threat, suddenly you must solve two problems instead of one. And you may not be able to cope with both threats on your next play. So don't give perfunctory checks. "Be not careless in deeds . . . nor rambling in thought"—Marcus Aurelius.

177

PIN

Ruy Lopez

1. e4	e5
2. Nf3	Nc6
3. Bb5	Nd4
4. Nxd4	exd4
5. d3	c6
6. Bc4	Nf6
7. 0-0	d5
8. exd5	Nxd5
9. Re1 +	Be6
10. Qh5	Be7

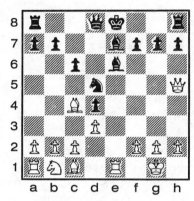

WHITE TO MOVE

Scenario: Black's last move prepared castling and broke the pin on the e6-Bishop by the e1-Rook to Black's King. But there was another pin also in full operation: by White's Queen along the h5-e8 diagonal. White capitalizes with 11. **Rxe6!.** Black probably should try 11. . . . g6, when 12. Rxe7 + Qxe7   13. Qd1 still leaves White ahead, two minor pieces against a Rook. If Black sallies 11. . . . **Nf6** instead, to drive away White's Queen from the h5-e8 diagonal, then 12. **Rxf6!** gxf6 (to take with the Bishop permits White's Queen to mate at f7) 13. **Qxf7 + Kd7**   14. **Bf4,** threatens 15. **Be6** mate. Black goes down.

Interpretation: Black was doing reasonably well until he played 10. . . . Be7. He should have added support to his e6-Bishop instead. The development Qd8-d7 satisfied that requirement easily. Innocuous developing moves are no guarantee of achieving a satisfactory game. They may even lose quickly. "What we plan we build"—Phoebe Cary.

178

KING HUNT

Ruy Lopez

1. e4	e5
2. Nf3	Nc6
3. Bb5	Nge7
4. 0-0	f6
5. Nh4	a6
6. Bxc6	Nxc6
7. Qh5 +	g6

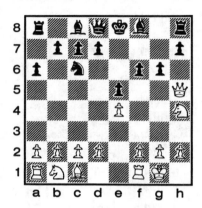

WHITE TO MOVE

Scenario: Black is dreadfully weakened on the e8-h5 diagonal from moving up his f-pawn. Despite blockage on the diagonal by the g6-pawn, White crashes through with 8. **Nxg6**, when White's Knight is immune to capture because Black's h-pawn is pinned to the h8-Rook by White's Queen. Black unpins with 8. . . . **Rg8**, and White gives a discovered check by 9. **Ne5 +**. Mate follows after 9. . . . **Ke7** 10. **Qf7 + Kd6** 11. **Nc4 + Kc5** 12. **Qd5 + Kb4** 13. **c3 + Ka4** 14. **b3** mate.

Interpretation: Game after game, variation after variation, the defensive pawn move f7-f6 bombs out. It deprives the King-Knight of its best square, f6; it weakens two diagonals by removing their pawn cover, a2-g8 and h5-e8; it's passive. Once Black does it, however, he should proceed super carefully. Instead of capturing on move 6 with his e7-Knight, he should retake with his b- or d-pawn. If then called upon to block a Queen-check at h5 with his g-pawn, his e7-Knight would lend a hand upholding g6. Black's real failing here was that he had no coherent plan. His moves were not woven together but rather stitched willy-nilly. That helps to guarantee a lost game. "These unhappy times call for the building of plans"—Franklin Delano Roosevelt.

179

MATING ATTACK

Ruy Lopez

1. e4	e5
2. Nf3	Nc6
3. Bb5	Nge7
4. c3	d6
5. d4	Bd7
6. 0-0	Ng6
7. Ng5	h6
8. Nxf7!	Kxf7
9. Bc4 +	Ke7
10. Qh5	Qe8

WHITE TO MOVE

Scenario: Given one more move, Black will play his King to d8, and then ply it to safety on the Queenside. White has no time to bargain. After 11. **Qg5 +** (11. Bg5 + hxg5 12. Qxg5 is also mate) 11. . . . **hxg5** 12. **Bxg5** is definitely mate. Because the diagonals of White's two Bishops cross each other's paths, the tactic is called a "criss-cross mate."

Interpretation: The slow defense 3. . . . Nge7 is supposed to give Black a cramped but solid position. However, it, invites attack on f7, especially by giving White a free hand in the center. If Black had played 10. . . . Be8 instead of 10. . . . Qe8, he would still lose, this time after 11. Bg5 + hxg5 12. Qxg5 + Kd7 13. Qf5 + Ke7 14. Qe6 mate. The real error was 7. . . . h7-h6. This pierced Black's Kingside edifice. A better try was 7. . . . Be7 or 7. . . . Na5, both avoiding mate. In the opening, be chary about making pawn moves. Their effects can be permanent and devastating. "The moving finger writes; and, having writ, moves on"—Edward Fitzgerald, *Rubáiyát of Omar Khayyám.*

180

UNPIN

Ruy Lopez

1. e4   e5
2. Nf3   Nc6
3. Bb5   Nge7
4. Nc3   a6
5. Ba4   b5
6. Bb3   h6
7. d4   d6
8. a4   b4
9. Nd5   Bg4
10. dxe5   Nxe5?

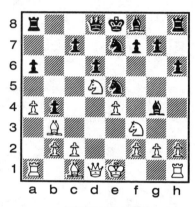

WHITE TO MOVE

Scenario: Black intends to intensify the pressure on the pinned f3-Knight. But the pin is only relative. White can move the Knight if he's willing to accept the consequences—and he is: 11. **Nxe5!**. If Black then takes White's exposed Queen, 11. . . . **Bxd1**, then 12. **Nf6+ gxf6** 13. **Bxf7** is mate.

Interpretation: Black's development of the c8-Bishop to g4, pinning White's f3-Knight, both increases the pressure against d4 and induces White to relieve the central tension with d4xe5. But such a situation—of a Queen-Bishop pinning the enemy King-Knight to the enemy Queen—compels the pinner to be alert to counteracting combinations. If Black had been on the ball, he would have captured on e5 with a pawn, not with his Queen-Knight. "A little pin bores through his castle wall, and farewell king!"—William Shakespeare, *Richard II*.

181

DEFLECTION

Ruy Lopez

1. e4   e5
2. Nf3   Nc6
3. Bb5   Nge7
4. d4   exd4
5. Nxd4   Nxd4
6. Qxd4   c6
7. Bc4   d5
8. Bb3   dxe4??

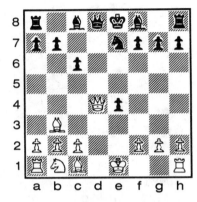

WHITE TO MOVE

Scenario: Black's blundered. His last move loaded too many tasks on his King, forcing it to guard the f7-pawn and the Queen at d8. White deflects Black's King off the e8 square, leaving the Black Queen undefended. After 9. **Bxf7+ Kxf7** 10. **Qxd8**, White has a Queen for a Bishop, and a win.

Interpretation: Once Black exchanged off his center-pawn on move 4, he was ill positioned to strike back quickly in the center, as he attempted with 6. . . . c6 and 7. . . . d5, for White was better developed. A slower approach was in order, such as 6. . . . Nc6, getting out a piece. Of course, Black's eight move is an outright blunder. He should have brought his light-square Bishop to e6, though after 9. Nc3, mobilizing his forces is still a problem. Don't make elaborate preparations in the opening. Your pieces are there to work. Get to them in a no-nonsense fashion.

182

PIN

Ruy Lopez

1. e4   e5
2. Nf3   Nc6
3. Bb5   a6
4. Ba4   Bb4
5. 0-0   Nge7
6. d4   exd4
7. Nxd4   d5
8. exd5   Qxd5

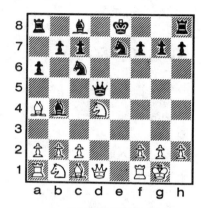

WHITE TO MOVE

Scenario: Black seems on the right track. He's ahead in development and attempting control of the center. The problem is that his King is stuck in the middle, menaced by White's a4-Bishop. White capitalizes with 9. **Nxc6**. Though Black has three lip-service protectors for c6, they cannot recapture. Taking on c6 with the Black Queen loses Her Mightiness directly to the a4-Bishop. Capturing with the e7-Knight abandons the Queen to White's Queen. And taking with the b7-pawn loses to a trade of Queens on d5 and a follow-up capture—with check—on c6, forking Black's King, d5-Knight, and a8-Rook. Even if Black trades Queens, 9. . . . **Qxd1**, there is the in-between check, 10. **Nxb4+**, which after 10. . . . **Bd7** 11. **Rxd1 Bxa4**, places White a piece ahead.

Interpretation: The characteristic Lopez move, 3. Bb5, sets up a potential pin on Black's c6-Knight, which happens once Black advances his d-pawn. Black must dissolve this hampering pin if he is to complete his development and salvage to a middlegame. In order to play d7-d5 successfully, Black should precede the central thrust with one on the flank, b7-b5, a pawn block on the pinning a4-Bishop once and for all.

183

MATING ATTACK

Ruy Lopez

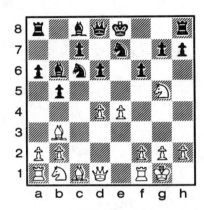

WHITE TO MOVE

1. e4	e5
2. Nf3	Nc6
3. Bb5	a6
4. Ba4	b5
5. Bb3	Bc5
6. 0-0	Nge7
7. c3	d6
8. d4	exd4
9. cxd4	Bb6
10. Ng5	f6

Scenario: White can win two ways. He can enter f7 with his Knight (11.Nf7) forking Black's Queen and Rook. Or he can interpose 11. **Qh5+**, answering 11 . . . **g6** by entering f7 with his Bishop, 12. **Bf7+**. Now 12 . . . Kf8 allows 13. Qh6 mate, so Black should continue 12 . . . **Kd7** when 13. Qh3+ f5 14. **Ne6** catches Black's Queen. third row rather than to the second.

Interpretation: The development of Black's dark-square Bishop to c5—natural in some other openings—wallows in danger in the Ruy Lopez. It encourages White to central expansion with c2-c3 and d2-d4, the latter gaining time because it also attacks the susceptible c5-Bishop. The problem is heightened when Black later places his g8-Knight on e7. It grants White carte blanche on the Kingside, for White's Queen may soon enter the fray safely at h5. This would be undesirable if Black's g8-Knight were instead positioned on f6, also guarding the square h5 and deterring the entrance of White's Queen. Knights are generally more assertive when developed to the third row rather than to the second. Gilbert Keith Chesterston's "lean and foolish Knight forever rides in vain."

184

DOUBLE ATTACK

Ruy Lopez

1. e4	e5
2. Nf3	Nc6
3. Bb5	a6
4. Ba4	b5
5. Bb3	Bc5
6. 0-0	Nf6
7. Nxe5	Nxe5
8. d4	Bb6?

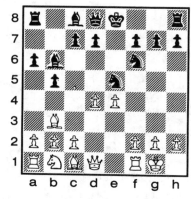

WHITE TO MOVE

Scenario: White is positioned to get back his sacrificed Knight with interest. After 9. **dxe5**, he has regained a Knight and is attacking Black's remaining one. If Black retreats his Knight to g8, control of d5 falls to White's Queen, which unleashes a winning double-attack: threatening the a8-Rook and mate at f7. Black "can't dance at two weddings at the same time."

Interpretation: White's little combination at move 7 (7. Nxe5 Nxe5 8. d4) is a sham sacrifice called the "fork trick." White's advance d2-d4 recoups his earlier loss. White makes this trade-off to get rid of Black's e-pawn, and thereafter has a freer hand in the center. Thus Black enables White to advance his e-pawn, drive away Black's f6-Knight, and score with the d5 double-attack. To avoid this, Black should have played 8. . . . Bxd4 instead of 8. . . . Bb6. After 9. Qxd4 d6, Black would then be able to deter White from advancing his e-pawn because Black now guards that square with the d6-pawn.

185

FORK

Ruy Lopez

1. e4   e5
2. Nf3   Nc6
3. Bb5   a6
4. Ba4   b5
5. Bb3   Bc5
6. 0-0   Nf6
7. Nxe5   Nxe5
8. d4   Bd6
9. dxe5   Bxe5

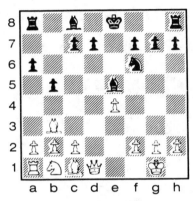

WHITE TO MOVE

Scenario: White's pseudo sacrifice, 7. Nxe5, set up the "fork trick," 8. d2-d4, whereby White's d-pawn fork regains the sacrificed piece after Black's center has been blooeyed. Without his e-pawn, Black loses his center foothold. The counter 10. **f4** exposes Black's central insecurity. His pieces go helter-skelter after 10. . . .**Bd6** 11. **e5 Bc5 +** 12. **Kh1 Ng8** 13. **Qd5**, forking Black's a8-Rook and c5-Bishop, while threatening mate at f7.

Interpretation: Timing in the opening is critical. Black's c5-Bishop placement is fine, but not on move 6. And if White didn't have a fork trick setup on move 7, he could still look to fruitful centerland prospects with c2-c3. In the variation Black chooses, where he advances his b-pawn, Bf8-c5 ought to be preceded by Bc8-b7, securing the a8-e4 diagonal first. Even after allowing the fork trick, Black could have cut losses by a Bishop capture on d4 instead of withdrawing it to d6, which turned out to be a blunder. In the Ruy Lopez, if you advance b7-b5, make sure you can deal with tactics along the a8-e4 diagonal.

186

REMOVING THE GUARD

Ruy Lopez

1. e4   e5
2. Nf3   Nc6
3. Bb5   a6
4. Ba4   b5
5. Bb3   Bb7
6. d4   Nxd4?

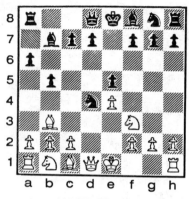

WHITE TO MOVE

Scenario: Black hopes to win a pawn after 7. Nxd4 exd4   8. Qxd4 c5 9. Qe5+ Qe7 10. Qxe7+ Nxe7, when the threat to trap White's b3-Bishop by 11. . . . . c4 forces White to save his Bishop and abandon the e-pawn to menace. White has a triumphant combination, however. After **7. Bxf7+! Kxf7** (ruinous would be 7. . . . Ke7 8. Bxg8 threatening 9. Bg5+, winning Black's Queen). **8. Nxe5+ Ke8   9. Qxd4,** Black's pocket has been picked of a pawn.

Interpretation: Black has better than 6. . . . Nxd4. Either 6. . . . d6 or 6. . . . exd4 avoid material loss. The real problem was Black's fourth move, b7-b5, a premature pawn advance that gave White a birthday cake of many options. The weakness along the a8-d5 diagonal, and also White's ability to attack b5 with his a4-pawn, piles more worry on Black than before he advanced the b-pawn. The thrust b7-b5 could be useful, especially when Black must save his c6-Knight from White's light-square Bishop. But that move should be kept in reserve until actually needed.

187

TRAPPED PIECE

Ruy Lopez

1. e4	e5
2. Nf3	Nc6
3. Bb5	a6
4. Ba4	d6
5. d4	b5
6. Bb3	Nxd4
7. Nxd4	exd4
8. Qxd4?	

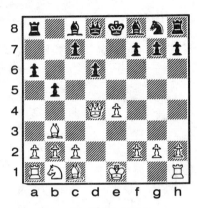

BLACK TO MOVE

Scenario: Black snares a Bishop with 8. . . . c5 9. Qd5 Be6 10. Qc6+ Bd7 11. Qd5 c4. This is the Noah's Ark Trap. Anyone can fall for this, even a master, such as the Hungarian master Endre Steiner, who succumbed to it against Jose Capablanca at the 1929 Budapest tournament.

Interpretation: White's fifth move is sometimes criticized in that it allows Black to spring the Noah's Ark Trap. This is unfair. White's only real mistake is recapturing the eighth move with his Queen. White should instead play an in-between move—a *zwischenzug*—and then follow with a capture on d4. Thus, after 8. Bd5 Rb8 9. Qxd4, White's light-square Bishop does not get trapped. Still another approach is the gambit offer for development and activity: 8. c3 dxc3 9. Qd5 Be6 10. Qc6+ Bd7 11. Qd5. This gives White at least a draw. If a certain capture is baited, find a *zwischenzug*. It might save the day.

188

DEFLECTION

Ruy Lopez

1. e4 e5
2. Nf3 Nc6
3. Bb5 a6
4. Ba4 d6
5. c3 f5
6. d4 fxe4
7. Ng5 b5
8. Bb3 d5
9. dxe5 Nce7

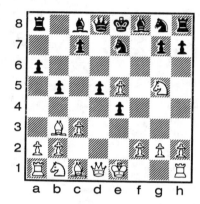

WHITE TO MOVE

Scenario: Black's last move, Nc6-e7, was meant to keep his pawn chain, e4 and d5, intact. It actually precipitates the loss of the e4-pawn. With 10. Nxe4, White garners a valuable pawn. If Black replies 10. . . .dxe4, his Queen goes down by 11. **Bxf7+ Kxf7** 12. **Qxd8.**

Interpretation: The Siesta Variation of the Ruy Lopez, 1. e4 e5 2. Nf3 Nc6 3. Bb5 a6 4. Ba4 d6 5. c3 f5, is much better than this trap indicates. instead of 7. . . .b5, Black should try 7. . . .dxe4. The onus is then on White to rebalance the position. The thrust b7-b5 actually drives White's light-square Bishop to a commanding position at b3. From there, in conjunction with the g5-Knight, the Bishop threatens to invade, or support invasion of f7. Thus Black closes the a2-g8 diagonal by d6-d5, but after 9. d4xe5, White's Queen and b3-Bishop team up on d5. Black might have tried 9. . . .Nge7 instead of Nce7, but White is still top dog after 10. e6, when the incursion Ng5-f7 is menaced. If you're going to play sharp variations, you'll win some exciting games, but you'll take some lumps, too. "A man gazing on the stars is proverbially at the mercy of the puddles on the road"—Alexander Smith.

189

DISCOVERY

Ruy Lopez

1. e4	e5
2. Nf3	Nc6
3. Bb5	a6
4. Ba4	f5
5. Bxc6	dxc6
6. Nxe5	Qd4
7. Qh5 +	g6
8. Nxg6	Nf6
9. Qh4	Ng4
10. Nxh8	

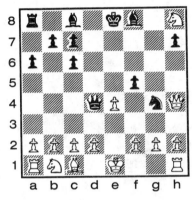

BLACK TO MOVE

Scenario: White has just picked off Black's h8-Rook, but Black gets counter-action with 10. . . .Qxe4 +, forcing White's King to budge. Whether the King flees to d1 or f1, his Queen is lost to 11. . . .Ne3 +, uncovering a discovery to her ladyship at h4. However White answers, Black's Queen takes over White's.

Interpretation: The delayed Schliemann Defense (3. . . .a6 and 4. . . .f5) is a risky way to steal the initiative. But White, with his Queen-check at h5, tried violently to refute Black's hair-raising play. Black could have defended himself by answering 8. Nxg6 and hxg6, since his h8-Rook is guarded by his Queen from d4. After Black opted to attack White's Queen by Ng8-f6, White's Queen should have retreated to h3, not h4. At least that avoids the discovery demolishing along the 4th rank. An excellent way to lose is to put your head on the chopping block.

190

FORK

Ruy Lopez

1. e4   e5
2. Nf3   Nc6
3. Bb5   a6
4. Ba4   Nf6
5. Qe2   Bc5
6. c3   b5
7. Bc2   d5?

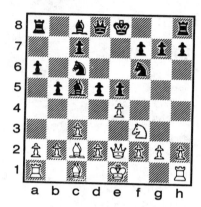

WHITE TO MOVE

Scenario: Black's last move is sharp but leads to exposure of the e-pawn to White's Queen and f3-Knight. White's 8. **exd5** compels 8. . . .**Qxd5** so that Black's Queen adds protection to his King-pawn. White applies more pressure with 9. **d4!**, and if Black answers 9. . . .**Bd6**, also to guard e5, White conquers by 10. **Bb3 Qe4** 11. **Qxe4 Nxe4** 12. **Bd5**, forking both Black Knights.

Interpretation: Since Black starts the game a move behind White, if he plays as aggressively as White, he incurs risk. Black's moves have to conform to the shots that White, the first mover, calls on the position. Here Black gambled with 5. . . .Bc5, figuring that if White tried to knock off a pawn by 6. Bxc6 bxc6 7. Nxe5, he would provoke counterplay after 7. . . .0-0   8. 0-0 Re8   9. Nxf7 Qe7 (not 9. . . .Kxf7 because of 10. Qc4+)   10. Ng5 d5. Black indeed gets more action after sacrificing a pawn. But since his 7. . . .d5 opened the game too soon, he gave White the chance to attack Black's uncastled King. "There's a time for all things," says the Bible. Don't open the center till you've castled your King.

191

TRAPPED PIECE

Ruy Lopez

1. e4	e5
2. Nf3	Nc6
3. Bb5	a6
4. Ba4	Nf6
5. Nc3	d6
6. d4	b5
7. Bb3	exd4
8. Nxd4	

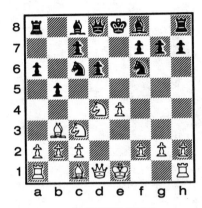

BLACK TO MOVE

Scenario: Black's Knight is attacked at c6, and the simplest solution is 8. . . . Nxd4. This exchange has two side benefits: (A) it draws White's Queen to d4, open to attack; and (B) it clears the road for the c-pawn to advance. After 9. Qxd4 c5, White saves his exposed Queen and Black advances c5-c4, trapping White's light-square Bishop.

Interpretation: This is another example of the Noah's Ark Trap, where White's light-square Bishop is corralled by pawns. White had chances to save his Bishop from move 6 through move 8 and didn't: (A) on move 6 he could have traded his light-square Bishop for the c6-Knight, then advanced his d-pawn two squares; (B) on move 7 he could have exchanged the d-pawn for the e-pawn; and (C) on move 8 he could have inserted Bb3-d5 before recouping his pawn shortly after. As in baseball, three strikes and you're out.

192

PIN

Ruy Lopez

1. e4	e5
2. Nf3	Nc6
3. Bb5	a6
4. Ba4	Nf6
5. 0-0	Bc5
6. Nxe5	Nxe4
7. Qe2	Nxe5
8. Qxe4	Qf6

WHITE TO MOVE

Scenario: Black's e5-Knight is pinned by White's Queen. Pinned pieces should be attacked without compunction until defense breaks down. White can't attack Black's Knight by moving the f-pawn, which is pinned by the c5-Bishop to White's King. Nor does moving the f1-Rook to e1 work, for Black's c5-Bishop takes on f2 and then e1. The advance d2-d4 looks promising, but Black answers Bc5xd4; and if White's Queen captures it, Black takes the Queen with a discovery, Ne5-f3 +. Still, the correct move is 9. **d4!**, but after 9. . . .**Bxd4**, White should continue 10. **c3**, driving the intruder back. After 10. . . .**Bc5** 11. **Bf4 Bd6** 12. **Re1**, Black's Knight finally falls.

Interpretation: After 6. Nxe5, Black should have played 6. . . .Nxe5. If White then continues 7. d4, Black answers 7. . . .Nxe4. But Black did otherwise and had to answer 6. . . .Nxe4 7. Qe2 Nxe5 8. Qxe4 with 8. . . .Qe7, at least breaking the pin on his Knight. However, Black would not be totally out of the woods, for 9. d4 Ng6 10. Re1! Bxd4 11. Bd2! keeps him on the lookout for a clearing.

193

PIN

Ruy Lopez

1. e4   e5
2. Nf3   Nc6
3. Bb5   a6
4. Ba4   Nf6
5. 0-0   Nxe4
6. d4   b5
7. Bb3   d5
8. a4   b4
9. a5   Be7

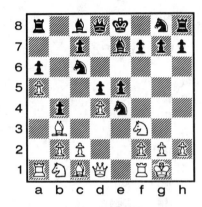

WHITE TO MOVE

Scenario: Black's light-square weaknesses are exposed by 10. **dxe5**, threatening 11. Bxd5, forking the Knights at e4 and c6. If Black tries to defend himself by 10. . . . **Be6**, White sets up a winning pin with 11. **Ba4**. Regardless of Black's defense, he then loses a piece: (A) 11. . . . Qd7 fails to 12. Nd4, increasing c6-pressure unanswerably; (B) 11. . . . Bd7 crumbles before 12. Qxd5, and Black's Knights are, as Nietzsche put it, on "a rope over an abyss."

Interpretation: The first five moves of this example, closing with Black's 5. . . . Nxe4, signal the Open or Tarrasch Defense to the Ruy Lopez. It obtains counterplay for Black, but he must keep a careful watch over the square d5. If that strong point falls, his position dismantles. Black should answer White's eighth move, a2-a4, with 8. . . . Rb8 or 8. . . . Nxd4, but not by his actual choice, 8. . . . b4, which weakens the a4-e8 diagonal. The final *faux pas* was 9. . . . Be7, which ignores White's assault plans. On the ninth move, Black should instead play Nc6xd4, though his position still remains a little worse because of earlier sins. Once Black commits himself to opening the center by exchanging a couple of pawns, he must prepare himself for White's attack, for opening the game generally favors the better developed side. "Unto you is paradise opened"—Apochrypha.

194

UNPIN

Ruy Lopez

1. e4   e5
2. Nf3   Nc6
3. Bb5   a6
4. Ba4   Nf6
5. 0-0   d6
6. Qe2   b5
7. Bb3   Na5
8. d4   Bg4
9. dxe5   dxe5

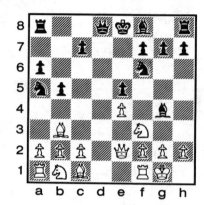

WHITE TO MOVE

Scenario: The e5-weakness hands White the mechanism to break the pin on his f3-Knight: 10. **Bxf7 +!** draws the Black's King to a vulnerable square, 10. . . . **Kxf7.** White then follows with 11. **Nxe5 +,** forking Black's King and g4-Bishop. Black's King moves to safety; White takes the Bishop, and discovers he is two plans ahead.

Interpretation: With 7. . . . Na5, Black shunts his Knight from the center just to eliminate White's light-square Bishop. White correctly answers the flank attack by a center thrust, d2-d4. Black should then exchange his Knight for the Bishop, following the plan he started and defending his e-pawn afterwards by Nf6-d7, upholding his center. With his eighth move, Bc8-g4, Black's logic goes caflooey, for he will probably have to exchange his light-square Bishop for Black's f3-Knight. Why work for two Bishops if you'll have to surrender them on the spot? In fact, Black's best is 9. . . . Bxf3, to keep material equality. If he had tried 9. . . . Nxb3, then 10. axb3 dxe5 11. Rxa6! Rxa6 12. Qxb5 + wins for White. Don't play without a plan. Stay with the one you've chosen unless you are forced to change or a better idea develops. "Chances change by course"— Robert Southwell.

195

REMOVING THE GUARD

Ruy Lopez

1. e4   e5
2. Nf3   Nc6
3. Bb5   a6
4. Ba4   Nf6
5. 0-0   Be7
6. Qe2   0-0

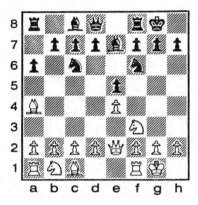

WHITE TO MOVE

Scenario: White gains the vital e-pawn by the simple expedient of removing its protector: 7. **Bxc6 dxc6**   8. **Nxe5.** If Black persists in trying to regain the pawn by 8. . . .**Qd4**, then 9. **Nf3 Qxe4**   10. **Qxe4 Nxe4**   11. **Re1 f5**   12. **d3** wins either Black's e4-Knight or his e7-Bishop. Note how White's Rook attacks both minor pieces along the same line, the e-file.

Interpretation: In the early stages of the Ruy Lopez, Black's e-pawn is indirectly defended, so he can afford to play 3. . . .a6, apparently ignoring White's pseudo threat to the c6-Knight, removing the guard for the e5-pawn. Thus 4. Bxc6 dxc6 (capturing away from the center for tactical purposes, in contradistinction to the axiom recommending capture toward the center)   5. Nxe5 is answered most effectively by 5. . . .Qd4, hitting White's e5-Knight and e4-pawn and subsequently winning back the pawn. (The counter 5. . . .Qg5 attacks the e5-Knight and g2-pawn, but overall is less good.) But White's sixth move, Qe2, protects the e-pawn and vitiates Black's counterattack, so that he must put off castling to instead guard his e-pawn, 6. . . .d6, or drive away White's a4-Bishop, 6. . . .b5. Either way, he avoids losing his e-pawn. "Use power with power, and slay me not by art"—William Shakespeare, "Sonnet 139."

196

FORK

Ruy Lopez

1. e4   e5
2. Nf3   Nc6
3. Bb5   a6
4. Bxc6   dxc6
5. 0-0   f6
6. d4   exd4
7. Nxd4   Bc5?

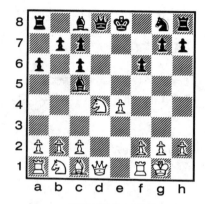

WHITE TO MOVE

Scenario: Black's last move tries to remedy his backward development, bringing out his dark-square Bishop and attacking White's d4-Knight. But Black succumbs to the cure, for White's Queen checks at h5, forking Black's King and c5-Bishop. Whatever way Black gets out of check, White captures his ill-placed Bishop on the next turn.

Interpretation: The f7-f6 defense of Black's e-pawn in double King-pawn openings has certain liabilities. Mainly it weakens two critical diagonals: a2-g8 and h5-e8. Nevertheless, it's all right for Black to essay f7-f6 as in this example, for White cannot exploit it. The a2-g8 diagonal is hard to capitalize on once White has exchanged his light-square Bishop. And potential dangers along the h5-e8 diagonal may be rebuked by forcing an exchange of the piece most suited to traveling it: White's Queen. This is done by attacking White's d4-Knight with Black's c-pawn rather than his dark-square Bishop. After 7. . . .c5   8. Nb3 Qxd1   9. Rxd1, Black's King is home free. As in Shakespeare's *Hamlet,* "That skull had a tongue in it and could sing once more."

197

MATING ATTACK

Ruy Lopez

1. e4   e5
2. Nf3   Nc6
3. Bb5   a6
4. Bxc6   dxc6
5. 0-0   Bg4
6. h3   h5
7. hxg4   hxg4
8. Ne1

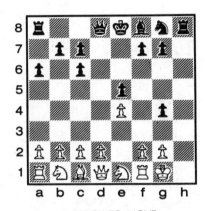

BLACK TO MOVE

Scenario: Black offered his g4-Bishop as bait and White unwisely took it. Using the h-file, Black now musters a blitz attack, first threatening mate at h2 or h1 with 8. . . .Qh4. White's best try is to create a loophole at f3 with 9. f3, but the retort 9. . . .g3 shuts the escape hatch for good. Mate cannot be stopped.

Interpretation: White erred in seizing the g4-Bishop. Instead, he should have continued building his game until he can capture on g4 with safety. Analysis suggests White will be ready for a g4-capture after 7. d3 Qf6   8. Nbd2 Ne7   9. Re1 Ng6   10. d4 Bd6. One line continues: 11. hxg4 hxg4   12. Nh2 exd4 (12. . . .Rxh2 favors White after 13. Qxg4)   13. e5! Nxe5   14. Ne4 Qh4   15. Nxd6+ cxd6   16. Bf4, and White is winning. Preparation is everything; don't engage the enemy without it.

198

PIN

Ruy Lopez

1. e4	e5
2. Nf3	Nc6
3. Bb5	a6
4. Bxc6	dxc6
5. 0-0	Bg4
6. h3	Bh5
7. g4	Bg6
8. Nxe5	Bxe4
9. Re1	Qd5

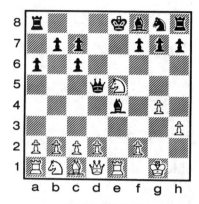

WHITE TO MOVE

Scenario: Black's position is critical because of the open e-file. Just look at the e1-Rook's threat to Black's King. Black's last move, Qd8-d5, endeavors to keep the file at least temporarily blocked until he can secure his King's position. But he never gets the chance. After **10. Nc3 Qxe5   11. Rxe4**, White's Rook pins and wins Black's Queen.

Interpretation: Black's early pin, 5. . . .Bg4, begins a chain reaction after 6. h3. Rather than retreat the Bishop to h5, Black should settle for exchanging Bishop for f3-Knight. A riskier try is 6. . . .h5!?, sacrificing a piece for attack. If White then plucks the Bishop, h3xg4, Black plucks back on g4, opening the h-file and regaining the f3-Knight. If White tries to move this harried piece to safety, Black's Queen thunders in on h4 with a threat of deadly invasion via the h-file. Once Black chooses to retreat his Bishop to h5 instead, he must follow White's 8. Nf3xe5, not by 8. . . .Bxe4, but by 8. . . .Qh4, trying to undermine White's weakened Kingside pawns. A risky line will breed a game of surprises, so be prepared for its contingencies and for its consequences.

199

UNPIN

Ruy Lopez

1. e4   e5
2. Nf3   Nc6
3. Bb5   a6
4. Bxc6   dxc6
5. 0-0   Bd6
6. d4   Bg4
7. dxe5   Bxe5

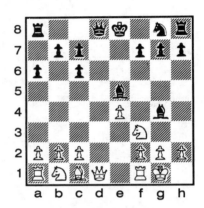

WHITE TO MOVE

Scenario: Black hopes that by pinning the f3-Knight with his g4-Bishop he will safeguard his e5-Bishop. But he's overlooked something elementary: 8. **Qxd8+ Rxd8** 9. **Nxe5**, winning the Bishop. Black failed to realize that once Queens are traded, his g4-Bishop no longer pins the f3-Knight to White's Queen because the Queen is gone.

Interpretation: When Black plays the c8-Bishop to g4, pinning the f3-Knight, he commits the Bishop to an exchange of minor pieces on f3. If he is not prepared for this, he shouldn't develop his c8-Bishop to g4. After White's d-pawn takes on e5, Black must interpolate Bg4xf3 before recapturing on e5. At least then he doesn't lose anything, though White still has better Kingside chances, since his four pawns there can do more than Black's three. Don't fall asleep at the wheel. Tactics may need revision from move to move if they are to continue to reap success. Keep your concentration up throughout a game and be alert to changing fortunes.

200

FORK

Ruy Lopez

1. e4	e5
2. Nf3	Nc6
3. Bb5	a6
4. Bxc6	dxc6
5. 0-0	Bd6
6. d4	f6?
7. dxe5	fxe5

Scenario: Black's e-pawn is attacked by White's Knight but defended by Black's Bishop. A standoff, right? Wrong! After 8. **Nxe5! Bxe5,** White regains his sacrificed piece with a forking Queen-check at h5. The smoke clears, and White has pilfered a valuable pawn.

Interpretation: A bad move can be a good move, at the right time. Instead of Bd6 on the fifth move, Black can safely deposit his pawn on f6, though it opens the h5-e8 diagonal. There is no way to exploit this weakness right away. If White advances his Queen-pawn two squares, Black exchanges pawns. Black can even play f7-f6 in the line chosen if he first trades pawns on move 6 and then pushes his f-pawn on move 7. But if he chooses f7-f6 on the sixth move, to uphold his e-pawn, he actually loses his goal of protection through a combination. In chess, so much is a matter of timing.

201

PIN

Ruy Lopez

1. e4   e5
2. Nf3   Nc6
3. Bb5   a6
4. Bxc6   dxc6
5. d4   Nf6?
6. Nxe5   Nxe4

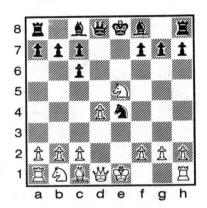

WHITE TO MOVE

Scenario: Black perhaps thought he was simply trading pawns but he floats into a sea of trouble after 7. **Qe2.** If he withdraws his Knight, 7. . . .Nf6, his Queen goes down in a discovered check, 8. Nxc6+. If Black defends the Knight with his Queen, 7. . . .**Qxd4,** then 8. **Nf3 Qd5** (or 8. . . .Qb4+   9. Nfd2)   9. **Ng5** followed by 10. f3 knocks off his Knight. Black will lose a piece.

Interpretation: Black's fifth move, Ng8-f6, is an error costing him his e-pawn. He compounds the mistake by capturing White's e-pawn, losing the ill-placed Knight. After White played 5. d4, Black should have exchanged pawns, leading to a Queenless middlegame (5. . . .exd4   6. Qxd4 Qxd4   7. Nxd4), which offers chances for both sides. White has a mobile four-to-three pawn majority on the Kingside, but Black's game is more dynamic because he has two Bishops, usually a greater attacking force than a combination of Bishop and Knight.

202

DISCOVERY

Ruy Lopez

1. e4   e5
2. Nf3   Nc6
3. Bb5   a6
4. Bxc6   bxc6
5. d4   exd4
6. Qxd4   Qf6
7. e5   Qg6
8. 0-0   Bb7
9. e6

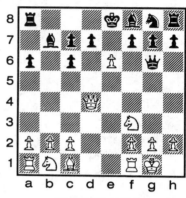

BLACK TO MOVE

Scenario: White's last move is a sacrifice bringing danger to both sides. The immediate threat is mate at d7. If Black's Queen defends by taking the e-pawn, it gets pinned to her King by White's Rook. And if Black captures on e6 with a pawn, White's Knight invades at e5, menacing Black's Queen and mate at d7 simultaneously. Black could castle, 9. . . . 0-0-0, but that loses to 10. exd7+ Rxd7 11. Qxd7+! Kxd7 12. Ne5+, resulting in the gain of the exchange. Black can cut through "the forest of the Knight" with 9. . . . fxe6 10. **Ne5 Qxg2+!** 11. **Kxg2 c5+**, discovering an attack to White's King and directly stabbing his Queen. Black ends up two pawns ahead.

Interpretation: White's ninth move is a stumblebum. A better plan is 9. Qc3, to be followed by 10. Nbd2 and 11. Nb3. Perhaps White could even play 9. Nbd2, sacrificing his c-pawn, 9. . . . Qxc2, for this seizure costs Black valuable development time. White may have been misled by Black's fourth move, bxc6, capturing so that his pawn takes toward the center. In the Ruy Lopez, to facilitate developing, Black usually captures away from the center, dxc6. White realized this was an inaccurate capture, but he overreacted by sacrificing his e-pawn. He should have played it steadily and positionally, not riskily. "Keep cool," Emerson advised, "it will be all one hundred years hence."

Glossary

ACTIVATE—To develop, improve the position of, mobilize, or make more aggressive.

ACTIVE—Aggressive, with regard to a move, variation, or placement.

ADVANCE—To move a pawn. A pawn move.

ADVANCED PAWN—One that has reached its 5th rank or farther.

ADVANTAGE—Superiority in development, space, material, pawn structure, or King safety; or in any combination thereof.

ATTACK—A move or series of moves to mate, gain material, or obtain advantage. To make such moves. To threaten.

ATTACK AT THE BASE OF THE PAWN CHAIN—A strategy first articulated by Aron Nimzovich (1886–1935). When two sets of connected, fixed pawns for each side confront each other, blocked and interlocked, generally the most effective attack should be directed at the base of the pawn chain (the enemy pawn closest to the enemy's back rank). If the base falls, the head pawn becomes weaker. For example, in the pawn chain where White has pawns on d5 and e4 blocked by Black pawns at e5 and d6, White will try to attack the enemy base at d6 by advancing his c-pawn to c5. Black in turn will aim to attack White's base at e4 by advancing his f-pawn to f5.

BACK RANK—The rank occupied by all eight enemy pieces in the original position.

BACKWARD DEVELOPMENT—Having several unmoved pieces that should have been already developed.

BACKWARD PAWN—A pawn whose neighboring pawns are too far advanced to protect it. Usually a weakness, generally restrained by enemy pieces and pawns, often subject to frontal attack along the file it occupies.

BAD BISHOP—A Bishop blocked by its own pawns, whose mobility is therefore obstructed.

BASE OF PAWN CHAIN—The pawn closest to its own back rank, when two or more pawns for each side block and immobilize their enemy counterparts, for either side.

BATTERY—Two or more pieces of like power attacking together along the same line of squares in any direction. Two Rooks or a Rook and Queen can form a battery along a rank or file, and a Bishop and Queen can establish one along a diagonal.

BIND—A grip, usually held by pawns, from which the opponent cannot easily free himself.

BISHOP PAIR—The advantage of having two Bishops against a Bishop and Knight or against two Knights. This superiority is pronounced in open, unblocked positions.

BISHOPS OF OPPOSITE COLORS—A situation in which each player has only one Bishop—one traveling on light squares, the other on dark. They can never attack each other or guard the same squares. Also called OPPOSITE-COLOR BISHOPS.

BLOCKADE—A term made popular by Aaron Nimzovich (1886–1935). A defensive strategy aimed at preventing the advance of an enemy pawn, especially a passed pawn, by stationing a piece directly in front of it and guarding that square with other pieces and pawns.

BLUNDER—A bad mistake resulting from oversight, miscalculation, or violation of principle.

BOOK—The overall body of published theory. A book player is one who relies on published analysis rather than on his own ideas.

BOOK MOVE—A move recommended by current books and theoretical articles on the openings as best, or playable, in a given position.

BREAK—A freeing move or maneuver, usually involving the advance of a pawn.

BREAKTHROUGH—Usually a pawn move (or moves) to clear lines and penetrate enemy terrain, often by means of a sacrifice.

BREVITY—A short game, usually about ten moves, containing interesting or brilliant tactics based on exploiting violations of principles or mechanical play.

CASTLING—Moving the King and one of its Rooks on the same turn. Shifting the King out of the center, along the back rank, to the g-file or the c-file, and then moving the Rook from the same side to the f-file or the d-file, respectively. Neither King nor castling Rook may have moved earlier, nothing must occupy the squares between King and Rook before castling, and no enemy man may guard squares passed over or landed on by the King. In games where central pawns are likely to be exchanged, one should develop the minor pieces between the King and Rook right away, especially those on the Kingside, to be able to castle in the first five or six moves.

CENTER—The four squares known as e4, e5, d4, and d5, taken as a block. Loosely defined, the sixteen squares in the middle of the board, or any of them in particular: c3, c4, c5, c6, d3, d4, d5, d6, e3, e4, e5, e6, f3, f4, f5, and f6.

CENTRALIZE—To place the pieces and pawns so that they exert maximum effect on or at the center, by guarding, occupying, or influencing the center squares or enemy men that could utilize the center.

CLASSICAL—A school or style of play that favors direct occupation of the center and a systematic, often dogmatic approach to strategy.

CLASSICAL PAWN CENTER—Two friendly pawns aligned on the 4th rank: for White, pawns on d4 and e4; for Black, pawns on d5 and e5. A typical goal for those playing in classical style.

CLEARANCE—Evacuating a square or line so that another piece can use it. The clearance piece is often sacrificed to gain time.

CLOSED CENTER—A center blocked by pawns for both sides, so that movement through the center is impossible. In double King-pawn openings, the two most typical closed centers are White pawns on e5 and d4 versus Black pawns on e6 and d5, arising, for example, from the French Defense; and White pawns on d5 and e4 versus Black pawns on d6 and e5, from, for example, the Ruy Lopez.

CLOSED FILE—A file containing pawns for both players, so that neither side's heavy pieces may freely develop along it.

CLOSED GAME—A type of position characterized by few exchanges and a dense or interlocked pawn structure. Closed openings are those generally reached after any other first move than 1. e2–e4.

COLOR WEAKNESS—Inability to successfully guard, occupy, or influence squares of a particular color, generally because one's pawns are fixed on squares of opposite color and one's minor pieces are unable to compensate the weak-color squares, especially because the Bishop guarding those squares has been exchanged or is out of play. A pronounced case is the condition of having Bishops of opposite colors, so that each side is weak on the squares guarded by the other side's Bishop.

COMPENSATION—A counterbalancing advantage. An advantage in one element (such as material) approximately equivalent to the opponent's advantage in another element (such as time or pawn structure). Also, equivalence within the same element. For example, three pawns compensate for a Bishop.

CONNECTED—Pertaining to two pieces of the same color that can move along the same rank, file, or diagonal and therefore protect each other, as in "connected Rooks." For pawns, it means occupying adjacent files so that as the pawns advance, they can protect each other, as in "connected passed pawns."

CONSOLIDATE—To stabilize a loose or uncoordinated position. For example, in winning material, one may expend several tempi and remove pieces from the main playing area. One consolidates by bringing pieces back into the game so that they are working together, guarding and attacking harmoniously, cooperating, safeguarding the King, and thereby are ready to exploit the material advantage.

CONTROL—Domination by one player of an important square or group of squares (such as the center), or a file.

COORDINATION—A state of having one's pieces positioned so that they enhance each other's capabilities, where each one performs duties suitable to itself without interfering with the actions of others.

COUNTERATTACK—An attack mounted by the defender or a player who is apparently defending. Also a description of an opening variation begun by Black.

COUNTER-GAMBIT—Generally, an opening gambit offered by Black in response to White's offer of a gambit; thus, an attempt to seize the initiative and blunt White's attack.

COUNTERPLAY—The possibility of the defending side's undertaking aggressive action on his own, usually by opening another front. When a player is said to have counterplay, the usual implication is that his overall chances are roughly equal to his opponent's.

CRAMP—A disadvantage in space from a lack of mobility. A position in which pieces get in each other's way.

CRITICAL POSITION—That point in a theoretically important line, usually in the opening and more or less forced from the preceding moves, the evaluation of which determines whether that previous sequence favors White or Black. Also, any decisive turning point in a game.

DEFENSE—A move or series of moves designed to meet enemy threats or attacks, whether immediate or long range. Also used in names of openings, when the characteristic positions are determined largely by Black.

DEFLECTION—Luring a defending piece away from its post.

DEVELOPMENT—The process of increasing the mobility of pieces by moving them from their original squares.

DISCOVERED ATTACK—An attack given by one piece when another friendly piece moves out of its way. Also called DISCOVERY.

DOUBLE-ATTACK—A simultaneous attack directed against two separate targets, which may be enemy men or squares. The most common type is a FORK, whereby one man attacks two or more enemy men on the same turn.

DOUBLED PAWNS—Two pawns of the same color lined up on the same file as a result of a capture.

DOUBLED ROOKS—Two Rooks of the same color lined up on the same rank or file, each protecting the other and capable of attacking or defending with the other's support.

DOUBLING—The act of placing two heavy pieces (usually Rooks, though sometimes a Rook and Queen) on the same rank or file. A rarer use of the term describes placement of a Queen and a Bishop along the same diagonal.

EN PRISE—"In take"; a French term designating a piece or pawn that is unprotected and subject to capture.

EQUALITY—A situation in which neither side has any overall advantage.

EQUALIZE—To reach a position of dynamic equilibrium or material equality.

ERROR—Any mistake, regardless of degree—a blunder, oversight, miscalculation.

EXCHANGE—A trade or swap of no material profit to either side.

EXCHANGE, THE—A term expressing the difference in value between a Rook and an enemy Bishop or Knight. You win the exchange if you gain a Rook for a Knight or Bishop, and you lose the exchange if you give up a Rook for a Bishop or Knight.

EXCHANGE SACRIFICE—To sacrifice a Rook for a Knight or Bishop.

FAMILY FORK—A Knight fork to the opponent's King, Queen, and Rook. Also called a ROYAL FORK.

FIANCHETTO—An Italian word meaning "on the flank"; in chess, it is the development of a White Bishop to b2, a3, g2, or h3, or a Black Bishop to g7, h6, b7, or a6.

FIXED—Blocked, or held in place. Usually referring to pawn formations. A "fixed pawn center" is one that contains two pawns, one White and one Black, which occupy the same file and block the other's advance.

FIXED CENTER—A center consisting of two pawns, one White and one Black, where neither pawn can move, fixed in place by the other. For example, a White d4-pawn versus a Black d5-pawn, with no other pawns on the central files. The general plan therefore is to successfully occupy one's strong points, the squares guarded by one's center-pawn. Thus White would like to occupy c5 and e5, while Black utilizes c4 and e4.

FLANK—The three outer rows on either side of the board. On the Queenside, the c-, b-, and a-files; and on the Kingside, the f-, g-, and h-files. Also called the WING. Also, to *fianchetto* a Bishop.

FLANK OPENINGS—Openings where White defers moving his center-pawns, preferring instead to develop on the wings by *fianchetto* of a Bishop or both Bishops. Popular flank openings include the English Opening (1. c4) and Reti's Opening (1. Nf3).

FLIGHT SQUARE—Any square to which the King can flee in order to escape check.

FORCE—A general term for all the pieces and pawns, otherwise known as material. A major element in chess, along with space, time, pawn structure, and King safety.

FORCED—Referring to a move or series of moves necessary to avoid losing or incurring disadvantage.

FORCING MOVE—A move that compels the opponent to respond with a move or moves for which there are no satisfactory alternatives. A forcing move leaves the opponent no practical choice.

FORK—A double-attack by one man in two directions. One subcase is a pawn fork, whereby a pawn advances or captures to attack two enemy men (usually pieces) simultaneously. Another is a Knight fork, whereby a Knight attacks two or more enemy men on the same turn. Generally, the most effective Knight forks are also checks. A Knight fork to the enemy King, Queen, and Rook is also called a FAMILY FORK or a ROYAL FORK.

FORK TRICK—A combination that either wins a pawn or trades center-pawns favorably. A minor piece, usually a Knight, captures an apparently protected center-pawn. If the opponent recaptures the minor piece with his own minor piece, a pawn advance then forks two enemy minor pieces simultaneously. When this tactic doesn't gain a pawn, it is played to break the enemy pawn center.

FREEING ADVANCE—A pawn move that unblocks a cramped position and activates one's pieces. Often an equalizing move or the start of meaningful counterplay.

FRONTIER LINE—An imaginary division across the middle of the board, between the 4th and 5th ranks, that separates the two armies.

GAMBIT—A voluntary opening sacrifice, usually of a pawn, which is offered in order to gain an attack, increase the initiative, or further development.

GOOD BISHOP—A Bishop not impeded by its own pawns, with excellent mobility on either side of the board. As a general rule, pawns should be placed on squares different in color from one's Bishop, so that neither pawns nor Bishop interfere with each other and squares of both colors are guarded.

GRANDMASTER DRAW—A quick draw out of the opening, agreed to by both players, without a fight. Usually used derogatorily.

HALF-OPEN FILE—A file occupied only by pawns of one color, so that the opponent is able to use it as a conduit for heavy pieces.

HANGING—Referring to an unprotected piece or pawn exposed to capture. A related term is EN PRISE.

HANGING PAWNS—Two adjacent same-player pawns on their 4th rank, separated from other same-player pawns and subject to frontal attack from heavy pieces along one or two half-open files. They are weak or strong depending on their dynamic capabilities.

HEAD PAWN—A term of Hans Kmoch's. The most advanced pawn in any formation.

HEAVY PIECE—A Queen or Rook. Also called MAJOR PIECE.

HOLD—To survive an attack, to defend successfully.

HOLE—A key square, on the 3rd rank or beyond, indefensible by pawns, which the enemy may be able to occupy advantageously.

HYPERMODERN—A school or style that advocates several ideas opposed to classical principles, such as controlling the center from the flank rather than directly occupying it. The term was first used by Savielly Tartakover in the 1920s.

IN-BETWEEN MOVE—One move that interrupts an apparently forced sequence. Often a finesse played with a gain of time. Also called ZWISCHENZUG.

INDIRECT DEFENSE—Defense of a piece, pawn, square, or position that doesn't involve the actual protection of what is being threatened. It may be a counterthreat, the removal or dislodging of the enemy strike force, or the exploitation of a sudden vulnerability in the opponent if he follows through with his original threat.

INITIATIVE—An advantage in time, usually a developmental lead, that enables a player to control somewhat the flow of action. White starts the game with a natural initiative because he has the first move. Thus generally White attacks and Black defends.

INNOVATION—A new move in an established opening, defense, or variation that often has theoretical value.

INTERFERENCE—A tactic that blocks the line of movement of an opponent's piece by putting something in the way, often with a counterattack gaining time.

ISOLATED PAWN—A pawn with no same-player pawns on either adjacent file. Generally, a weakness that needs to be supported by pieces.

ISOLANI—A term created by Aron Nimzovich (1886–1935) for the special case of isolated Queen-pawn, which often is as much a strength as it is a weakness. Sometimes describes any isolated pawn.

KING HUNT—A series of moves chasing a King around the board until it is mated.

KING SAFETY—A main element of chess, generally based on an evaluation of the other four main elements: material, time, space, and pawn structure; the degree to which the King is secure from danger of enemy attack.

KINGSIDE—The e-, f-, g-, and h-files taken as a block. Half the board, consisting of the files that the King, King-Bishop, King-Knight, and King-Rook occupy at the game's start.

KNIGHT FORK—Any double-attack by a Knight. See FAMILY FORK and ROYAL FORK.

LEGAL'S MATE—A mate with two or three minor pieces, usually combined with an unpin combination. The following short game illustrates: 1. e4 e5 2. Nf3 d6 3. Bc4 Bg4 4. Nc3 g6 5. Nxe5 Bxd1 6. Bxf7+ Ke7 7. Nd5 mate.

LEVER—A pawn attack at the base of an opponent's pawn chain. More often, any pawn advance leading to breakthrough pawn exchanges.

LIGHT PIECE—A Bishop or Knight. Also called MINOR PIECE.

LINE—A rank, file, or diagonal, or any number of consecutive squares along these rows.

LIQUIDATION—Exchanging to reduce the intensity of your opponent's attack and/or simplify to a superior, manageable endgame.

LUFT—A German term meaning an escape hatch for the King, usually created by moving a pawn.

MAJOR PIECE—A Queen or Rook. Also called HEAVY PIECE.

MAN—A piece or pawn for either side. Also called CHESSMAN. Note that chessplayers distinguish between pieces and pawns. All chessmen occupying each player's first rank at the start are pieces. Pawns are never called pieces.

MANEUVER—A redeploying series of moves, transferring a piece to a better position.

MATERIAL—Pieces and pawns, whether collectively, individually, or in some portion, excluding the King. You can be even, up, or down material. Material can be balanced (the same kind and number for pieces and the same number and relative placement for pawns) or imbalanced.

MATING ATTACK—A general assault against the enemy King with concentrated material that should lead to mate.

MIDDLEGAME—The second phase of a chess game, coming after the opening and preceding the endgame, where the superior side (usually White) tries to convert his initiative into concrete advantages while his opponent tires to neutralize or negate those efforts.

MINOR EXCHANGE—A term signifying the difference between a Bishop and Knight. In many situations, a Bishop tends to be slightly stronger than a Knight. Generally, a Bishop is especially better in open games, and only marginally stronger in most other cases. A Knight may get the edge in some closed positions, or if it can occupy an unassailable central square, or when squares of both colors must be guarded. You win the minor exchange if you trade your Knight for your opponent's Bishop.

MINOR PIECE—A Bishop or Knight. Also called LIGHT PIECE.

MINORITY ATTACK—An attack by several pawns against a larger group of pawns, usually supported by pieces, and designed to inflict attackable pawn weaknesses on the opponent.

MOBILE PAWN CENTER—A center where one side has two connected, supportable, advanceable pawns, usually aligned on their 4th rank, opposed by a single enemy pawn, usually on its 3rd rank.

MOBILITY—Freedom of movement. A piece has good mobility if it influences many squares, is not impeded by its own pawns, and the enemy counterpart is less effective and/or cannot neutralize it.

NOAH'S ARK TRAP—A famous trap in the Ruy Lopez, where Black snares White's light-square Bishop with three Queenside pawns. One version is 1. e4 e5   2. Nf3 Nc6   3. Bb5 a6   4. Ba4 Nf6   5. 0-0 d6   6. d4 b5   7. Bb3 Nxd4   8. Nxd4 exd4   9. Qxd4 c5, when Black traps the Bishop next move by advancing c5 to c4.

OPEN CENTER—A pawn center in which pieces can move freely, unhindered by pawns. The center is open if it contains no pawns, a lone pawn, or just one pawn for each side (such as a White pawn on e4 and a Black pawn on d6), placed so that the 4th or 5th rank is clear of pawns. To create an open center, at least one pawn for each side must be exchanged or captured.

OPEN FILE—A file containing no pawns of either color. A HALF-OPEN FILE contains a single pawn. Rooks should be positioned on open files or half-open files (for the side without the pawn) or on files containing advanced pawns that are likely to be exchanged.

OPEN GAME—A game in which at least a pair of central pawns, one for White and one for Black, have been exchanged, so that some pieces can move through the center more easily, often stemming from openings with a two-square advance of White's e-pawn.

OPENING—The initial phase of a chess game, followed by the middlegame and endgame. Generally, the first ten to fifteen moves, where forces are mobilized, generally to influence the center; the King is castled; and the players grapple for the initiative.

OPENING A FILE—Generally, clearing a file for your own use by exchanging away a pawn blocking it.

OPEN LINE—A rank, file, or diagonal clear, or nearly clear, of pawns. A Queen, Rook, or Bishop posted on such an open line enjoys increased mobility.

OPPOSITE-COLOR BISHOPS—See BISHOPS OF OPPOSITE COLORS.

OUTPOST—Usually an entrenched, supported piece occupying a square in the enemy part of the board; very difficult to drive away.

OVERLOAD—To tax with too many tasks, such as a chessman unable to follow through on a superficial defense of two different squares.

OVERWORKED PIECE—A piece unable to perform two or more required tasks simultaneously. See OVERLOAD.

PASSED PAWN—A pawn whose path to the last rank cannot be stopped by any enemy pawn. Thus it has "passed" opposition pawns that might have blocked or captured it.

PAWN CENTER—A distinctive arrangement of central pawns that determines the game's character. If the center is clear of pawns, for example, then tactics and quick attacks reign. If the center is impeded by interlocked friendly and enemy pawns, then play develops more slowly and both sides generally have more time for maneuvering and planning.

PAWN CHAIN—The same number of pawns for each side on adjacent files, obstructing each other's advance and generally slowing the play, especially in the central zone. Two typical pawn chains are White pawns at d4 and e5 opposed by Black pawns at d5 and e6, and White pawns at e4 and d5 opposed by Black pawns at e5 and d6. Also, two or more pawns connected diagonally.

PAWN FORK—A simultaneous attack by one pawn against two enemy chessmen.

PAWN GRABBING—Capturing insignificant pawns, usually at the cost of position, often wasting time while removing one's pieces from the main action.

PAWN ISLAND—A block of pawns, separated from supportive pawns by at least one file. Usually, the fewer pawn islands, the easier it is to defend one's pawns.

PAWN MAJORITY—Over any consecutive group of files, having more pawns than the opponent. Generally, one should use a pawn majority for attack.

PAWN STRUCTURE—The overall arrangement of pawns, usually resistant to change and affecting the nature of the ensuing play.

PAWN WEAKNESS—One or more pawns difficult to defend and/or vulnerable to attack.

PERPETUAL CHECK—A type of draw by threefold repetition, whereby the same exact position is forced or simply occurs on three separate occasions in the same game. Loosely, an unending series of checks that cannot be stopped but cannot force mate. Thus, for practical purposes, the game is drawn, for neither side can progress.

PIECE—A King, Queen, Rook, Bishop, or Knight.

PIN—A tactic preventing an enemy piece or pawn from moving off a rank, file, or diagonal because that would expose another enemy unit or key square to attack.

PIN BREAKING—Ending a pin by putting a piece or pawn in the line of the pinner's attack. Also, capturing or driving away the pinner.

PRINCIPLE—A general truth, often a maxim, frequently expressed as a "do" or a "don't," serving as a guide for reasonable play.

PROBLEM BISHOP—A Bishop generally blocked by its own pawns, resulting from a specific opening. Thus, in the French Defense, 1. e4 e6, Black's c8-Bishop—immediately obstructed by placing the King-pawn on e6—is a problem Bishop, and Black must find a way to develop or exchange it, to get rid of the problem it poses.

PROTECTED PASSED PAWN—A passed pawn defended by another pawn and generally protected from capture.

PSEUDO SACRIFICE—An offer of a piece or pawn that cannot be accepted without incurring disadvantage or immediate loss. Therefore, a sacrifice in name only, for the sacrificer knows his opponent cannot safely take the offered material. Also called a SHAM SACRIFICE.

QUEEN FORK—A fork given by the Queen.

QUEENSIDE—The half of the board containing the Queen at the game's start, including all the squares on the a-, b-, c-, and d-files. The KINGSIDE combines the e-, f-, g-, and h-files.

QUEENSIDE PAWN MAJORITY—The advantage of having more Queenside pawns than one's opponent. If the majority produces a passed pawn, it may lure the enemy King to stop its advance, leading to abandonment of the enemy's Kingside pawns.

REAL SACRIFICE—The opposite of a PSEUDO or SHAM SACRIFICE. A material sacrifice whose consequences cannot be seen or evaluated precisely. The sacrificer is taking a calculated risk, for he's not sure the sacrifice will work. Also called a TRUE SACRIFICE.

RELEASE OF TENSION—A pawn exchange, usually in the center, that gives the game a more or less fixed character. Often it would be better to maintain the tension, with the possibility of exchanging later, so that one retains options and hides intentions.

REMOVING THE DEFENDER—A tactic making a chessman vulnerable by capturing, luring away, or immobilizing its protector. Also called REMOVING THE GUARD and UNDERMINING.

REMOVING THE GUARD—See REMOVING THE DEFENDER.

REPETITION OF POSITION—A situation in which the player on the move may claim a draw if he intends to repeat for the third time a position that has occurred twice before. The repetitions need not be on consecutive moves and everything must be as it was on the previous two cases (all men on the same squares with the same powers) for the rule to apply.

SAC—An abbreviation for SACRIFICE.

SACRIFICE—Generally, the offer of material for other advantages. For example, one might sacrifice a pawn to gain the initiative or a piece to attack the enemy King.

SEVENTH RANK—One's own 7th rank or the enemy's 2nd rank. The term implies the attempt to occupy the 7th rank, especially with Rooks, in order to attack a row of enemy pawns and/or minor pieces, while fueling powerful assaults on the opposing King.

SHAM SACRIFICE—The opposite of a REAL SACRIFICE. See PSEUDO SACRIFICE.

SIMPLIFICATION—Exchanging to guard against potential enemy attacks, to clarify a position so that it becomes more manageable, to reduce enemy counterplay, or to reach a suitable endgame.

SKEWER—A double-attack on two enemy pieces along a rank, file, or diagonal, where the front piece usually is forced to move so that the one behind is subject to capture.

SPACE—One of the main elements of chess, generally based on mobility and number of squares controlled or influenced.

STRATEGY—An overall, long-term plan.

SWINDLE—A trap that wins or draws an otherwise lost game, if one's opponent falls for it.

SYMMETRICAL OPENING—A opening by which both players make a series of essentially the same moves, not necessarily in the same order. At some point, generally the player with the initiative, usually White, will break the symmetry by playing a move that cannot be copied, stamping the game with character.

SYSTEM—A set of related opening variations branching from a particular move or group of moves, in which pieces and pawns are positioned for harmonious purposes, with corresponding logic, and in which definite middlegame plans emerge.

TACTICS—Generally, short-term, immediate attacks and threats.

TEMPO—A unit of chess time. A move. (*pl.* tempi)

THREAT—Generally, a direct or indirect attack on an enemy man.

TIME—One of the main elements of chess, usually evaluated in terms of initiative and development.

TRADE—An even exchange. To make such a transaction.

TRANSPOSE—In a possible series of moves, to reverse the order so that a later move or plan is played earlier than another.

TRAP—A baited variation to lure a careless opponent into error.

TRAPPED PIECE—A piece that is attacked and cannot be saved, either by moving it away or defending it.

TRUE SACRIFICE—Another name for REAL SACRIFICE.

UNDERMINING—See REMOVING THE DEFENDER.

UNPIN—A tactic by which a pin is broken, either by moving another piece or pawn in the way, or by capturing or driving away the enemy pinner.

VARIATION—A sequence of moves, particularly in the opening. An alternative to the main line of play.

WEAKNESS—A square inadequately defended, generally no longer capable of being guarded by pawns. A tactical vulnerability.

X-RAY—A SKEWER attack or defense along a rank, file, or diagonal. Either it drives away an enemy man in front of another enemy man to expose the back one to capture, or it protects a friendly man through an enemy man in the middle along the same line of power.

ZWISCHENZUG—An IN-BETWEEN MOVE. Generally a finesse, played instead of a more obvious, inferior move.

Sources

PERIODICALS

1. British Chess Magazine
2. Chess
3. Chess Life
4. Inside Chess
5. Players Chess News

OPENING REFERENCE BOOKS (GENERAL) & (DOUBLE E-PAWN)

1. Botterill-Open Gambits
2. Collijn-Larobok I Schack
3. Estrin-Gambits
4. Estrin—Three Double King Pawn Openings
5. Fine-Ideas Behind the Chess Openings
6. Fine-Practical Chess Openings (PCO)
7. Freeborough & Ranken-Chess Openings Ancient & Modern
8. Hartston, Mednis, Peters, & Soltis-Understanding the Open Games
9. Harding-Counter Gambits
10. Horowitz-Chess Openings
11. Keres-Drei-Springerspiel bis Konigs Gambit
12. Keres-Vier-Springerspiel bis Konigs Gambit
13. Keres-Spanisch bis Franzosisch
14. Korn-Modern Chess Openings (MCO)
15. Kasparov & Keene-Batsford Chess Openings (BCO)
16. Matanovic-Encyclopedia of Chess Openings, Volume C (ECO)
17. Pachman-Open Games
18. Schlechter-Handbuch des Schachspiels

OPENING TRAPS

1. Cherney-Winning Chess Traps
2. Greig-Pitfalls of the Chess Board
3. Horowitz—New Traps in the Chess Openings

COLLECTIONS-MINIATURES

1. Bachmann & Huther-Sonell Matt!
2. Barden & Heidenfeld—Modern Chess Miniatures
3. Chernev—The 1000 Best Short Games of Chess
4. Clark—100 Soviet Miniatures
5. Du Mont—200 Miniature Games of Chess
6. Reinfeld—Win in 20 Moves or Less
7. Richter—Kurzgeschichten um Sohachfiguren
8. Wall—500 Italian Game Miniatures
9. Wall—500 King's Gambit Miniatures
10. Wall—500 Ruy Lopez Miniatures

COLLECTIONS-GENERAL

1. Becker & Grunfeld-Teplitz-Schonau 1922
2. Informants 1–43
3. Levy & O'Connell—Oxford Encyclopedia Of Chess Games, 1885–1866
4. The New Chess Player 1–10
5. Tarrasch-Die Moderne Schachpartie
6. Tartakover-Die Hypermoderne Schachpartie
7. Tartakover & Du Mont-500 Master Games
8. Tartakover & Du Mont—100 Master Games of Modern Chess
9. Bronstein—200 Open Games
10. Hooper & Whyld—The Oxford Companion to Chess

SPECIFIC DOUBLE E-PAWN OPENINGS (BOOKS/PAMPHLETS)

1. Barden—The Ruy Lopez
2. Bhend—Konigs Gambit
3. Botterill & Harding—The Italian Game
4. Cafferty & Hooper—A Complete Defence to 1. P-K4, A Study of Petroff's Defence
5. Du Mont—The Center Game & Danish Gambit
6. Estrin—The Two Knights Defence
7. Florian—The Schlilemann Variation of the Ruy Lopes
8. Forintos & Haag—Petroff Defence
9. Harding—Bishop's Opening
10. Harding—Ponziani Opening
11. Harding—Vienna Opening
12. Konstantinopolsky & Lepeshkin—Vienna Game
13. Korchnoi & Zak—The King's Gambit
14. Larson—Why Not the Philidor?
15. Levy—The Siesta Variation
16. McKormick & Soltis—Bird's Defence to the Ruy Lopez

17. Pickett—The Delayed Exchange Ruy Lopes Deferred (DERLD)
18. Pickett—Philidor's Defence
19. Pickett & Swift—Scotch Game
20. Pickett & Swift—Scoth Gambit
21. Pickett & Swift—Goring Gambit
22. Thimann-King's Gambit
23. Schwartz-Spanisch II
24. Shamkovich & Schiller-Spanish; Schliemann (Jaenisch)
25. Yudovich-Spanish without . . .a6.

Tactical Index

NOTE: Numbers listed refer to example numbers, not page numbers.

DEFLECTION	16, 181, 188 (3)
DESPERADO	74 (1)
DISCOVERY	30, 31, 45, 60, 96, 100, 108, 111, 114, 138, 142, 149, 161, 163, 170, 189, 202 (17)
DOUBLE-ATTACK	10, 34, 87, 113, 115, 164, 176, 184 (8)
FORK	5, 14, 17, 18, 33, 35, 51, 53, 61, 67, 69, 72, 81, 84, 107, 126, 134, 140, 146, 147, 155, 160, 162, 165, 167, 172, 173, 185, 190, 196, 200 (31)
KING HUNT	19, 43, 48, 50, 57, 59, 62, 63, 64, 101, 178 (11)
IN-BETWEEN MOVE	1, 3, 28, 37, 125, 144 (6)
MATING ATTACK	4, 8, 9, 13, 23, 26, 27, 32, 36, 38, 39, 40, 42, 44, 46, 47, 49, 52, 58, 65, 66, 68, 71, 90, 93, 98, 99, 104, 106, 116, 118, 119, 120, 122, 124, 127, 129, 131, 132, 136, 139, 143, 145, 148, 154, 169, 179, 183, 197 (49)

MULTIPLE ATTACK   20, 92 (2)

OVERLOAD   82, 89, 95, 133 (4)

PIN   2, 29, 77, 79, 80, 85, 86, 88, 97, 121, 150, 151, 153, 157, 168, 177, 182, 192, 193, 198, 201 (21)

PROMOTION   24, 56, 141 (3)

REMOVING THE GUARD   6, 70, 73, 91, 105, 123, 152, 156, 158, 186, 195 (11)

SAVING BY CAPTURING   12 (1)

SKEWER   11, 15, 21, 55, 110, 174 (6)

TRAPPED PIECE   7, 25, 75, 76, 78, 83, 128, 130, 137, 159, 166, 171, 175, 187, 191 (15)

UNPIN   22, 41, 54, 94, 102, 103, 109, 112, 117, 135, 180, 194, 199 (13)

Opening Index

CENTER GAME

1. **e4 e5** 2. **d4 exd4** 3. **Qxd4**
   3. . . Nf6 [Ex. #1]
   3. . . Nc6 4. Qe4 *(Hall Variation)* [Ex. #2]
      4. Qe3 *(Paulsen Attack)* [Ex. #3, 4, 5, 6]

CENTER GAMBIT

1. **e4 e5** 2. **d4 exd4**
   3. Bc4 [Ex. #7]
   3. Nf3 [Ex. #8]

DANISH GAMBIT

1. **e4 e5** 2. **d4 exd4** 3. **c3 dxc3**
   4. Bc4 Bb4 *(Danish Declined)* [Ex. #9]
   . . . cxb2 *(Danish Accepted)* [Ex. #10, 11, 12, 13, 14, 15]
   4. Nxc3 *(Half Danish)* [Ex. #16]

GORING GAMBIT

1. **e4 e5** 2. **Nf3 Nc6** 3. **d4 exd4** 4. **c3** [Ex. #17, 18]

SCOTCH GAMBIT

1. **e4 e5** 2. **Nf3 Nc6** 3. **d4 exd4** 4. **Bc4** [Ex. #19, 20, 21, 22]

SCOTCH GAME

1. **e4 e5** 2. **Nf3 Nc6** 3. **d4 exd4** 4. **Nxd4**
   4. . . Nge7 [Ex. #23]
   4. . . Be7 [Ex. #24]
   4. . . Qh4 *(Pulling Counter-Attack)* [Ex. #25, 26]
   4. . . Bc5 *(Classical Variation)* [Ex. #27, 28, 29, 30]
   4. . . Nf6 *(Schmidt Variation)* [Ex. #31]
      5. Nc3 *(Scotch Four Knights)* [Ex. #32]

BISHOP'S OPENING

1. e4 e5   2. Bc4
  2. . . Bc5 *(Classical Variation)*   [Ex. #33]
  2. . . Nf6 *(Berlin Defence)*
    3. d3 Be7   4. f4   [Ex. #34]
    3. d3 c6   4. Qe7   [Ex. #35]
    3. d3 c6   4. Nf3   [Ex. #36]
    3. d4 exd4   4. Nf3 *(Urusov Gambit)*   [Ex. #37, 38, 39]

VIENNA GAME

1. e4 e5   2. Nc3

  2. . . Bc5 (Anderssen Variation)   [Ex. #40]
  2. . . Nc6   3. f4 (Vienna Gambit)   [Ex. #41, 42, 43]
    3. Bc4 Bc5 (Bishops Variation)   [Ex. #44, 45]
  2. . . Nf6 (Falkbeer Variation)   [Ex. #46]
    3. Bc4 Nxe4 (Frankenstein-Dracula Variation)   [Ex. #47, 48, 49]
    3. f4 exf4   [Ex. #50, 51]
    . . . d5   [Ex. #52, 53]
      4. fxe5 Nxe5   5. d3 (Oxford Variation)   [Ex. #54]

KING'S GAMBIT ACCEPTED

1. e4 e5   2. f4 exf4

  3. Kf2 (Irregular)   [Ex. #55]
  3. b3 (Orsini Gambit)   [Ex. #56]
  3. Bc4 (Bishop's Gambit)   [Ex. #57, 58]
  3. Nf3 (King's Knight Gambit)
  3. . . Be7 (Cunningham Defence)   [Ex. #59]
  3. . . d5 (Abbazia Defence)   [Ex. #60]
  3. . . Nf6 (Schallopp Defence)   [Ex. #61]
  3. . . g5 (Classical Defense)
    4. Bc4 Bg7   [Ex. #62]
    4. Bc4 g4   5. d4 (Ghulam Kassim Gambit)   [Ex. #63]
    4. Bc4 g4   5. Nc3 (McDonnell Gambit)   [Ex. #64]
    4. Nc3 (Quaade Gambit)   [Ex. #65, 66]
    4. h4 g4   5. Ne5 (Kieseritzky Gambit)   [Ex. #67]

KING'S GAMBIT DECLINED

1. e4 e5   2. f4

  2. . . Nf6 (Bernstein Defense)   [Ex. #68]
  2. . . d6 (Nimzovich Defence)   [Ex. #72]
  2. . . Bc4 (Classical Defence)   [Ex. #69, 70, 71, 73, 74]

FALKBEER COUNTER-GAMBIT

1. **e4 e5**   2. **f4 d5**
   3. Nf3 (Anti-Falkbeer)   [Ex. #75]
   3. Nc3 (Hoffmann Variation)   [Ex. #76]
   3. exd5 Qxd5 (Greco Variation)   [Ex. #77, 78]
   3. . . . e4 4. Nc3 (London Variation)   [Ex. #79]
      4. Bb5+ (Nimzovich Variation)   [Ex. #80]

DAMIANO DEFENCE

1. **e4 e5**   2. **Nf3 f6**
   3. Nxe5 Qe7   [Ex. #81]
   . . . fxe5   [Ex. #82, #83]

LATVIAN COUNTER-GAMBIT

1. **e4 e5**   2. **Nf3 f5**
   3. Nxe5 Qf6 4. Nc4   [Ex. #84, #85]
      4. d4   [Ex. #86]

QUEEN'S PAWN COUNTER-GAMBIT

1. **e4 e5**   2. **Nf3 d5**
   3. Bd3   [Ex. #87]
   3. Nxe5   [Ex. #88, 89, 90]

ALAPIN OPENING

1. **e4 e5**   2. **Ne2**
   2. . . d5   [Ex. #91]
   2. . . Bc5   [Ex. #92]
   2. . . Nf6   [Ex. #93, 94, 95]

PONZIANI OPENING

1. **e4 e5**   2. **Nf3 Nc6** 3. **c3**
   3. . . d5   [Ex. #96, 97, 98]
   3. . . Nf6   [Ex. #99, 100, 101]

PHILIDOR DEFENCE

1. **e4 e5**   2. **Nf3 d6**
   3. Bc4   [Ex. #102, 103, 104, 105]
   3. d4   [Ex. #106, 107]

PETROFF DEFENCE

1. e4 e5   2. Nf3 Nf6
3. Nxe5   [Ex. #108, 109, 110, 111]
3. Bc4 *(Boden-Kieseritzky Gambit)*   [Ex. #112]
3. d4 *(Steinite Variation)*   [Ex. #113]

THREE KNIGHTS GAME

1. e4 e5   2. Nf3 Nc6   3. Nc3
3. . . Bc5   [Ex. #114, 115]
3. . . f5   [Ex. #116]

FOUR KNIGHTS GAME

1. e4 e5   2. Nf3 Nc6   3. Nc3 Nc6
4. Bc4 Bb4 (Vienna Four Knights)   [Ex. #117]
4. Bb5 *(Spanish Four Knights Game)*   [Ex. #118, 119, 120]

HUNGARIAN DEFENCE

1. e4 e5   2. Nf3 Nc6   3. Bc4 Be7
4. d4   [Ex. #121, 122]
4. Nc3   [Ex. #123]

PARIS DEFENCE

1. e4 e5   2. Nf3 Nc6   3. Bc4 d6
4. 0-0   [Ex. #124]
4. d4   [Ex. #125]
4. c3   [Ex. #126]

GUIOCO PIANO

1. e4 e5   2. Nf3 Nc6   3. Bc4 Bc5
4. d3 d6   [Ex. #127, 128]
4. Nc3 Nf6 *(Italian Four Knights Game)*   [Ex. #129, 130, 131, 132]
4. c3 *(Greco Variation)*
4. . . d6   [Ex. #133, 134]
4. . . Qe7   [Ex. #135]
4. . . Nf6   [Ex. #136, 137]
4. Bxf7 + *(Jerome Gambit)*   [Ex. #138]

EVANS GAMBIT

1. **e4 e5**   2. **Nf3 Nc6**   3. **Bc4 Bc5**   4. **b4**
    4. . . . Bxb4 *(Accepted)*
       5. c3 Bc5   [Ex. #139, 140]
        . . . Ba5   [Ex. #141]
    4. . . . Bb6 *(Declined)*   [Ex. #142]

TWO KNIGHTS DEFENCE

1. **e4 e5**   2. **Nf3 Nc6**   3. **Bc4 Nf6**
    4. 0-0   [Ex. #143]
    4. d4   [Ex. #144, 145, 146]
    4. d4 exd4   5. 0-0 Bc5   6. e5 *(Max Lange Attack)*   [Ex. #147]
    4. Ng5 Bc5 *(Wilkes Barre Variation)*   [Ex. #148]

RUY LOPEZ

1. **e4 e5**   2. **Nf3 Nc6**   3. **Bb5**
    3. . . d6 *(Steinitz Defence)*
       4. 0-0   [Ex. #149, 150]
       4. d4   [Ex. #151, 152]
       4. Bxc6+   [Ex. #153]
       4. d3   [Ex. 154]
    3. . . Nf6 *(Berlin Defence)*
       4. d3   [Ex. #155*, 156]
       4. 0-0   [Ex. #157, 158, 159, 160, 161, 162, 163]
    3. . . Bc5 *(Cordel Defence)*
       4. d3   [Ex. #164]
       4. c3   [Ex. #165, 166]
       4. Nxe5   [Ex. #167]
       4. 0-0   [Ex. #168, 169, 170, 171]
    3. . . f5 *(Schliemann Defence)*
       4. Nc3   [Ex. #172, 173, 174]
       4. Bxc6   [Ex. #175, 176]
    3. . . Nd4 *(Bird Defence)*   [Ex. #177]
    3. . . Nge7 *(Cozio Defence)*   [Ex. #178, 179, 180, 181]

RUY LOPEZ with 3. . .a6

1. **e4 e5**   2. **Nf3 Nc6**   3. **Bb5 a6**
    3. . . a6 (Morphy Defence)
    4. Ba4 Bb4 *(Alapin Defence Deferred)*   [Ex. #182]
    4. Ba4 b5   5. Bb3 Bc5 *(Graz Variation)*   [Ex. #183, 184, 185]
          5. Bb3 Bb7 *(Tchigorin Variation)*   [Ex. #186]
    4. Ba4 d6 *(Steinitz Defence Deferred)*   [Ex. #187, 188*]
    4. Ba4 f5 *(Schliemann Defence Deferred)*   [Ex. #189]

4. Ba4 Nf6   5. Qe2 *(Wormald Attack)*   [Ex. #190]
   5. Nc3 *(Tarrasch Variation)*   [Ex. #191]
   5. 0-0 Be5 *(Moller Defence)*   [Ex. #192]
   5. 0-0 Nxe4 *(Open Defence)*   [Ex. #193]
   5. 0-0 d6 *(Russian Defence)*   [Ex. #194]
   5. 0-0 Be7   6. Qe2 *(Worrell Attack)*   [Ex. #195]
4. Bxc6 *(Exchange Variation)*
   5. 0-0 f6   [Ex. #196]
   5. 0-0 Bg4   [Ex. #197, 198]
   5. 0-0 Bd6   [Ex. #199, 200]
   5. d4   [Ex. #201]
4. . . bxc6   [Ex. #202]

*#155 Mortimer's Defence is 4. . . Ne7 and the whole of #156 is known as Mortimer's Trap.
*#188 The moves 5.c3f5 constitute the Siesta variation.

About the Author

BRUCE PANDOLFINI is the author of eight instructional chess books, including *Bobby Fischer's Outrageous Chess Moves, Principles of the New Chess, Pandolfini's Endgame Course, Russian Chess, The ABC's of Chess, Let's Play Chess, Kasparov's Winning Chess Tactics,* and *One-Move Chess by the Champions.* He is also editor of the distinguished anthologies, *The Best of Chess Life, Volumes I and II.* Perhaps the most experienced chess teacher in North America, and the Executive Director of the Manhattan Chess Club, Bruce Pandolfini lives in New York City.